A New Model of the Economy

A New Model
of the Economy

BRIAN HODGKINSON

SHEPHEARD-WALWYN (PUBLISHERS) LTD
IN ASSOCIATION WITH
THE SCHOOL OF ECONOMIC SCIENCE, LONDON

First published in 2008 by
Shepheard-Walwyn (Publishers) Ltd
15 Alder Road
London SW14 8ER
in association with
The School of Economic Science
11 Mandeville Place
London W1U 3AJ

British Library Cataloguing in Publication Data
A catalogue record of this book
is available from the British Library

ISBN-13: 978-0-85683-250-5
ISBN-10: 0-85683-250-2

Typeset by Alacrity,
Winscombe, Somerset
Printed and bound through
s | s | media limited, Wallington, Surrey

Contents

Acknowledgments

THIS BOOK is largely the product of innumerable discussions, formal and conversational, with a great many people over many years. To all of them I am deeply grateful. However, I must name some whose contribution has helped to enlighten specific areas of the subject or who have played a part in bringing the book to fruition. They are John Allen, Leslie Blake, Haydon Bradshaw, Judith Clarke, Martin Cuss, Alex Godden, Margaret Godden, Peter Green, Ian Mason, John Pincham, Roger Pincham, David Smith, John Stewart, Professor Paul Streeten, David Triggs, Tony Vickers, Robert Watson, and Bernard White. I am particularly grateful to Professor Patrick Minford for some valuable suggestions and encouragement, which he gave despite disagreeing with the central thesis of the book. My thanks are especially due to Anthony Werner as the publisher, to Veronica Daniels for the diagrams, and to my son David and his wife Catherine for help with computers. Above all, I am grateful to my wife Catherine for her interest and patience, and indeed for her professional advice on some aspects of finance and company organisation.

Preface

THIS BOOK is the outcome of many years study of Economics from two rather different standpoints. On the one hand, my study of modern academic Economics began at Balliol College, Oxford, and continued through a long career of teaching the subject and editing an economics journal. On the other hand, I have studied and taught for almost as long at the School of Economic Science in London and Oxford, where the fundamental principles of the subject, rather than its ever-changing theories and multitudinous empirical facts and statistics, have been the central issue.

An analogy may help to put these two standpoints into perspective. Building a house requires both firm foundations and a well designed, aesthetically pleasing superstructure. Modern academic Economics provides the latter, but not, in my view, the former. It is a fine house, built upon foundations which are askew. Hence it leans dangerously, and might even collapse in a welter of broken theories and dubious 'facts'. One hopes that the real economies which it purports to explain do not similarly come to grief. Cracks are certainly appearing at the time this book is published. Over half a century of research and teaching by the School of Economic Science, however, has yielded a set of principles revealed by reason and by careful examination of economic thinkers in the tradition of natural law. Upon the foundation of these principles this book attempts to construct a new house of Economics from the materials offered by modern analysis.

A growing awareness of the inadequacy of existing economic orthodoxy is evident from a number of books and articles that have appeared in recent years, such as *A Guide to What's Wrong with Economics* (ed. E. Fulbrook, Anthem Press, 2004). It is in response to this need for a new kind of economic model that this book is offered. The model presented is not mathematical; it is rather an amendment of the present framework of micro and macro economic analysis by changing the assumptions. In particular, it removes the 'flat-earth' assumption of homogenous land. As Eaton and Lipsey – two economists who have realised the importance of land in economic theory

– have written, 'many phenomena that appear inexplicable when inserted into a spaceless model are explicable in a spatial model.' (*On the Foundations of Monopolistic Competition and Economic Geography*, Edward Elgar, 1997). *The New Model of the Economy* hopes to restore the spatial model that the founders of Economics, such as Ricardo, had in mind.

BRIAN HODGKINSON
November 2007

Summary

PART ONE affirms some fundamental principles, which underpin the main arguments, although they are not always explicitly recalled. They are, in brief, that the purpose of the study of Economics is to enhance human freedom, that natural law underlies all economic phenomena, and that land, as defined by economists, is a prime factor of production, not just in the third world, but in all advanced industrial economies, alongside the natural forces of the universe and human labour.

Human freedom has a variety of aspects (Chapter 1). On the highest level it is spiritual or philosophical, and concerns the nature of the self and the very essence of humanity. On the political level it concerns one's relationship to the State and the forms of government most suited to particular peoples and times. On the civil level it is a matter of the individual's recognition of law, and the nature of laws that deal with violence, defamation, personal property and so on. But, on the level of the economy, freedom is above all the ability to use one's creative powers to the full. Productive work is the principal means of expressing oneself. Today such a concept of freedom tends to be limited to the fortunate few whose special talents and opportunities enable them so to express themselves – actors, artists, sportsmen, self-employed craftsmen and successful entrepreneurs, for example. The majority of people are assumed to be suited to be employees, often in repetitive or tedious occupations. Their principal motive for work degenerates into earning sufficient to maintain themselves and their families in a modest standard of living. What then so inhibits their natural freedom? The study of the limitations on human creativity through work, and how they might be removed, is the theme of this book.

The second principle, which is also given scant recognition in modern economic thought, is that economic activity is subject to natural law (Chapter 2). Whilst modern physical sciences are largely built upon the idea that phenomena are governed by laws, the social sciences have been beset by apparent difficulties in establishing laws and a resulting recourse to statistical generalisation. However, in Chapter 2 I have attempted to show that some of the simplest and least controversial operations of any economy are governed by natural law. The argument is not philosophical. It is just that certain highly predictable and regular forms of behaviour occur so commonly as to be suitably categorised as law-like. They follow from human nature, which is itself a controversial concept if examined in depth, but for the purposes of Economics can be quite well known by observation. There is, for example, a division of labour in all modern societies, however they are organised politically and socially. Plato and Adam Smith observed it before we did. What is more controversial, of course, are the implications drawn later in this book that such matters as the general level of wages and the impact of taxation are similarly law-like.

The third principle under discussion is the significance of land in the economy (Chapter 3). This is the first major point of departure from conventional economic analysis. When that economy is not a typical capitalist one, then land tenure may become an important ingredient in its analysis, but when it is the economy of the UK or the USA, for example, then the present system of private property in land is indeed taken for granted or ignored. Yet this system literally and conceptually underlies the whole operation of the economy built upon it. To give but one instance from many that are explored in detail later in the book: consider what kind of competitive relationship exists between two firms in the same industry, one of which owns a freehold site in the centre of a large city and the other rents a site nearby. The former pays nothing to a landowner. The latter pays a large annual rent. Yet they must sell their products at similar prices. Is this competition; if so, of what kind? Any analysis that ignores this is futile. Yet the standard economic analysis does ignore it.

Another aspect of the current neglect of land in economic theory is that too often land is subsumed under the heading of capital. Yet, at least since Ricardo, it has been clear that the part played by land in any economy is radically different from that of capital, either in its proper sense of produced means of production or in its looser sense of money loaned for the purchase of capital goods or other assets. Why is this? As Ricardo so carefully explained, land gives rise to rent. But so does capital in certain circumstances, says the conventional wisdom. This spurious reply is dealt with in Chapter 8 below; here it is sufficient to say that the concept of rent in modern economic thought is thoroughly ambiguous.

Part Two follows closely the pattern of micro-economic analysis found in textbooks (Chapters 4-7). Its *modus operandi* is simple. The firm is redefined as a one-site productive unit (sometimes this condition is relaxed to deal with multi-site enterprises.). The economic rent of land is explicitly shown in each of the four cases of perfect competition, monopolistic competition, monopoly and oligopoly. This is not merely the extraction of rent payments to landlords. For the whole point is to show how economic rent, properly defined as the potential annual value of a site i.e. Ricardian rent, enters into economic activity, profoundly affecting the competitive situation of firms. This inevitably involves distinctions being made between firms with freehold or leasehold land and those paying a full rent to landlords, crucial facts usually ignored in economic analysis. A striking example of the impact of making economic rent explicit is the case of firms holding mineral-rich land, such as oil companies. Once the land is acquired – which historically may have been by force or fraud – nothing is charged against their profits for land costs. Hence their recorded profits are substantially economic rent, a return to land, not a return to either capital or entrepreneurship. There are many similar examples of the failure of micro-economic analysis to trace correctly the proper economic source of streams of income. Oddly enough present-day economic conditions are revealing this in strange ways. For example, private equity firms are becoming aware that supermarkets have property interests that are more valuable than their goodwill as retailers.

One conclusion of this fresh analysis of the theory of the firm is that perfect competition can be seen to have much wider application that is currently thought, if it is taken to be a 'level playing field' after the proper charging against profits of the full economic rent of land. In other words, if all firms, not just those without freeholds or beneficial leases, paid a full economic rent, then they would be left in a truly comparable situation as regards economic efficiency and the ability to make profits, properly defined as a return to entrepreneurs. Moreover, the extent to which monopoly power of varying degrees relies on ownership of land would become evident if economic rent were shown explicitly in the analysis of monopolistic competition, monopoly and, perhaps most interestingly, oligopoly. The tendency towards oligopoly in many key industries, such as oil and retailing, in the UK and other advanced economies could then be seen as not so much a financial and technological phenomenon, but rather one founded largely on unconditional land ownership.

Part Three on factor incomes begins with the law of rent itself (Chapter 8). The classic statements of this, of course, were in Ricardo, John Stuart Mill, Alfred Marshall and, with less orthodoxy, in Henry George. In the twentieth century it was largely ignored, except as a very minor and isolated part of micro-analysis. Why this happened is a matter for historians of ideas and sociologists. Vested interests in land have undoubtedly played a part, particularly since the widespread movement of Georgists to introduce a land tax. Yet there can be little doubt about its relevance to the present day economy. Most obviously the housing market is almost dominating economic policy, through the need to adjust interest rates to control housing demand. What is rarely noticed is that it is the land element in house prices that causes the problem, not the price of 'bricks and mortar' (see Chapter 19 on Housing).

There is, however, an intellectual reason why the law of rent has been downgraded. This is the outright mistake in analysis perpetuated by generations of textbook writers, which identifies it with 'rent' defined as the excess of earnings of a factor over its transfer earnings (Chapter 9). Economic rent of land is the difference between the potential output from a particular site and the potential output using the same inputs on the least productive site in use i.e. the marginal one. This is totally distinct from any excess over transfer earnings; in the case of land, transfer earnings from a change of use. Economic rent takes the use to be the same in calculating the excess output on the superior site. Neither concept of rent is wrong. The problem is that they are confused, with the result that the economic rent of land is grossly underestimated in its scale and impact on the economy.

Wages are dealt with within this context (Chapter 10). Thus the general level of wages is determined by what happens at the margin of production. This is not the margin as used in marginal productivity theory, but the margin as defined by the law of rent. This means that wages are in general set by what labour can produce on the least productive sites in use. Of course, actual wages vary a great deal around this norm, owing to both equilibrium and disequilibrium differentials. Such a generalisation, which no doubt could be studied empirically at much greater length, exemplifies the natural law approach, for it is a consequence of the law of rent. Production on the margin sets an absolute upper limit to wages, though these may be reduced further by charges on marginal firms, such as a landlord's claim or taxation.

The analysis of capital that follows is, no doubt, even more controversial, since it argues that only in a diminished sense is there such a

thing as 'capitalism' (Chapter 11). This turns upon the point that capital only receives its supply price i.e. cost of production. Any apparent
return above this is either a short term quasi-rent, or is a result of
monopoly power of some kind. What is commonly regarded as
capital is, in fact, money loans. Economists make the distinction
between capital goods and financial capital, and then often follow the
layman's practice of identifying the two. In this book they are kept
strictly distinct. Financial capital is consistently treated as money loans,
which usually receive interest. Hence Chapters 11 and 13 should be
read as a continuous argument. The question of profits, however,
intervenes (Chapter 12). Here the analysis originating with Schumpeter
is used, with his brilliant account of the role of the entrepreneur as
the creative element in a free economy.

Part Four deals with the complex issues of money and value. Credit
is seen as the natural feature of society that underlies the use of money,
on the grounds that money itself is no more than a principal form of
credit, enhanced by the trustworthiness of bankers and central governments (Chapter 13). The radical aspect of this discussion, however,
lies more in the analysis of interest. Historical theories, such as those
of Bohm-Bawerk and Marshall are briefly considered, but the conclusion reached – that banks could provide credit in the form of advances
at the supply price of money i.e. at an almost zero interest rate – is
based on argument. A key point is that there is a vital distinction
between money created by banks giving advances on one hand, and
money lent by money lenders to borrowers on the other. The latter
may well need to be charged at interest, depending on the supply and
demand for funds, but the former need not charge interest above the
supply price, which is the cost of a banking service. Needless to say,
were banks to follow this practice, the market for loanable funds would
move hugely in favour of borrowers. In which case Keynes' famous
'euthanasia of the rentier' might be a practical possibility!

Value is demarcated from price, by defining the latter as whatever is
given, or promised, in a transaction, whilst the former is an entirely
subjective concept (Chapter 14). Nevertheless it is shown that value
can be given an ordinal, but not a cardinal, measurement. The result
is that value so measured can be directly related to supply and demand
analysis. This is important for the consistency of the book, since the
revised theory of the firm retains a faith in supply and demand curves!

Part Five, entitled Public Revenue, is admittedly somewhat of a rag-
bag collection of topics, united by the single, overriding idea of rent
of land as public revenue. Present day taxation is analysed in terms of

the primary division of output between rent and wages (Chapter 15). This yields a rather different view of the impact of both direct and indirect taxes from that conventionally given. The main reason for this is that the impact is viewed essentially as occurring on the margin of production. Thus taxation which is levied on the margin closes down firms and creates unemployment, whilst taxation proportional to the rent of land has a nil impact on the margin. This is one major rationale for collecting rent as tax. The other is based upon the proposition that factors of production in an efficient economy receive income pro rata with their ability to create it. Landowners create no income – except in so far as they manage land – whereas society creates economic rent by its activity and infrastructure. Hence it is the community, not landowners, which attracts rent in an efficient economy.

A very brief historical analysis is introduced to give a fresh slant on how the UK economy has developed since the main period of land enclosure (Chapter 16). This is not at all intended to recommend a return to a pre-enclosure past. Rather it is to emphasise that the current payment of rent of land into private hands distorts economic efficiency and denies the Exchequer what should be its principal source of revenue. Chapter 17 on Externalities is an attempt to show how the greatest measure of externalities is – guess what! – rent of land. A landowner receives rent as a result of all the external benefits created by surrounding firms, public infrastructure and other economic activity. Similarly landowners may suffer, to a lesser extent, from negative externalities, such as pollution. Rent is a precise measure of both types of externality. A notable example of this is the huge increase in land prices when a railway is built, as in the case of the Stratford extension of the London Underground, or the new London Crossrail. Some observers have been shrewd enough to see this and call for the introduction of a land tax to recoup these externalities. But why should this not be a general conclusion, rather than one related only to particular projects?

Chapter 18 on Natural Monopoly, like that on the theory of the firm, seeks to make explicit the rent of land element in most natural monopolies. This has been largely ignored in debates over privatisation, even though the commercial interests involved have often been quick to draw appropriate conclusions about the land values obtainable from privatised utilities, like rail and public buildings. The monopoly aspect of utilities is usually intimately tied to ownership of land, simply because they naturally use large and valuable sites. Were the rent of these charged in their accounts, their real viability as public or private enterprises would be revealed. Moreover, such utilities create particularly large external economies. Transport systems, for example, raise land values enormously, yet only receive revenue from transport users as passengers. Their fixed costs, at least, could easily be financed out of a land tax, which would merely represent the uncollected value that they create.

Housing as a topic sits uneasily under the heading of Public Revenue (Chapter 19). The justification for its position is that house prices are very easily divisible into building costs and land prices. Since the latter are the capital value of annual rent, housing could be a suitable subject for a land tax in substitution for existing rates. This distinction goes some way to explain the present housing crisis in the UK, whereby accelerating house prices lead to a generation gap between older house owners and young people unable to afford homes. Building costs are subject to a relatively free market in materials, labour etc. Land costs are determined by a fairly fixed supply of suitable land, rising demand and competition with other land uses, especially in urban areas. Were rent collected as public revenue, the land element in 'house' prices would diminish. (Chapter 27 deals with problems of adjustment.)

Part Six begins with a straightforward 'textbook' account of the theory of income determination, in the expectation that this is less familiar to some readers than other areas of economic analysis (Chapter 20). It is followed by three chapters (21-23) which form a critique of the whole theory. These apply the preceding concepts of rent, money and credit, and taxation to the assumptions and deductions of the theory, concluding with a reformulation. Chapter 24 'The Model Reformed' shows that the existing theory has implied limitations, which if withdrawn reveal an economy with greatly enhanced productivity, efficiency and fairness. The limitations are restrictions on the use of land, restraints on the availability of credit, especially for productive investment, and the destructive impact of taxation on labour and enterprise. The reform of the theory reveals the possibility of a reformed economy, in which wages are determined by the full product of marginal land, rent of land becomes entirely public revenue, and secondary claims on output, such as interest, taxation on labour and enterprise, and monopoly profits have disappeared. Such a reformed economy is, of course, an ideal. But economic thought is sadly in need of a new ideal. Socialism has long ceased to be one. So-called free market economics is proving itself a poor substitute, even if some of its tenets are well-founded. Why not then consider free men and free land as a new vision to be attained? We in Britain have some conception of what it is for people to be free, but historically we have little idea of what free land means. The subtext of this book is a definition of free land, meaning land free for the whole of society and not for a minority.

How a reformed economy would behave in an international context is briefly considered in Chapter 25. Much more needs to be said about this. As always confidence would play a large part, but confidence is itself mainly attributable to the type of economy in which one lives. Chapter 26 takes a brief look at business cycles. It does not quarrel greatly with the existing method of treating them as functions of variables, such as the levels of consumption and saving, investment, government expenditure and the trade balance. Predictably, however, it emphasises the role of land in their generation. The existence of a market in land, and especially the creation of bank advances for the purchase of land, are seen as adding to the virulence of cycles, which otherwise could be accommodated more easily by price and wage changes. Needless to say the reformed economy would adapt itself to cycles by a much greater flexibility upwards and downwards of prices and wages.

Finally, the concluding Part Seven deals first with some practical problems that would arise were the principle of collecting rent of land as public revenue carried out (Chapter 27). These are partly transitional problems, partly problems associated with radically changing existing rights. Harold MacMillan once wisely said that there is never any real reform without a change in property rights. There can be little doubt that the great majority of people would benefit from the reform of land law in the UK. Existing rights of tenure could be maintained, even strengthened. Perhaps existing inheritance rights could remain unaltered. The key reform is, of course, the transference of rights to economic rent from private landowners to public authorities, be they central and/or local. Yet even those landowners who surrendered the right to rent might, in the course to time, come to appreciate the general rise in physical and moral well-being of the community in which they live, and to find their own place in it as productive and enterprising individuals, as some have already.

Plato is quoted near the beginning of this book. His great theme of justice in the *Republic* returns to complete it (Chapter 28). Nowadays Economics is rarely studied in relation to justice. If this book contributes even slightly to a closer connection between them in the minds of readers then it has well satisfied the purposes of the author.

PART ONE

Principles

CHAPTER 1

Economic Freedom

ECONOMICS as a subject of serious study has grown up within modern societies that have been deeply affected by land enclosure and the industrial revolution. In Britain the work of Adam Smith, Ricardo and Malthus achieved fame during the decades when a final great wave of land enclosure gathered pace and the new industrial towns forged weapons for the Napoleonic wars and capital for the railway age. Such an origin has coloured the development of economic thought ever since. The apparent diminution in the part played by land in the economy, the accumulation and enhanced productivity of capital, the need for an expansion of financial resources and for the growth of limited liability companies, and above all the idea of labour as primarily employed rather than autonomous, all these outstanding features of the new industrial economy gave rise to concepts in the study of Economics which have become entrenched. It is time that such concepts were re-examined.

The ideas that have emerged from 200 years of intellectual advance in Economics centre upon the question of production. After an initial period, especially associated with the writings of Ricardo, when distribution of the product between economic classes or factors was the major concern, most economists accepted the conclusion that production was the key issue. How could it be measured? What inhibited its growth? What determined its composition? Why did it fluctuate in cycles? After all, both political conservatives and political radicals have finally agreed that it is better to have a bigger cake than to quarrel over much about shares in a smaller one. Production has become the yardstick by which almost every economic policy is assessed, even though science and technology have more or less solved the technical problems of how to produce. And yet economic unease remains, sometimes amounting to disease, in the economic organisms of advanced economies. Could it be that to look almost exclusively at

3

production is to fail to understand the many-sided aspects of human economic behaviour, including non-technical ones about production itself?

To what then should economists turn as the central issue of their subject? Where better to look than to the genius of Plato, whose initial outline of the State is that of a single economy. For the theme of the *Republic* is justice, which is surely the touchstone for any economic study that might arrive at conclusions of permanent benefit to all.

> You remember the original principle which we were always laying down as the foundation of the State, that one man should practise one thing only, the thing to which his nature was best adapted; – now justice is this principle or a part of it ...
>
> Plato, *Republic*, Book IV, p.433, trans. B. Jowett, Random House, New York, 1937

Many of the ills of modern society, extending beyond those strictly economic, flow from the disregard of this root concept of the work appropriate to each person's nature. So accustomed have we become to the idea of work as an unfortunate necessity, as a means to earn a living, as wage-labour, that we forget its essential character as the prime means of self-expression for most people in society, whether employees, employers, unemployed or owners, men and women alike. Frustration, depression, even neurosis accompany its neglect; greed, laziness, carelessness invade the workplace; unemployment, inefficiency, loss of production beset the economy.

No one doubts that the small minority of people who are able, for whatever reason, to practise what they love doing, what they are naturally talented to do, are happy in their work and usually in their lives. Self-employed workers who are artists, craftsmen or members of a learned profession, for example, usually exhibit a degree of commitment, interest and enjoyment in their work rarely found amongst employees, especially those with little opportunity to choose the type and conditions of their employment. Few indeed are those who would claim to find a deep and lasting freedom through work. Yet such economic freedom, which is distinct from the civil freedom under laws which prevent assault, imprisonment or defamation, should be available to everyone in a well-governed society.

Were people thus free to create with hands and heart and mind whatever they choose to offer to society in return for their own share in its wealth, there would be few problems of production. The economics of society would become the economics of abundance.

History abounds with examples of the much greater productivity of free labour compared with that of slaves. Freedom is the one great incentive to produce, exceeding by far the paltry 'rewards' offered to workers in unfree conditions in the form of overtime, bonuses, perks or promotion. Nor do men and women who find fulfilment in work usually seek to accumulate riches beyond their reasonable needs. They do not have the inclination, or even the time, to exploit others; they do not wish to live off the labour of others, for that would be to deny their own economic freedom, found in the pursuit of what they love. Devotion would characterise their work, as it does even now for some to whom service to the community transcends hard and often unrecognised effort.

The ideal of economic freedom of this kind is not a dream, though it may be a vision. Indeed, it is an economy in which people are treated as a means to others' ends, such as profits, that is the dream. How such a state of illusion originated and grew is a matter for historians of ideas; but what conditions enable it to be perpetuated now is a proper subject for economists. Let our enquiry then be, 'Under what conditions is economic freedom at present denied, and under what conditions may it be, in the course of time, fulfilled?'

CHAPTER 2

Natural Law

But when we Stoics say that the universe is formed and governed by nature, we do not mean that it is just stuck together mechanically, like a lump of earth or a piece of stone or something of that sort, but organically, like a tree or an animal in which there is nothing haphazard but an appearance of order which is akin to art.

Cicero, *The Nature of the Gods*, pp.156-7; trans. H.C.P. McGregor, Penguin, London, 1972

IT IS A MARKED feature of the scientific culture that has emerged in the Western world since the 17th century that the physical sciences have discovered natural laws of great scope and explanatory power, whilst the social sciences have achieved less. This has led to much debate about whether they are sciences at all and to the formulation of statistical generalisations to fill the gap. Laws are both universal and necessary; statistical generalisations or correlations do not meet such strict requirements. Hence Economics in particular has become a 'soft' science characterised by a great deal of opinion, vagueness, and disagreement. As one American President said, he wanted a one armed economist as an adviser, because all the economists he ever met kept saying 'on the one hand ... but on the other hand ...'.

Too often economists look to the outer manifestations of their subject matter, rather than to its inner qualities. Natural scientists do not so often make this mistake, as the immense growth of such subjects as nuclear physics and biochemistry demonstrates. Since natural laws are expressions of the nature of things, be they physical objects or human beings, it is to human nature that any social scientist should look in order to find the laws that govern both individual action and social phenomena. Since the investigator is a man himself, the student of human nature has the advantage of looking both within himself, as well as at the behaviour of others, for evidence.

6

Of course, this raises problems of subjectivity, but a detached observer is in principle able to observe both inner and outer phenomena with an impartial eye. It may be difficult to turn aside from, say, entrenched political attitudes and from deep personal feelings when investigating social phenomena, but the opportunity is there. Thus the social scientist needs to train himself to observe the concepts, beliefs and prejudices in his own mind. Thereby he may obtain at least a valid degree of objectivity. Ultimately, he relies upon the truth that Man's nature is universal, that all men and women are fundamentally the same, so that the more he avoids identifying his own personal attitudes with objective facts, the more he penetrates towards the truth about himself and therefore about humanity. This is the greatest blessing of social science, not its greatest bane, as is often supposed. Other problems, like the impossibility of precise experiment and the inexhaustible range of variables beloved by modern social scientists, remain. Yet such problems often arise from ignoring certain fundamental and incontrovertible facts about mankind. One example illustrates clearly that this ignorance may stem from vested interests, which directly or indirectly influence economists' investigation. It is an unquestionable fact that everyone needs land to live on and – for most people – to work on. However, the economic consequences of this fact, such as its effect upon the distribution of income, are substantially overlooked.

What then do we mean by natural laws that arise from human nature? We may begin our analysis with a brief discussion of seven examples fundamental in any economy, which enter into the discussion developed in later chapters. They concern work, land, co-operation, capital, credit, surplus and freedom.

Work

First and simplest is that people desire to express themselves through work. Every human society at all times and places exhibits this desire. The conditions under which work takes place are manifold; they range from peasant coffee bean growers of South America to the Princeton laboratory of Albert Einstein, but everywhere at all times the vast majority of people work from an inner necessity. Particularly since the industrial revolution, work has become associated with wage-labour. Even so the unemployed man or woman often becomes desperate to work again, not just for an income, but for personal satisfaction. Even those whose work is of a frustrating and unsuitable nature retain a strong desire for work itself, unless they are finally driven into a state of abject hopelessness. Modern technology may reduce hours of work and years of employment, but those who acquire more leisure time are often singularly keen to take on productive and creative activities. We all recognise how, in the film *The Bridge on the River Kwai*, British prisoners of the Japanese, forced to work in appalling conditions on the notorious 'Burma Road', became proud of the bridge they built. Except for a philosopher perhaps, it is acutely distressing to do nothing at all.

Land

Human nature also requires land. Indeed all the elements of earth, air, water and fire, in the form of sunlight, are essential. Questions now arise in modern Economics about the availability of unpolluted air and access to water, but the freedom of the latter three elements has generally been beyond dispute. It is the earth, or land, which is most contentious. As economists have long recognised, land is best defined to include both the dry surface of the earth and natural resources within, on and above it. These include such vital products as oil and metal deposits. Land in this inclusive sense is needed for all productive processes, in short for work, but equally it is needed as living space. These primary requirements of human existence – work and space – make the conditions under which land is available of fundamental significance to individuals and to society. Variations in those conditions shape the economic development of a community. If, for example, land is held under absolute private ownership, the economy usually exhibits the accumulation of vast wealth in the hands of a minority; if, on the other hand, it is held absolutely by the government authorities, as in the Soviet Union, the power of the State over individuals' lives becomes overwhelming. These consequences are the operation of natural law. Economic historians are aware of this, as their analysis of societies like feudal Europe exhibit, but for whatever reason – vested interest is one – economists regard conditions of land tenure as legal studies or, at best, land economy, and fail to see the implications. The effect upon the distribution of income, for instance, is largely obscured by leaving capital payments for freehold land out of account, even though these are, in fact, merely the capitalisation of a series of annual rents. Similarly the differential between urban and rural land values is mainly ignored, although crucial in understanding a modern economy.

Co-operation

Work on land is the basis of every economy, but natural law extends also to the character of work. By nature people vary greatly in their inherent talents, capacity for learning, and adaptation to circumstances. Social conditions, education, training, personal wealth and much else determine what kind of work an individual may choose or be compelled to follow; yet by nature each will be urged in particular directions. As Adam Smith – or perhaps Plato – was the first to emphasise, such specialisation by ability is greatly enhanced by constant practice. Smith himself argued that an inherent desire to exchange generated the need to specialise, rather than the reverse (*The Wealth of Nations*, Volume I, Chapter 2, p.12, Everyman, London, 1953). Whatever the direction of causality, however, it is certain that specialisation and exchange are interdependent. Exchange is a form of co-operation, which leads to organisation in working groups, like firms and other bodies. Within organisations, as the word implies by analogy with a living body, there is an exchange of products. Human gregariousness strengthens this process. Natural sympathy and the desire for company underpin the economic phenomena of co-operation.

Capital

Human nature finds expression also in each individual's attempt to satisfy his or her desires with the least effort. Everyone walks from A to B by the least arduous route, unless there is a special reason for choosing otherwise, such as scenic beauty; nor will someone dig a field twice when once is sufficient, or write two cheques when one is enough. Upon this principle rests the oft-quoted definition of Economics as the study of the allocation of scarce resources to alternative uses. Why not allocate them irrationally? Reason demands the most efficient use of means to given ends. Waste is unreasonable and defies the principle of least effort. Co-operation, however, gives to the desire for efficiency a special and most influential means, namely the use of capital. For mankind's ingenuity long ago discovered the use of tools, which embody the intention to economise on effort. A spade saves the labour of hands, a telephone the labour of travelling, an atomic power station the labour of mining and transportation. Capital as the use of produced wealth in the production of further wealth is the natural progression of this principle of least effort. Roundabout ways of producing are intended to be, and often are, efficient in human labour. So the existence of capital is merely the natural consequence of a universal desire. The present day confusion of real capital with financial instruments, like shares, bonds and so on, greatly obscures this fact.

Credit

All production, of course, takes time, even if it is not roundabout. Using capital tends initially to extend the time of production, if the creation of capital goods is included in the measurement. Growing a crop takes a season; manufacturing agricultural machinery adds time to the production cycle. What follows from this is that all production of necessity requires credit. What does the producer eat and wear whilst he produces? He is fed and clothed by others, with whom he exchanges his product either directly or indirectly via the use of an intermediary like money. Exchange itself involves credit, for who hands over his product first? One must wait and trust the other party to deliver his product in return. Even the use of a stakeholder to hold the goods on behalf of both parties means that the stakeholder himself must be trusted. Giving credit indeed means extending belief that the other party will pay. Without such belief production would cease, for society depends upon exchange and all productive processes take time.

Surplus

There remains one example of natural law which concerns whole societies and not individuals as such. Except in quite exceptional periods of social distress during war, plagues or other far-reaching disasters, an economy produces a surplus over and above what individuals need to support themselves and their dependants. Even in disaster a society retains this potential creative power. The surplus does not include capital formation, since this is a cost of production attributable to the period for which the capital is in productive use. But social infrastructure may be created out of a surplus; so also may 'non-productive' projects like cathedrals, monasteries, works of art, space probes and nuclear weapons. Culture, religion and warfare are perhaps historically the main contenders for the use of the surplus. In Periclean Athens a large share went into the provision of public works of art; medieval Europe built huge churches; in the twentieth century many countries accumulated massive armaments.

One question, especially, arises concerning this surplus. Is it the property of the whole community or is it private property? The answer depends primarily upon each society's beliefs about the origin of the surplus. When general belief, for example, credits private landowners with creating the value of land, then they are usually allowed to keep this part of the social surplus. Or when the belief was that God is the source of all creation, including economic output, the surplus was used to construct great cathedrals to his glory. In every case beliefs about how the surplus arises and to what use it should be put are fundamental tests of the values and quality of life of that society. A recent newspaper article highlighted the question of the respective claims of individuals and the community upon the use of the surplus.

> What is still lacking, even in the highest political circles, is a fair conceptual understanding of the difference between the public and private sectors ... it [the public sector] is concerned with the universal ends of society rather than with the particular ends of individuals.
>
> Michael Prowse in the *The Financial Times* (weekend) 26/27 May 2001, p.xxii

And as a recent book by two leading American economists says:

> It is the legitimacy of the public sector within capitalism that lies at the core of the contemporary crisis of vision.
>
> R. Heilbroner and W. Milberg, *The Crisis of Vision in Modern Economic Thought*,
> p.120, CUP, 1995

Freedom

Finally, let us return to economic freedom. Freedom of self-expression, or freedom to be creative, is a gift of nature and of God. It is not the privilege of a few. The 'dismal science' that has followed the teaching of Malthus, and which emphasises the concept of scarcity, would have us believe that only a minority can find fulfilment in rich and rewarding work. Human nature speaks otherwise when it commands men and women to search within for the source of their creativity, and to ask from one another and from those who govern them that they be ruled, not by power or opinion but by justice. Ideals are not unrealistic, though illusions are. One of the greatest idealists of the Florentine Renaissance, Marsilio Ficino, grounded his beliefs upon an understanding of human nature, which offers a vision to economists of the new millennium:

> It was not for small things but for great that God created men, who, knowing the great, are not satisfied with small things. Indeed it was for the limitless alone that He created men, who are the only beings on earth to have rediscovered their infinite nature and who are not fully satisfied by anything limited, however, great that thing.
>
> *The Letters of Marsilio Ficino*, Vol. 4, p.10,
> trans. School of Economic Science, Shepheard-Walwyn, London 1988

To search for the unlimited within oneself is to plumb the depths of one's own capacity. The craftsman who seeks perfection in wood carving, the nurse who tends her patient with love and care, the manager who aims at efficiency with benefit for customers and workers alike, all find freedom through work. For to realise the potential of one's nature is freedom. The recognition of that law is essential to a well-founded science of Economics.

These seven examples of natural law, concerning work, land, co-operation, capital, credit, economic surplus and freedom are not selected at random. All lie at the core of the subject of Economics. They are, needless to say, in no way a definitive list of natural laws pertaining to the subject. Others are perhaps as fundamental, such as the long established laws of diminishing returns and supply and demand, and more contentious ones concerning rent, the role of money and the level of wages. The formulation of natural law is fraught with difficulties. Counter examples are evident, which on examination are in fact law-like, as in physical science when a change in conditions leads to quite different observation of effects. For all laws operate within sets of conditions. Citing cases of men not working, living in outer space, failing to co-operate and so on is a challenge to explain why.

Nor are laws known directly by sense perception or by superficial introspection, for their force is derived from an inner power, inherent in nature. Hence they are a potential, a necessity to act rationally in ways which may be outwardly inhibited or obstructed, but which remain potent and effective. The twentieth century, influenced both by Freud and by a narrow concept of consciousness as immediate aware-ness, has generally thought of inner powers as irrational and even brutish. But perhaps they are in truth rational, creative and even divine. Perhaps, like St Paul, we should all come to see ourselves, not as prisoners, but as free men and women. For freedom is found, not in opposition to natural law, but in recognition of it.

CHAPTER 3

The Significance of Land

This earth is *pushan* (he who nourishes), for it feeds everything everywhere.
Brihadaranyaka Upanishad I, iv, 13, in *Ten Principal Upanishads*, p.122,
trans. Shree Purohit Swami and W.B. Yeats

Land is the factor of production that nature supplies ...
Begg, Fischer and Dornbusch, *Economics*, p.200, McGraw-Hill, UK, 1997

THIS DEFINITION by modern economists is very comprehensive, for it includes all that nature offers in the form of the
earth, whatever is found on it, growing and living upon it in a
wild state and even what is above it in the form of water, air and light.
In short, it includes the natural elements of earth, air, water and
sunshine; in other words, our whole natural environment. The depend-
ence of humanity upon these is, of course, absolute. What matters for
the subject of Economics is the question of access to them, which is
in practice a matter of access to the dry surface of the earth, where
people live for more or less the whole of their lives. Indeed, it could
be said that Economics is especially concerned with a fifth element,
namely space itself.

Plato was well aware of the primary importance of laws regarding
land to the welfare of the State:

But they to whom God has given, as He has to us, to be the founders
of a new State as yet free from enmity – that they should create themselves enmities by their mode of distributing lands and houses, would
be superhuman folly and wickedness.
Plato, *Laws*, Book V, 737, trans. B. Jowett, Random House, New York, 1937

Nor did he abandon hope for States which had allowed such enmities
to develop. The way of escape, the only way, he warned, was to hold
to 'freedom from avarice and a sense of justice' (Plato, *ibid.*, Book V,
737).

No one can reasonably argue that land is unimportant. Without land a nation cannot exist. Individuals of necessity use land for their work and homes. Man is a territorial animal. So much is indisputable. What is less obvious is the emphasis given by Plato to 'the mode of distributing lands'. Intuitively it may be evident that the method of distribution of such an essential requirement for human life is bound to have serious implications for society. Equally an intuitive 'sense of justice' may tell us that some distributions will be just and others unjust. Some obvious examples confirm what intuition tells us.

In the Soviet Union the State, under Communist Party control, owned and administered almost all land, including collective farms, which nominally were vested in the collective farmers. Effectively this meant that virtually all workers were under State control. Soviet power was not just a matter of political dictatorship; it demonstrated also how economic freedom is denied if land monopoly exists, even if exercised by the State in the name of the people. For the ownership of land carries with it the right to deny access to it; hence if the State, or an individual, or a class or group, own all or much of the land the majority of the people may be excluded from its use or benefit.

Nearer home, vast areas of Scotland are owned by a small minority of landowners, many of whose claims arose from the breaking up of the clan system after 1745 and from the vast enclosures, largely for sheep pasturing, forced through with violence and suffering in the following century. The resulting huge concentrations of population in Glasgow and other cities are now accepted as a normal state of affairs. The associated problems of housing, employment, public services and crime are rarely related to the question of the 'mode of distributing lands', yet this indeed is their origin.

The huge expansion of London in the past 200 years has the same basic cause, although, of course, as the metropolis it was bound to grow. Land enclosure, associated with the agrarian revolution, especially from about 1760 to 1850, was responsible for the mass migration of population from the rural areas, as in Scotland. Today the present state of this land distribution has a constant effect of profound significance. Urban land values have risen in real terms by very large amounts since the Second World War. Whoever owns freehold property in London has grown relatively rich compared to non-owners. Often this means that the older generation has grown very much richer than the younger. Whatever the age or class distribution of ownership the fact is that there has been an immense shift in favour of owners. Housing the non-owners, mortgage problems, the inability of essential workers, like nurses, to afford homes, and many related

issues are consequences of this land distribution. So is the problem of
land needed for public services, like transport and recreation. The high
cost of urban roads is also a direct function of land prices.

Conditions of Land Ownership

Such examples demonstrate the importance of the distribution of land
in terms of who owns it. Are the shares of land owned by individuals
or institutions, including the State, fairly equal or not in quantity and,
more pertinently, in value? But distribution of land involves much
more than the issue of who owns it. To ask who does, or should, own
land assumes that the whole matter concerns ownership, whereas the
conditions under which ownership is exercised have an even greater
impact on society. Unconditional, or absolute, ownership of land is
very different from ownership subject to duties to others.

As a recent writer has put it;

> Land owners became increasingly hostile to constraints upon their
> exclusive use of property; they wished to reduce ownership to a single,
> pre-eminent right to the use of the property which would allow them
> to exploit 'their' land without restraint ...
>
> M.J. Daunton, *Progress and Poverty*, pp.69-70, OUP, 1995

Moreover, an analysis of the concept of ownership soon makes clear
that the rights which constitute it each have separate effects. For
example, the right to hold valuable land out of use for long periods is
socially damaging. Further discussion of these complex questions of
principle is best left until later. Meanwhile they serve to illustrate that
Plato's assertion about the mode of distribution of lands is fully
justified. Exactly how land is distributed lies at the centre of any worthwhile study of Economics. Without it the subject becomes merely a
set of variations played upon the theme of the *status quo*, analogous to
the study of epicycles in Ptolemaic astronomy, where the overriding
principle of an earth-centred universe was left unquestioned. Let us
question the existing 'mode of distributing lands'.

Land as a Factor of Production

Reference to almost any modern text book on Economics reveals a
serious neglect of land as a factor of production. *Economics* by Begg,
Fischer and Dornbusch devotes 8 pages out of 605 to the subject.
Such an enormously influential book as Keynes' *General Theory of
Employment, Interest and Money* refers to land briefly four times. More-
over, information concerning the value of the land and, in particular,

its rental value is seriously deficient. In the United Kingdom national accounts (Office for National Statistics, *The Blue Book*) rent is greatly undervalued for a range of reasons. It does not include the value of the beneficial rent of owner/occupiers, both householders and commercial. Firms that hold freehold or leasehold property may be receiving a large part of their income in rent, which is disguised in their turnover. In addition, when freehold or leasehold land changes hands for a capital payment, this does not appear as rent in the national accounts, because of accounting conventions about measuring income, yet in economic terms the capital payment is a once and for all premium paid for the right to receive all or some future rent. Hence, for the seller of the freehold or lease it is simply an advance payment of rent. In short, accountants, including national accountants in government service, generally measure money flows and not economic categories. Text books are quick to point this out in principle – for example, see Begg, etc. *Economics*, p.94 – but rarely include rent of land as a separate category in their subsequent analysis.

In modern economic theory land is more or less excluded, though its importance in early theorists, like Ricardo, is acknowledged. It is usually taken initially to be a distinct factor of production alongside labour, capital and, sometimes, entrepreneurship; but then largely drops out of the analysis. This is justified on two grounds: that it is no longer a major factor in production, and that it can be subsumed in theory under capital. The misleading consequences of both of these assumptions are discussed in detail later, but a few indications are given now.

'Investment' in the theory of income determination is defined as 'the purchase of new capital goods by firms' (Begg, *ibid.*, p.326). This item then enters the circular flow chart and plays a crucial role in the analysis which demonstrates equilibrium when savings equal investment, or when all withdrawals equals all injections in models that include foreign and government sectors. Expenditure by firms on land is thus effectively ignored. Yet when a firm buys a new office or factory the cost of the land often exceeds the capital cost of the buildings. This would not matter greatly if expenditure on land had the same effect as that on capital, but since land is not produced, its purchase does not create a stream of income payments to workers. Hence there is a dissimilar multiplier effect. Furthermore, expenditure on land tends to raise land prices, since land has an inelastic supply. Further implications arise if one considers that borrowing to finance 'investment' may be for land or for capital purchase. Money created by the banking system to finance land purchases may be highly inflationary.

Land in the Theory of the Firm

The whole subject of micro-economics also suffers from a failure to include a rigorous analysis of the role of land. It is usually assumed that firms operate in a non-spatial economy, where differences of location are excluded from the analysis. Yet location may be the most important influence on costs and/or revenues. Economists, for example, recognise that the perfect competition model is rarely applicable, whilst not often noticing that differential location is what commonly invalidates it. Similarly the theory of monopolistic competition is careful to include differentials arising from branded goods, advertising etc. and careless about locational differences.[1] Likewise, oligopoly in practice often arises from causes related to land, as in the case of markets controlled by a few multi-national companies or of supermarkets dominating a retail market. As for monopoly itself, many monopolists are directly in control of the source of production, like a mine, or have acquired sites possessing monopoly power, such as the freehold land of a housing estate. As Eaton and Lipsey say:

> Our general conclusions then are that space matters; that space matters a great deal; that many phenomena that appear inexplicable when inserted into a spaceless model are explicable in a spatial model; that space deserves a central rather than a peripheral position (the metaphor is conscious) in neo-classical value theory ...   *Ibid*, p.65

Land and Factor Incomes

A third area of modern theory where confusion arises over land is in the analysis of factor incomes. Land is frequently treated as an homogenous factor, when in fact its non-homogeneity is both apparent and far reaching. 'Homogenous land requires that all natural resources be available in the same proportions in all land in the economy' (Eaton and Lipsey, *ibid.*, n.8, p.65), an utterly impossible condition. Land values reflect the huge degree to which land is heterogeneous. Central urban land in the UK may be valued at 100,000% of agricultural land. To treat land as homogenous in an analysis that allocates land between competing uses is therefore grossly misleading (Begg, *ibid.*, p.212).

---

1 This is not true of research by economists like B. Curtis Eaton and R.G. Lipsey, who have examined spatial implications at length. See their *On the Foundations of Monopolistic Competition and Economic Geography*, Edward Elgar, Cheltenham, 1997.

At best such an analysis should refer only to marginal land, where its value may be similar in competing uses. Incomes from land are liable to distortion in any case, owing to their misclassification as profits or capital payments (see above, p.16).

Why has Land been Overlooked?

Why then has land been rendered insignificant in modern economic theory? To explain this fully would require a thorough study of the history of economic thought, at least since Adam Smith. J.S. Mill was the last major economist to take serious account of land, if one excludes Henry George, who understood its importance thoroughly but remained outside mainstream analysis. Since Mill, economists have justified their virtual exclusion of land from models and theories in both micro- and macro-economics in various ways. Difficulties of definition have played a part. Again Begg is admirably concise: 'land is the factor of production that nature supplies' (Begg, *ibid.*, p.200). But such breadth leaves the elements of air, water and sunshine within the scope of land. Since these are free goods, effectively in infinite supply, a more useful definition would limit land to the surface of the earth and finite natural resources above and below it, like minerals and, perhaps, air space. When improvements are made to land in this sense, as in the case of irrigation or draining, problems arise about the distinction between capital and land. Hence much modern theory takes the easy way out by treating land as capital for the purposes of analysis.

A further reason is the misleading assimilation of rent of land to other kinds of surplus, such as rent of ability and, in general, to the excess of income over transfer earnings for any factor of production. Thus rent of land is treated as a sub-class of rent and quasi-rent, which seems to reduce its theoretical significance (see Chapter 9). Combined with the under measurement of rent of land, this enables most economists to relegate land itself to a minor aspect of the subject.

Thirdly, the accumulation of capital and associated technological growth have enabled capital as a factor to eclipse land in the imagination of economists. Were greater attention given to the real world, it would be evident that land remains paramount as the factor, which with labour, yields an output of goods and services. Capital, however extensive, is still merely the instrument of labour. Even in a most capital intensive industry, like car production, labour on land is what creates value by using 'bought-in' material of all kinds, which includes capital in the form of machinery and so on. However, the illusion that capital has superseded land in importance continues to dominate

economic thinking. Capital/labour models abound; production
functions ignore land. Capital/output ratios similarly are employed in
growth models, even for third world economies where the fundamental role of land is all too obvious.

An anecdote provided by a colleague illustrates the careless way in
which modern economists wrongly identify land with capital. Some
years ago a group of people, including some academic economists,
were visiting the area of east London where the docklands development was about to commence. One of the party, who was not a
professional economist but understood how enormously valuable the
land there would become as the development proceeded, exclaimed,
'Look at that land!' Whereupon an economist replied, 'Ah, yes, it's land
now, but soon it will all be buildings and roads!'

Beyond the technical reasons why the concept of land has been
largely excluded from theory, there is the more contentious question
of vested interests. Even Adam Smith may have withdrawn from
clearly advocating a land tax in view of his employment by the Duke
of Buccleuch, a great landowner in Scotland. More recently, the
general climate of opinion against examining objectively the economic
use of unconditional ownership of land has influenced economists as
much as it has politicians. Vested interests in land no longer consist of
a handful of great landowners, plus a few thousand country squires.
Major companies, including of course multi-nationals, control land of
unprecedented value in the centre of cities and in distant oil and
mining regions. Pension funds draw most of the populations of Western countries into indirect ownership of such land. Property-owning
democracies encourage every family to get a stake in the land, and
rises in its value tie them to a source of apparent wealth which may
outdo their own labour. 'My land' has become imbedded as a watch-
word of freedom and democracy. Yet nothing could be further from
the truth. It is incumbent upon economists, as students of natural law,
to set aside such influences and look objectively and clearly at how
things are.

Green Questions about Land
In apparent contrast to the issue of land in Economics, questions
about land use and the care of land have now become prominent as
a result of public interest in global warming and other 'green' matters.
Scientists assure us that there is every prospect of large areas of land
being flooded as polar ice melts. Land will thus become in shorter
supply, and hence its value will rise generally, with more economically

viable locations showing exceptional rises. At the same time, there is a growing outcry against the waste of resources, so that more efficient use of land, particularly sources of minerals, including fuels, is already demanded. The rate of extraction will become a vital issue as finite resources are depleted. As substitutes are found, the sites where they are mined or utilized will grow in importance. Renewable resources, like wind and tide power, hydro-electricity, even energy from the sun, all require sites for their exploitation, so that these might gradually replace mining sites as the most valuable resource locations.

On the other hand, pollution is also looming large in the public mind. In a country like the UK, significant amounts of land are now used for landfill. This removes it from other uses, thus putting greater pressure on non-polluted areas. Industrial pollution is now better controlled, which reflects greater concern for the environment generally, but more specifically for the overriding resource of land itself.

Yet there remains little awareness amongst both experts and public that all these issues – global warming, wastage, siting energy resources and pollution – cannot be properly dealt with in the absence of right thinking about the conditions under which land is held. They are all a function to varying degrees of the system of land tenure. Absolute private ownership carries the right to neglect, waste or pollute land, and, crucially, to hold it out of use. Absolute public ownership carries the right of the public authorities to do the same. Somewhere in between these extremes lies a natural balance between the rights of the individual and those of the community in relation to land. That balance can only be found by considering the duties attached to holding land, both of private and public land-holders. This book will say a great deal about the duty related to the rent of land. But it is of great importance also that the duty to keep the land in good condition is recognised as fundamental. This condition, that the land-holder should care for the land, by refraining from neglect, waste or pollution, is the key to many of the currently potent 'green' issues. For it is the land-holder upon whom such behaviour is incumbent. No amount of campaigning, exhortation or even legislation will succeed in actually changing people's behaviour towards land, unless the land-holders themselves – individuals and corporate or public bodies – take seriously their duties of care. However much the public may demand improvements, people themselves as land-holders have to take the requisite steps. Freeholders, leaseholders and occupiers all have to undertake to look after the land they hold.

It follows that changes in conditions of tenancy that are conducive to a new benevolent attitude towards land are central to any substantial economic reform. Who cares for land well – absentee landlords or owner-occupiers? Directors of public companies remote from the sites being exploited or self-employed workers whose livelihood depends on the welfare of the sites they use? Public authorities under centralised national control or those regionally or locally based? Such questions are not only matters of law and government. They are fundamental to the economy and how it works for the good of all. Economists can no longer treat the system of land tenure as a *datum*. How land is owned and used is as important for Economics as how labour is owned and used.

PART TWO

The Theory of the Firm
Re-Examined

CHAPTER 4

Perfect Competition

S INCE THE 'Keynesian revolution' of the mid 20th century, macro-economics has held the field as the most interesting and vital area of the subject, particularly because of an obvious connection with policy making. Micro-economic issues, such as 'What determines relative prices?', 'What is the optimum size of the firm?' and 'Do long-run costs within firms always rise?' have become academic. Yet micro-economics underlies the macro-economics. Concepts beloved by macro-economists, like aggregate supply and demand and the invest-ment/savings schedule, rest upon rarely questioned assumptions about individual firms. Supply curves are ultimately the summation of indi-vidual firms' cost curves, with allowances for external economies and diseconomies. Similarly aggregate demand has an impact on the economy only through individual firms' demand curves. The whole economy is more than the sum of its parts, as Keynes so effectively showed, but the nature of the parts profoundly influences the total outcome, even though it may not determine it. Physiologists may insist that the human body be studied as a whole organism, yet they do not neglect study of individual organs.

The following analysis of the firm begins with perfect competition, continues with monopolistic competition and monopoly, and con-cludes with oligopoly. The intellectual rigour of the traditional analy-sis is considerable, but it fails in one major respect. Starting from the premise that there are three factors of production – land, labour and capital, and perhaps a fourth, entrepreneurship – it proceeds to omit land from the analysis. Sometimes this is done deliberately on the grounds that land and capital exhibit identical characteristics within the theory, as though the benefits of simplicity are gained without loss of accuracy; sometimes unwittingly, when labour and capital are used throughout as a two sector model. It is, however, a serious error to subsume land under the heading of capital. Rent of land has fundamentally different characteristics from income derived from capital (indeed whether capital 'earns' any income at all is questionable. See Chapter 11). The following analysis re-introduces land as an independent factor in the theory of the firm in order to achieve greater realism. Nothing could be less realistic than a space-less firm or indeed a space-less economy. Only theorists who are engaged in logical analysis to the total neglect of ordinary empirical observation could seriously imagine that space-less theories offer realistic answers.

The Firm as a Productive Unit

What then is the firm? The obvious and conventional answer refers to the legal entities of the sole trader, partnership or limited company. Since companies, especially, may produce in many locations, problems arise about the shape of cost curves. A central difficulty is that economies of scale may be exhausted in one location, giving a rising long-run average cost curve and therefore a determinate solution to the question of size, but a firm may replicate its buildings, plant and machinery at other locations. Can it then expand indefinitely at constant long-run costs, leaving the question of size indeterminate? Experience suggests that this is possible. Equilibria for the firm and industry then seem impossible to establish and theories of oligopoly and monopoly become paramount as explanations.

Another approach is possible. Firms may be defined spatially. A firm then becomes a unit of production at one location only. If legal conditions are not set in stone as data which the economist does not question, the multi-plant limited liability company may no longer appear to be the most suitable and efficient kind of unit. Advantages like technical economies of scale at one location become more distinct from advantages of legal ownership, like financial benefits from jointly managing many sites. Gains for owners are often not gains for the economy, as much recent market failure analysis indicates.

Indeed from the standpoint of empirical observation firms defined by location are the obvious units of production. A factory or department store is obviously a workplace occupied by labour of many types, including managers, who receive input to the site and produce output which leaves the site. Work on the site yields value added. Stringing such units together under the title of one firm must make any analysis more complicated. Why should economists be bound by legal or accounting conventions? The definition of legal tender, for example, does not bind them to one definition of money. Nor do accountant's terms for costs and profits suit economists. The following analysis of the firm therefore adopts as a definition 'a unit of production located in one place'.

Differences between firms arising from location can now be more readily identified. Propositions like Begg's (p.147), 'in the long run all firms or potential entrants to any industry have access to the same cost curves' are shown to be extremely unrealistic. Though firms at locations with similar conditions may fulfil this requirement, most industries contain firms on sites of quite different quality. These differences of location within an industry (and between industries) have far reaching effects long ignored by conventional analysis.

Perfect Competition
The theory of perfect competition has held a key place in economic theory for a long time, despite increasing criticism of its application to actual firms or economies. Its resilience owes much to the simple logic of its arguments and to the apparently equitable nature of its conclusions, especially when compared with various degrees of monopoly power. If the factor of land is introduced fully into the analysis both these aspects remain, but with enhanced realism. Many phenomena about firms 'that appear inexplicable when inserted into a spaceless model are explicable in a spatial model' (Eaton and Lipsey above, p.17).

Briefly, the modern theory of perfect competition makes four main assumptions: that all products in the industry are homogenous; that there are many buyers and sellers, each small in relation to the industry, who act entirely independently of each other; that buyers have complete information about products and prices, and are not therefore deceived into thinking that a product is better or worse than another; and that there is free entry and exit for all actual and prospective firms in the industry. These conditions imply that each firm faces a horizontal demand curve for its output, although, of course, the industry demand curve slopes downwards. Each firm therefore makes an independent decision about how much to produce, but not about the price at which it sells. Each one is a price-taker. Marginal revenue (MR) for such a firm equals price. The short-run marginal cost curve (SMC) slopes upwards, as the law of diminishing returns operates in relation to fixed factors of production. Where SMC cuts the firms demand curve from below is the profit-maximising output, and therefore the equilibrium output for the firm. In the short run the firm will produce at any output above the intersection of SMC and its short-run average variable cost curve (SAVC), the shut-down point; hence the SMC above this point is its supply curve. The short-run industry supply curve is the horizontal sum of all firms supply curves. Supernormal profits are measured by output times average profit per unit sold (that is price minus short-run average total cost SATC). Normal profits are included in costs.

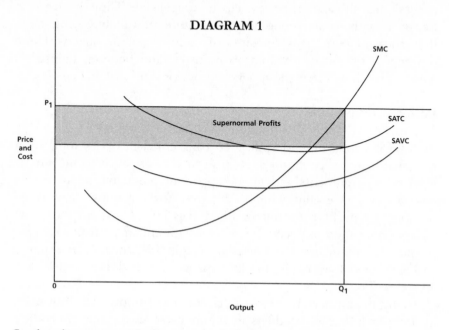

DIAGRAM 1

In the short run each firm in the industry may make different supernormal profits (or losses), because entry and exit to and from the industry is a long-run phenomenon involving a variation of fixed factors of land and capital. Since the scale of operations can change in the long run as land and plant size are varied, the long-run average total cost curve (LATC) becomes an envelope curve around the SATCs representing different plant sizes. Economies and diseconomies of scale give the characteristic U-shaped curve. Each firm then will maximise profits by producing at minimum LATC (equals minimum SATC for that scale). Any other size of output would yield a loss, as price is then tangential to LATC at its minimum point. Long-run marginal cost cuts LATC at the same point (see Diagram 2).

The horizontal summation of firms SMC curves above the SAVC gives the short-run industry supply curve, which therefore slopes upwards. If supernormal profits are available, firms enter the industry in the long run, driving down such profits to zero. Similarly losses are eliminated by the exit of firms. The long-run industry supply curve

DIAGRAM 2

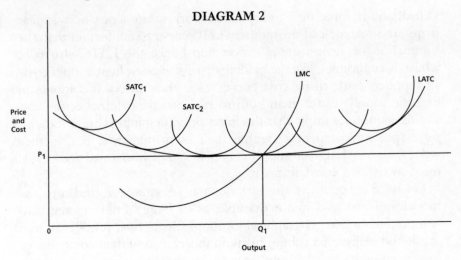

becomes horizontal, subject to external economies or diseconomies. Changes in supply along this curve depend entirely upon variations in the number of firms in the industry. All this is conventional theory (see Begg, Chapter 9 and R.G. Lipsey and K.A. Chrystal, *Positive Economics*, Chapter 12, 8th edition, 1995, OUP).

The long-run equilibrium condition does not necessarily show that all firms in the industry are identical in size or technical conditions of production. The only requirement is that they all operate at an output where LATC is minimum and that this minimum equals price.[1] The firm's U-shaped LATC curve is, of course, problematic. Why need it ever turn upwards? Management diseconomies in very large companies are often cited as a cause. In some industries LATC slopes downwards, owing to continuous increasing returns to scale, so that the demand curve cuts the LATC curve whilst the latter is falling. These are natural monopolies to which the theory of perfect competition does not apply. In other industries LATC would seem to be horizontal at all outputs above those for which economies of scale increase. Such cases raise problems about long-term equilibrium, which are discussed later (see Chapter 18).

In addition, external economies and diseconomies render incorrect the mere summation of individual firms cost curves to give the industry supply curve. External economies, like the gathering of a

1 An exception to this is when entry costs to an industry are significant and thus enable existing firms to make supernormal profits at a point on the upward slope of LATC to the right of minimum LATC, where diminishing returns to scale operate. See M. Blaug, *Economic Theory in Retrospect*, p.361, 5th edn, CUP, 1996.

skilled labour force or a transport network in an area where similar
firms are situated, lead the industry LMC curve to fall further than the
summation of firms supply curves and hence the LATC also falls,
whilst diseconomies, like the bidding up of wages, or higher input costs
as suppliers with rising cost curves raise their prices (i.e. inputs in
inelastic supply) cause them both to rise. Strictly, external economies
and diseconomies imply that the firms providing inputs are not themselves perfect competitors within their own industries. For, if they
were, their own long-run supply curves would be horizontal and enable
them to sell at a constant price.

Let us then consider the introduction of space or land into the
model, not just as a minor example, as in Begg's brief reference to
'a more favourable geographical location' (Begg, *ibid.*, p.129), but as a
major and realistic fact about firms, in this case in perfect competition.
Oddly enough the requisite analysis is already offered by current
theory, when it introduces the concept of the marginal firm. This is
taken to be the firm with the highest costs, indicated initially by higher
SMC, SAVC and SATC (Begg, *ibid.*, p.130; Blaug, *ibid.*, p.358).

DIAGRAM 3

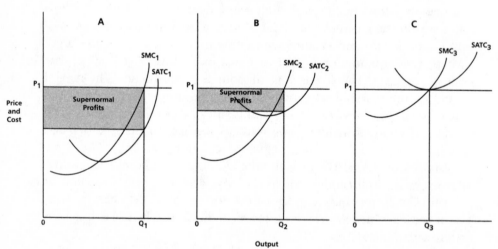

In Diagram 3 firm C is marginal in that it just breaks even in the short
run with SMC3 = SATC3 = P. The other two firms, A and B, are non-
marginal with positive supernormal profits. If demand rises or falls in
the industry, firms move along their SMC curves to a higher or lower
price and output expands or contracts, giving greater or smaller supernormal profits to all, including C. However, it is asserted, free entry

enables firms to enter or leave the industry in the long run. The price rises or falls again to its original level. The industry has moved along its horizontal long-run supply curve, if we ignore external economies and diseconomies.

The key question is whether costs can vary between firms in the long run. The state of technology in the economy at large is taken as a datum, even in the long run, but the innovation of existing technology is a function of the use of capital, including replacement of capital when the latest technology can be introduced. Hence, provided patents and other such restrictions on sharing innovation are ruled out, the latest technology will be a feature of all firms in perfect competition in the long run.[2] On the assumption of perfect knowledge and free access to technology, labour, materials and other inputs, how can any differential costs persist in the long run? As Lipsey says, 'in the pure abstract model of perfect competition, however, all firms are marginal firms in long-run equilibrium. All firms have access to the same technology, and all, therefore, will have identical cost curves when enough time has passed for full adjustment of all capital to be made' (Lipsey and Chrystal, *ibid.*, p.227).

This may be true of capital, but what of land? It is here that the omission of land from the theory, or its false assimilation to capital, gives rise to serious error. Location and the nature of land itself are relatively permanent characteristics, giving rise to persistent cost differentials, for most features of the land and its location do not change, except in relation to the evolution of the whole economy in a length of time usually in excess of any time period practical for analysis. The size and distribution of population, for example, must be taken as data, if any reasonable analysis of the firm is to be undertaken.

Examples of Land Differentials

Consider the following examples. In agriculture farms producing cereals operate on land of different fertility. Similarly, dairy farms may occur on lush Herefordshire pastures or on hilly land in north Wales. In mining, minerals may be dug out of shallow, easily accessible seams or deep, complex ones. In the fishing industry, some ports may be much closer to seasonal shoals of fish than others, or have more equable conditions of weather, tides etc. In manufacturing, some firms may be particularly close to raw materials, labour and power. Moreover, a firm may have monopoly power over local suppliers, or even

2 There may be 'waves' that cause firms to leave and enter the industry as capital wears out. See Lipsey and Chrystal, *ibid*, pp.227-9.

over local workers, if it is the sole buyer in a neighbourhood, enabling it to force down input costs. It then faces lower but more steeply rising cost curves (see Eaton and Lipsey, *ibid.*, p.65). In retailing, location affects transport costs. In all these cases, especially retailing, there may be differences of demand, arising from location, but these are ignored until later in order to consider the case of perfect competition where firm demand curves are horizontal i.e. identical. Such differences of cost attributable to location are persistent simply because land is not an homogenous factor of production. Every location is unique.

Agriculture perhaps exemplifies these persistent cost differences best in the case of perfect competition. The differences between an east Anglia cereal farm and a small marginal cereal farm in a less fertile region is not clearly recognised in agriculture policies in the UK and the EU. Guaranteed prices, or world prices, operate to make demand curves horizontal for all producers, though their choice of output may be limited by quotas. Whilst subsidies are unrelated to differential location costs, taxes, including those paid by employees, are identical. Hence some farmers make supernormal profits and others struggle to break even. The marginal farmer is a creature of location, yet subsidies and taxes make no attempt to acknowledge this. It might be argued that the marginal farmer is the least efficient one and therefore it is bad economic policy to subsidise the inefficient. But such an argument fails to comprehend the significance of location. Given equal efficiency in the use of factors of production – labour, land and capital – locational differences will still create different cost curves. A higher cost curve on a site with a relatively poor location does not imply less efficient production. It merely implies a lower economic rent of land. If this were not so a tenant farmer on the best land could undercut other farmers even if he were paying a full rent. Price, however, as Ricardo asserted, is set on the margin, meaning the marginal site, where costs are highest. The 'best site' farmer who undercuts would be unable to meet his rent charges, if he were a tenant. (If he were a freeholder, he would be giving away part of his rent in lower prices to consumers i.e. not charging the full market rent.)

Land in Perfect Competition Analysis
Spatial theory of perfect competition thus needs to adjust conventional analysis in order to make explicit the return to land as a factor of production. If the producer owns the freehold, then the persistence of cost differentials in the long run attributable to location appears as supernormal profits. These can be relabelled as rent of land. If, as

is commonly the case, land is rented from a freeholder, then rent payments need to be deducted from costs, thus reducing cost curves and enabling the new surplus to be also labelled as rent. If leases are involved, then part of the rent of the land appears as supernormal profit, to the extent that the annual payments under the lease are less than the full rent. Actual payments of ground rent under the terms of the lease then need to be deducted from costs. Regardless of who receives it, rent of land is then explicitly shown in the analysis. The conventional long-run analysis showing no supernormal profits is replaced by a realistic long-run analysis showing persistent rent for non-marginal firms (Diagram 4). In a competitive economy any site goes eventually to the firm who can pay the highest rent for it. Therefore the rent shown at the profit maximising output where $P = LMC$ is in principle equal to this competitively determined rent (see Appendix).

DIAGRAM 4

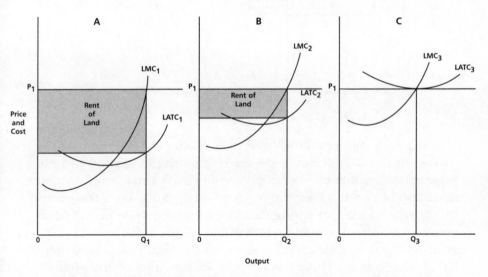

Cost curves have shifted downwards in elimination of any rent paid for the use of land. This removes a major source of error in the conventional theory of the firm (not just in the case of perfect competition) where rent of land is misleadingly treated as a cost when the firm is not a freeholder and as part of profits when it owns the freehold.[3] In conventional short-run analysis rent paid is a fixed cost, which may be shown separately from other costs. Average rent cost becomes

3 Similar confusion obscures the recorded figures in firms' annual accounts, where profit may be much inflated by what is strictly rent of land.

a rectangular hyperbola, but if rent is not paid it is ignored, and enters into supernormal profits. In Diagram 5 at any particular output the area made up of SATC1 minus SATC2, multiplied by the output, is constant and equals the fixed rent.

DIAGRAM 5

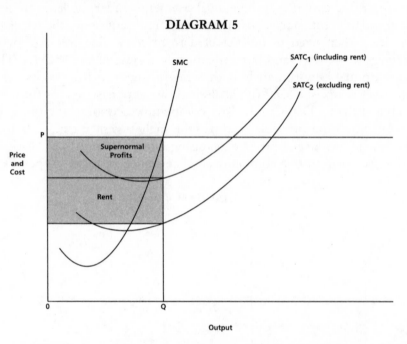

In the long run, economies and diseconomies of scale operate in relation to capital, but not, for a single site firm, in relation to land. Supernormal profits are competed away by new entry firms, so that rent appears as the whole surplus over other costs. Generally firms which have selected an appropriate site adjust the scale of capital to maximise returns on that site, which would only be at the lowest LATC, or minimum scale efficiency, for firms on marginal land with no rent (Q1 in Diagram 6). These firms would set the price of the product. Others, receiving rent, produce beyond this point at Q2.

In practice, firms may take over adjacent land, or reduce their site in the very long run in order to find an optimum size unit of land, but this represents marginal errors in initial decisions by firms, or changes, such as rapid growth of markets, which probably lead to replication of sites (see p.37). Moreover, obvious difficulties stand in the way of expansion to an adjacent site, such as the property rights of others, natural limits on suitable land, absence, or inelastic supply, of services and competition by other bidders for the extra land.

DIAGRAM 6

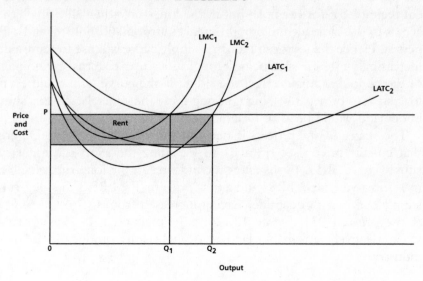

DIAGRAM 7

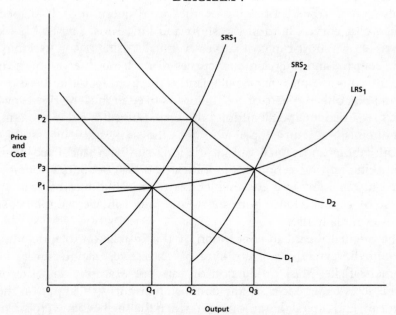

The implications of this analysis extend to the industry supply curve. In the short run this is derived from the marginal cost curves of firms under perfect competition. Short-run supply curves exclude payments

for the use of land, but include differential costs arising from different technology, for example; but in the long run, when all firms have
access to the same technology, differences attributable only to land will
persist. Hence the long-run industry supply curve will rise to represent
increasingly inferior sites being brought into use. External economies
or diseconomies might effect the slope of the curve (and could even
make it zero or negative), but ignoring these the general case on a shift
in demand would be as in Diagram 7.

The stages of the process if demand shifts out from D1 to D2 are
that initially price rises from P1 to P2 along the short-run industry
supply curve SRS1. Firms enter the industry in the long run, giving a
new short-run curve SRS2 and a new price of P3. LRS is the long-run
supply curve, with quantities having increased from Q1 to Q2 to Q3
(Lipsey, *ibid.*, p.231, Figure 12.12(ii)). In practice, LRS rises sharply
when relatively unsuitable land is brought into production in that
industry.

Long-run Average Cost Curves

The recognition of land as the one persistent cause of cost differentials has, of course, a bearing on the vexed question of U-shaped
average cost curves, both in the short and long runs. The text-book
analysis shows short-run cost curves eventually rising owing to diminishing returns, and long-run cost curves rising from diseconomies of
scale. But this assumes that capital/land is the fixed factor in the short
run and that only the state of technology is fixed in the long run. Once
land is regarded independently and the firm defined as a one-site unit,
then diminishing returns operate in both the short and long run. For
as both labour and capital vary in the long run with land fixed, then
diminishing returns to both act in a Ricardian fashion. Sooner or later
these outweigh any unit cost reductions from economies of scale in
the use of capital. Hence both short- and long-run average total cost
curves eventually rise.

The original Ricardian conception of this in relation to agriculture
undoubtedly extends to every kind of extractive, manufacturing or
commercial site. Mass production of cars, for example, on a site of
several acres experiences rapidly diminishing returns to labour (in the
short run) and capital (in the long run) when the site becomes crowded.
Commercial firms on sites in the City of London, for example, experience diminishing returns to investment in building of office space.
The height of the office block is a rough measure. If it were not, then
why stop at say, the 50th floor? Construction stops approximately

when the estimated cost of the operations on an additional floor are expected to fall short of the revenue from those operations.

For the purposes of this argument, however, we may drop the assumption of one-site firms in order to consider replication. Firms may expand on to new sites and replicate productive units. As Lipsey and Chrystal put it:

> Because the firm can replicate plants and have them managed independently, there seems no reason why any firm, faced with constant factor prices, should have a rise in LRAC at least for integer multiples of the output produced by the optimum-sized plant ...
> Lipsey and Chrystal, *ibid.*, p.233

Such a tendency for firms to become multi-plant operations may lead to horizontal LATC curves for individual firms and hence to no equilibrium firm size and no determinate number of firms in the industry i.e. economies/diseconomies of scale may cease. A perfectly competitive industry may change into a monopolistic one, as individual firms begin to face downward slopes in demand curves and to equate marginal costs with falling MR instead of price. Such a tendency is clearly widespread in modern industry.

Is this, however, an accurate analysis if it disregards permanent differences between sites i.e. if it wrongly regards sites as homogenous? A firm with the freehold of a superior site will make large 'supernormal profits' – in fact rent of land – which may be used to cross-subsidise a plant on an inferior site. Only if a full economic rent is measured on all sites can any real comparison between replicated plants be made. Whether (dis)economies of scale actually cease could then be ascertained. Moreover, if multi-plant firms occupy sites of different rental value, it is likely that they are misplacing other types of firms, which would be better users of the land if they were allowed to bid for it. Plants on land under freehold or beneficial leasehold would be getting 'a free ride'. Decisions to replicate, therefore, may yield a serious misallocation of resources. Other reasons for replication, such as economies of scope like reductions in selling and financial costs, raise issues discussed later (see p.61).

Even if rent is correctly identified, so that productive efficiency can be distinguished from advantages of land use and location, another distortion remains. In present conditions of land tenure, the price of land is kept up artificially by land being held out of use by planning regulations, for speculative purposes and for other reasons. High land prices operate as a fixed charge to firms paying rent, which must absorb it as overheads out of revenue. This exaggerates the extent to which minimum LATC (minimum efficient scale) requires a large output. Small firms are displaced, allowing larger ones to grow and dominate the market.

Were all these aspects of rent of land fully examined, the much maligned theory of perfect competition might be reinstated, at least as an ideal, for many industries, since where minimum LATC is reached at an output which represents a small proportion of the market, the industry would support a large number of firms (i.e. if minimum efficient scale is q and industry output Q, then Q/q would be large).

CHAPTER 5

Monopolistic Competition

TWENTIETH CENTURY economists developed micro-economic theory in the direction of greater realism by changing some of the assumptions of perfect competition. In particular, the American economist E.H. Chamberlin produced an analysis of monopolistic competition in order to explain the existence of firms in one industry where each produced goods or services that differed somewhat from others, yet were sufficiently similar for them all to sell at more or less the same price. The premises are that there are a fairly large number of small firms in the industry; that each firm's products are differentiated from others'; that costs are more or less the same for all firms; that free entry and exit are available in the long run; and that the effects of changes in industry demand and of firms' entry and exit is spread symmetrically amongst all firms.

Each firm has a demand curve for its own output, which slopes downwards because it can vary its price to some degree without losing more than a percentage of its customers. MR no longer equals P as in perfect competition, but is less than P. The theory then gives a long-run equilibrium for the firm with zero supernormal profits and production at a point of excess capacity (see Diagrams 8A and 8B).

Initially the firm is producing Q1 at price P1, which is above SATC, giving supernormal profits (Diagram 8A). Free entry in the long run enables new firms to take a share of the market from all existing firms, so that demand falls to D2. Equilibrium is reached at price P2 and quantity Q2, when D2 is a tangent to LATC, because only there will supernormal profits be zero (Diagram 8B).[1]

1 Even without free entry the same result is achieved if each firm acts as though its price cuts have no effect on other firms' decisions, and seeks to undercut its competitors to take a greater market share. In that case, since all firms in the same position act similarly, D1 also shifts downwards until supernormal profits disappear. Free entry would hasten this process towards equilibrium.

DIAGRAM 8A

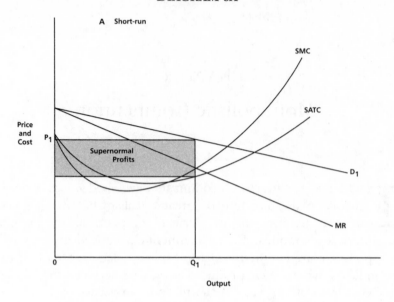

DIAGRAM 8B

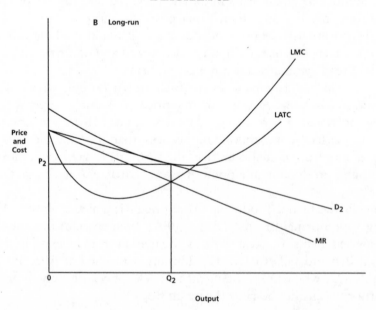

Several features of this analysis are confirmed by observation of the real world. Differentiated or branded products usually are produced with excess capacity. Such firms also develop selling departments, including advertising, which are excluded from perfect competition, where they would merely increase industry demand and only minutely raise the demand for the firm concerned.[2]

Land in Monopolistic Competition

In one respect Chamberlin's model of monopolistic competition seems to be realistic concerning space or land. The falling demand curve for a firm can be interpreted to mean a unique location with an associated market, the customers of which only move away when price rises substantially. In other words, location is a kind of brand, giving what is called an address model. This would seem to make the analysis relevant for such industries as retailing.[3]

However, can supernormal profits arising from location, which are in fact rent, be competed away? Eaton and Lipsey proved that, on reasonable assumptions about markets and location within an industry, they cannot. The market may be 'in free-entry equilibrium with positive pure profits for existing firms and negative expected profits for potential new entrants'.[4]

Their argument runs as follows. Given a collection of firms sharing a linear market equally i.e. spaced out equally along a line, then any new entrant can only gain a market half the size of existing markets. Since LATC curves slope downwards, at least initially, with existing firms making supernormal profits where LATC is below demand, at the same competitive price new entrants with half the demand will find price below LATC, giving losses (see Diagram 9).

There will be a density of customers per firm, C, such that if C0 is the density required to make existing firms break even and C1 is the density required to make new entrants break even, then: $C0 < C < C1$. Even if one argues that there may be some configurations of a real geographical market that do allow free entry to compete away all supernormal profits, there must be many that do not, which is sufficient to establish the long-run persistence of rent.

The address model can be replaced, however, in the following way. If we again extract rent from other costs by deducting all payments to landlords for land (not for buildings, which are capital), leaving all firms in the industry, including potential entrants, as though freeholders, the analysis reveals marginal and supra-marginal firms (see Diagram 10).

2 Such costs raise theoretical problems, because a fixed amount of selling expenses yields a rectangular hyperbola curve, which when added to average cost curves might prevent equilibrium at a point of tangency. See Blaug, *ibid.*, p.379.
3 See Begg, *ibid.*, p.150 re a grocer's shop.
4 Eaton and Lipsey, *ibid.*, p.71.

DIAGRAM 9

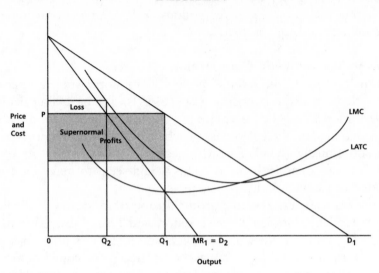

DIAGRAM 10

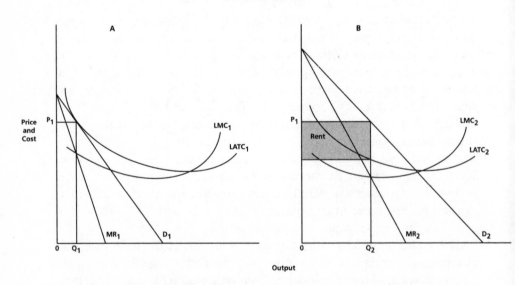

Firm A is marginal; at Q1 it breaks even. Firm B produces Q2 at the same price P, but there is a surplus arising from the better location, creating rent of the shaded area. B's location offers a bigger market than A's, but they have the same cost structures. This is a realistic distinction in an industry like retailing, for A competes not only with B, but with all other A-type firms, which are on similar sites to itself, though with their own local markets. B also competes with all or some A-type firms and with B-type firms on similar locations to itself. Concentric rings illustrate the situation.

DIAGRAM 11

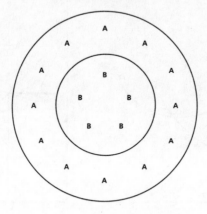

Central firms receive rent from their superior sites; suburban firms are marginal. All sell goods differentiated within a broad industry type. The key aspect of this analysis is that differentiation of goods by brand is indicated by the slope of all firms' demand curves, whilst differentiation by location is shown by lower or higher demand curves (D1 and D2). Of course, Chamberlin's analysis, renamed address models, may apply directly to locational differences whereby downward sloping demand represents locational differential, but it then fails to distinguish location from brand. If locational differentiation is separated clearly from brand, then rent is highlighted as a failure to achieve the tangency of demand and average costs, even in the long run.

Such an analysis clearly identifies rent as the return to land. Its application, especially to retailing, is probably wide. Shops of the same trade (e.g. shoe shops) are situated throughout suburbs and city centres. The latter attract huge rents; the former lower rents. Yet all charge very similar prices for similar but differentiated products. Grocery, hardware, electrical goods, restaurants and so on exhibit the same characteristics. Their trade costs are more or less the same; their markets on the other hand differ systematically with locational type.[5] Costs may in some cases vary with location more than trivially. Transport of inputs and provision of services to the site, for example, might be different,

5 Some industries may not use sites which are strictly marginal in relation to the whole economy, and therefore no firm in the industry experiences zero rent. This problem is dealt with later on pp.82-7.

even within one trade. Therefore an analysis holding demand curves constant is also required.

DIAGRAM 12

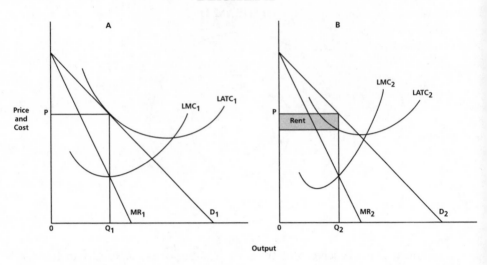

Since demand, and therefore MR, are the same for each firm and price is given as equal, it follows that their marginal costs are the same at an identical output Q1 or Q2. However, the shape of the costs curves may vary, enabling rent to arise at Q2. The site has a cost advantage, but no market advantage.

DIAGRAM 13

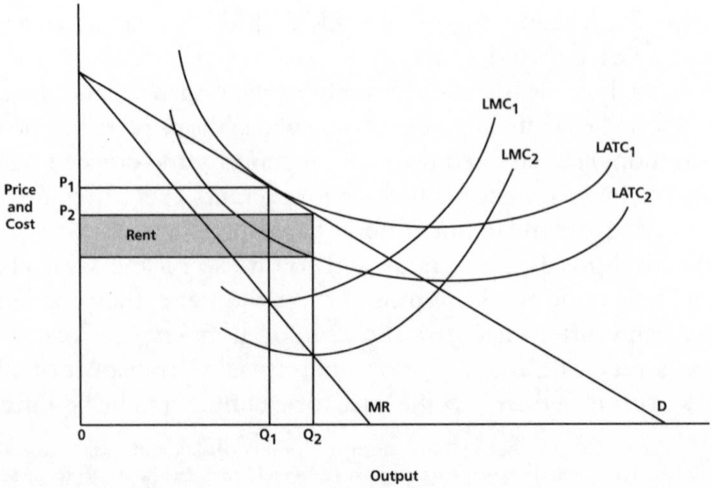

Sometimes cost differences may not offer an identical LMC at a single price. In which case price and output may differ slightly with some rent appearing on the lower cost site. The firm on the lower cost site sells slightly more at a slightly lower price. Of two suburban shops, one may have cheaper services, for example (see Diagram 13).

The Integer Problem

A more general question concerning monopolistic competition is the 'integer problem', when there are n firms in the industry, all of which may make supernormal profits, but when an increase to n + 1 firms would eliminate all such profits and give at least the entrant firm a loss. Thus entry stops short of eliminating supernormal profits. The existence of sunk costs, i.e. costs required for entry, which cannot be recouped on exit, such as preliminary advertising, may enhance this effect, making existing firms monopolistic. Suppose there are seven firms in a retailing industry, each with a downward sloping demand for its product. The entry of an eighth firm shifts all individual demand curves downwards by a significant amount. This shift may jump over the point of tangency with the firms' (identical) LATCs:

DIAGRAM 14

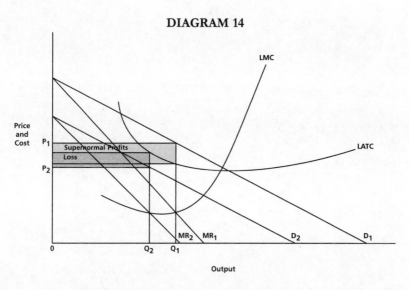

D1 is the demand for each of the seven firms, D2 for each of the eight. Seven make supernormal profits, eight make losses. There is no tangency solution, which in theory needs, say, seven and two-thirds firms. Integer problems clearly arise from indivisibility of firms. Why are firms indivisible? Increasing returns to labour through specialisation and co-operation within the firm, giving an initially falling LATC curve, accounts for this at low levels of output. If this occurs at high levels there may be a monopoly problem (see Chapter 18).[6] However, more commonly, as in retailing, indivisibility occurs for spatial reasons. Shops cannot get smaller and smaller as they get closer together; they need a minimum scale of space and equipment. Hence, once more, the use of land as a factor of production usually lies at the root of this problem. Minimum size land units must be used, with minimum spaces between the units also. Common sense tells us that there is a limit to the number of enterprises of a certain kind in one area. Thus the integer problem is yet another cause of rent of land.

6 The integer problem does not arise in the same way under conditions of perfect competition, because then the very large number of firms in the industry enable very small shifts in individual demand curves to take place, thus avoiding 'jumps' over the tangency point. For example, if the 1001st firm enters the industry, demand for each individual firm falls (shifts) by 0.1%. Hence the point of tangency at the lowest LATC can be achieved.

CHAPTER 6

Monopoly

MONOPOLY HAS two especially distinctive features. Firstly a monopolist, as the sole seller of a product, faces a downward sloping demand curve which represents both his own demand and the demand of the industry, since the firm is the industry. There is no separate firm demand curve, as in perfect competition where demand for the firm's product is perfectly elastic (horizontal), or in monopolistic competition where the firm views its own downward-sloping demand as distinct from the steeper sloping industry curve. Secondly, there is no free entry to the industry, for if there were monopoly would cease to exist in the long run, when such entry took place.[1] The monopolist then has a downward sloping demand curve,

DIAGRAM 15

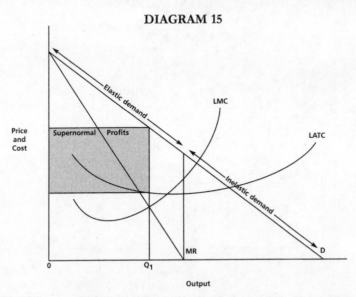

1 In theory a firm might maintain a monopoly position in the long run by having a permanent level of greater efficiency, but this is exceedingly unlikely in an economy with free movement of factors.

likely to be steeper than under monopolistic competition, for now an entire product is monopolised and not just a brand. Marginal revenue is, of course, less than price, and the equilibrium condition of profit maximisation occurs at MC = MR. Since MC must be positive, so too is MR, which means that production must be under conditions of elastic demand where total revenue expands with a lower price. The long-run situation is as shown in Diagram 15.

Supernormal profits are made provided LATC is below D at Q1 (MR = MC). Losses would lead to closure.

Monopolist Owning Land
The most basic case of monopoly power occurs when the monopolist owns a site (or sites) which is the only source of the product. This might occur in the mining industry, where a raw material like bauxite or gold could be monopolised, but other important examples include the site of a port uniquely serving a hinterland or that of an airport. In such cases intrinsic and locational advantages of the land held by the monopolist are the entire cause of the supernormal profits that can be made. It alone possesses the unique raw material source, or the site which uniquely enables users of the port or airport access to the transport facilities. Thus all supernormal profits are rent of land. The freeholding monopolist can capture all the revenue above total costs at the profit maximising output (Diagram 18).

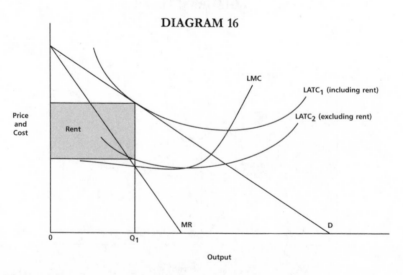

DIAGRAM 16

If, however, monopoly power arose entirely from a condition not related to land-holding, such as the grant of a legal monopoly for the sale of a product, the landlord could not capture all the supernormal profits and, indeed, might only receive an amount equal to the rent obtainable from a tenant using the site in its next best use. This assumes that the monopolist has alternative sources of the raw material or other product or service on the site. The result would be as shown in Diagram 17.

DIAGRAM 17

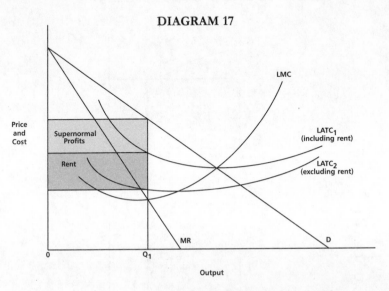

A third intermediate case occurs if the freeholder holds monopoly power over the raw material of a site, but another firm holds a legal monopoly in its further use and sale. Bargaining power then determines the division of the supernormal profits. Either side could close down the other, though the landlord has a bottom price from the second best use of his land. A monopoly oil company renting land from a public or private landlord would be in such a bargaining position for a lease. The outcome would look much like the previous case, with probably a greater share going to the landlord.

Multi-plant Monopolists

In order to discuss under the heading of monopoly the case of a monopoly firm controlling several sites, the concept of the firm adopted earlier is again dropped in favour of the multi-site firm. Assume a monopoly owns several sites all producing a good or service of the same kind with no product differentiation. Costs on each site, however, differ owing to the nature of the site. The most obvious example is a mining firm controlling all the sources. The long-run

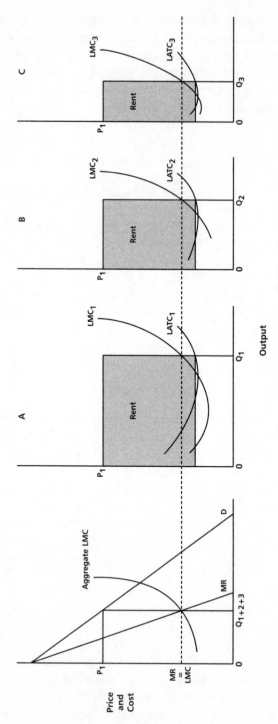

DIAGRAM 18

marginal cost curves can be horizontally summated to give a firm LMC curve, and where this aggregate LMC curve intersects MR will be profit maximisation, and therefore long-run equilibrium. Price and quantity are given on the aggregate diagram on page 50, which is not drawn to scale.

Such a monopolist derives his total output, and hence price, from equating MR to LMC on each site. Were he to allow LMC to differ between sites he would gain by raising output on one site and reducing it on another. His supernormal profits are all rent of land, because he is a freeholder and costs exclude rent.

A mining firm experiences this situation if, for example, workings are progressively harder owing to different depths, configurations and quality of seams at sites A, B and C. A nationalised mining industry is clearly in this situation also, though it may not be directed to maximisation of profits.

If all the sites were identical and could be replicated indefinitely – very unlikely conditions – individual site curves are unnecessary. LMC and LATC are then aggregates.

DIAGRAM 19

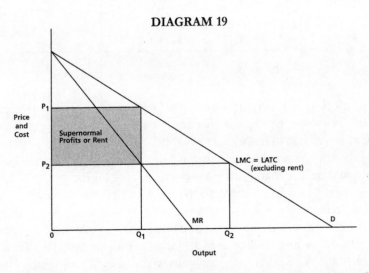

Unlimited replication means that LMC becomes the industry supply curve, does not rise and therefore equals LATC. A fully competitive industry would produce at Q2 with price of P2, but monopolisation reduces output to Q1 and raises price to P1. Since there are no cost differentials, there is no rent attributable to them. Such a case is very unrealistic, certainly in relation to extractive industries, where costs vary greatly with land conditions. The apportionment of the

surplus between P1 and P2 between landlord and firm would depend
upon bargaining power (Diagram 19).

The monopolisation of competing High Street firms demonstrates
the capture of rent by a move from monopolistic competition to
approximate monopoly. Suppose there are three High Street chemists
in one town, each operating as a monopolistic competitor with
similar costs, but with differentiation of product by location and name.
Each produces at Q1 (Diagram 20) and receives a small rent, which
persists in the long run:

DIAGRAM 20

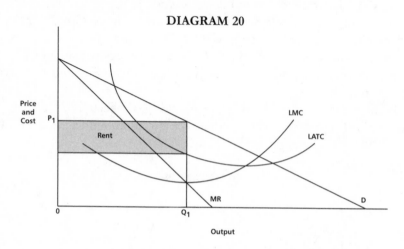

Output

The monopolist acquires all three sites and with them a new
element of power over price, for his nearest competitors are now in
the next town. His demand curve is much less elastic and his rent correspondingly greater than the sum of the three captured firms' rents.
Output will be less than before in order to force up the price. Whether
the monopolist keeps all three shops open or perhaps expands on one
site only, closing the others, matters little (if economies of scale were
available the change might have taken place earlier). Much High Street
'competition' is in fact disguised monopoly of this kind, for firms in
the UK can trade under several names and only Companies House
reveals the secrets of their monopoly power. Indeed, it is strange that
the current trend towards freeing markets has ignored this serious
impediment in the way of genuine choice by consumers.

Cartels

Cartels exhibit the chief features of monopoly by deliberately restricting industry output in order to raise price, where the industry supply

curve derived from the summation of individual LMCs equals MR for the industry. The most significant of modern cartels, OPEC, whose activities have greatly affected Western economies, is a clear example of monopoly power arising from control of land, i.e. oil wells. Unlike outright monopolies, cartels suffer from the incentive for individual members to break the agreement by selling more than their quotas at the mutually agreed price, as shown below:

DIAGRAM 21

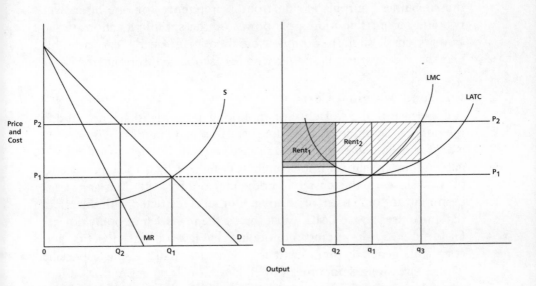

If the industry were fully competitive, which would require that all marginal wells were in use and the oil price was determined by costs of production at those wells, output would be at Q1 on the industry supply curve S at price of P1. Each marginal producer would produce q1 with no 'supernormal profits' (rent). Cartelisation brings industry output back to Q2 with price of P2 and marginal producers cutting back to q2, yielding them supernormal profits (rent) of Rent1. However, each one has an incentive to break the agreement and raise its output to q3, where LMC equals the new high price of P2, yielding Rent2. Hence cartels, like OPEC, are subject to breakdown. In practice, the oil industry is very much a differentiated cost case, like all extractive industries, so that there are many non-marginal wells already receiving rent, even at the market price without cartelisation. Forming a cartel simply increases their rent, whilst creating rent for marginal wells.

Discriminating Monopoly

Discriminating monopoly is yet another aspect of monopoly power that has wide implications.[2] It is no coincidence that many instances of it arise in industries where the root of the requisite monopoly is control of land, such as railways. Car park charges are an interesting example. Provided the car park owner knows the times for which people park by means of meters, inspection etc., he can differentiate between customers according to hours parked. Thus he gains some of the consumer's surplus arising from a preference for one hour over two and so on. The monopoly power of the specific location of the car park enables him to do this. Were there many nearby car parks, his demand curve would be flatter with less scope to discriminate.

Price and Marginal Cost

A good test of the existence of monopoly power is to ask how much the price of anything exceeds the cost of an extra unit of output. Why is it, for example, that if anyone discovers an oil well in their back garden they are almost immediately very rich? Why is the unit price of oil not close to the cost of producing more of it? The answer is monopoly in some form or another. Output is restricted with the effect that price rises above LMC. What then is the root of monopoly power? Governments may grant monopolies by law or fiat. Patents and copyrights generally grant justifiable rights to exclusive sale, especially if they are limited in time. Other kinds of legal monopoly might represent mere privilege or corruption, which is a matter for political action. Apart from these, monopoly power originates mainly in control of land.

Land Monopoly

Obviously anyone in control of all the land of a nation state would have almost absolute power over the inhabitants. This is not the point at issue in the UK today, though in Russia the Communist Party of the Soviet Union exemplified it for seventy years. Plato, however, was percipient when he referred to 'the mode of distributing lands'. For control of even one site gives a form of monopoly power, since no two sites, especially in a developed economy are identical. The specific advantages of a single site are at the disposal of whoever owns it. Land monopoly need not mean, therefore, all land being in one person's or

2 See, for example, Begg, *ibid.*, pp.142-3.

institution's hands; it can mean unlimited control over a particular piece of land.[3] Since all production of goods and services takes place on particular sites, either by using the materials available on the site, like mineral wealth, or by occupying space in productive work, every productive enterprise has some degree of monopoly power arising from its location, unless the site is marginal in relation to the whole economy and other such marginal sites are freely available – a condition not found in any developed economy today. This locational monopoly power is partly, but not wholly, measured by what a landlord can obtain for the site. Other claims on the production on the site, especially taxation, may obscure this relationship; nevertheless what a landlord receives reflects the inherent value of his monopoly power, whether he is an absentee, a firm holding a freehold, or a public authority.

The distinction between natural resources (which are included in the economist's definition of land) and man-made or produced things is fundamental. Economic activity begins with the gift of natural resources. From these, production arises by human effort – labour. To claim ownership of what is produced is one thing; to claim ownership of the free gifts of nature is another. In principle what is produced can be re-produced, so that monopoly of produced things can only be temporary, whereas monopoly of natural resources can be permanent. Moreover, monopoly of natural resources strikes at the source of economic activity, its starting point in space and substance. From there other forms of monopoly power can arise. Free access, as opposed to monopoly, at that critical point would establish the ground for a free economic system. What such free access means is discussed later; suffice it to say here that it certainly excludes land monopoly.

Monopoly Arising from Control of Land

How then may land monopoly create other forms of monopoly power? Unregulated ownership of a port enables the owner not only to charge a monopoly price for its use, but also gives a large measure of control over the industrial hinterland. Discriminatory pricing of port facilities would transfer the profits of even the most successful firms to the port owner. Businesses bought by the port owner could enjoy preferential trading facilities. They might become monopolies

3 There is a close analogy here with unlimited freedom extended to individuals in civil society. Freedom for a society requires the limitation of individual power to do as one pleases. Such limitation, when voluntarily accepted by the individual, is a higher form of his own freedom, as well as constituting that of society.

themselves as a result. Similarly the landowner of a housing estate, who may also be the developer, can have a large measure of control over businesses on the estate. He may grant exclusive rights under restrictive leases offering monopoly power to, say, a publican or a grocery store. Such a trader would share the monopoly rents received with the landowner, on the latter's terms, of course. Landowners in shopping areas of a city, town or village may create local monopolies in the same way by means of restrictive leases, or simply by allocating leases in such a way as to allow only a single seller of each product or service. The local monopolies of the village greengrocer, village hardware shop, village tea-shop and so on might all reap 'superprofits' for the landowner to whom the rent is paid, though the proprietors might be seen wrongly as the chief beneficiaries.

From ownership of the source of a raw material a firm may extend its control vertically through the industries that depend upon it. Oil based products, metallurgical and chemical industries, and food-processing firms may be subsidiaries of the landowner at the source of their product. So-called vertical integration, often justified in terms of technical efficiency, may thus conceal the power of land monopoly. Horizontal integration similarly may be the integration of separate sites to acquire monopoly power, rather than the mere pursuit of management or marketing or financial economies.

The whole question of natural monopolies as currently discussed is in danger of missing the point that control of land is often the key aspect. Long-run average cost curves that fall over the whole range of demand for the product owing to economies of scale are, of course, the technical reason for natural monopoly. However, it is no coincidence that the great public utilities – railways, water, gas and electricity, for example – are literally rooted on land. Their fixed assets, such as railway lines, signalling equipment and stations, gas pipes and electricity pylons, are permanently attached to land. Siting of such assets is crucial. Utilities are natural monopolies because land is their prime asset and their other, usually highly specific (i.e. immobile), assets are fixed to it. This important question is discussed later (see Chapter 18).

CHAPTER 7

Oligopoly

THE MARKET STRUCTURE that is the most widespread in several sectors of the British economy at present is oligopoly, where a few large firms either comprise or dominate an industry. This is especially so in many consumer goods industries, such as supermarkets, cars, petrol and alcoholic drinks. The N-concentration ratio measures this by assessing the percentage of the market controlled by N number of firms. For example, five firms may control 80% of the market.

Oligopoly, like monopolistic competition, lies between the market structures of perfect competition and monopoly, but unlike the monopolistic competitor, who faces a large number of producers of similar branded goods, the oligopolist confronts a small number. He also, however, has a downward sloping demand curve for his product, distinct from the industry demand curve, unlike the monopolist for whom these are identical. What chiefly characterises the oligopolist is that he must take into account the reaction of competitors to any changes he may make to price and quantity. As a price-maker, like the monopolist, he can choose his own price and therefore quantity sold (or vice versa), but his choice will be influenced by competitors' reactions. They in turn are in the very same situation of interdependence. How then does the oligopolist proceed?

Collusion

If collusion within the industry is legally permissible (or at their own risk, if it is not), oligopolists may together agree on the price which maximises industry profits. If so, they must also agree on market shares, in order to ensure that the quantity sold is at the level determined by the maximising price. That price will be at, or near, the price that a monopolist would set i.e. at MC = MR with both below price. (Unless the industry is in short-run equilibrium at a loss-making

monopoly price.) Cartels are a form of such collusive oligopolistic
behaviour and any such collective arrangement is subject to the pressure that all cartels experience of disciplining members to restrict their
output to the agreed levels. Any one firm gains, at least in the short
run, if it alone raises output and sells at the agreed price but above
MC. Such inherent pressure may induce the group of oligopolists to
agree on a policy of 'punishments' for rule-breaking members, or
to act individually to 'punish' them by themselves expanding output.
A dominant member, like Saudi Arabia within OPEC, may be a
powerful 'policeman' in this respect by greatly increasing its sales
if other members fall out of line, thus causing a collapse of market
price. In the long term the surviving members may gain from such
'punishment' behaviour.

Kinked Demand Curves

If collusion is ruled out, as it is by law in the UK, oligopolists call upon
other strategies. They may notice that competitors follow a price cut,
but do not follow a price rise, since firms may not allow themselves
to be undercut but hope to gain by undercutting others. This asymmetric behaviour generates a kinked demand curve for the oligopolist
concerned. If he raises price, his demand becomes much more

DIAGRAM 22

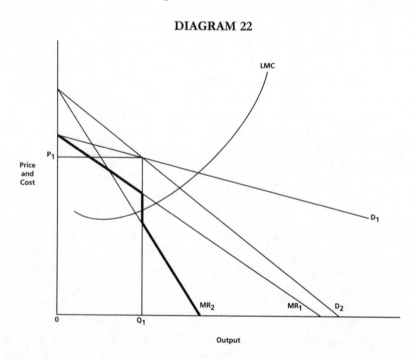

elastic, if he reduces price, it remains fairly inelastic as others follow suit. This produces two different MR curves, with a discontinuity at the initial price (see Diagram 22).

LMC may cut the discontinuous MR at any point where the latter is vertical, without the oligopolist having an incentive to change price or output, so that fluctuations in LMC within that range may occur without a price adjustment for them. This is consistent with some behaviour by oligopolists, though there are other explanations of this price stickiness as well, such as the cost of altering price lists and the aggravation of customers. Fluctuations in the industry LMC may nevertheless produce price adjustments. If so, this suggests that the industry price is near the collusive price, so that all firms are aware of the loss of industry profits when LMC changes and respond appropriately.

Equilibria in Oligopoly

Other answers may be given to the problem of the oligopolist's price and output. The kinked demand is an example of so-called Nash equilibrium,[1] under which each firm in the industry reaches a point where it has no incentive to change price or output given the present behaviour of other firms. There are other Nash equilibria based upon different assumptions about competitors' reactions. Some of these may involve what are called dominant strategies, whereby each firm will behave in a certain way whatever the reaction of other firms. For example, in certain market conditions it may pay a firm facing only one competitor (duopoly) to produce two-thirds of the collusive (monopoly) output, whatever output the other chooses.[2] This non-co-operative equilibrium obviously yields a price below, and an output above, those of the monopolist.

The French mathematician Cournot discovered an equilibrium condition below the collusive price by assuming that a duopolist took his competitor's output to be held constant whatever he – the first duopolist – did.[3] This also yielded a price below collusion price. Modern theory suggests that oligopolists may invest in capital equipment to the point where their output produces a Cournot equilibrium but falls short of creating a price war by the need to sell any larger output at LMC. (See Bertrand equilibrium, p.66.) These theories all focus on price determination within the limits of collusive

1 Named after the American mathematician, John Nash.
2 See example in Lipsey and Chrystal, *ibid.*, p.265, Fig. 14.2.
3 See Lipsey and Chrystal, *ibid.*, Appendix to Ch. 14.

(monopoly) price at one extreme and perfectly competitive price, where $P = LMC$, at the other. They all, however, concentrate on a group of oligopolists within an industry where new entrants are ignored. The more crucial issue is that of entry and exit from the industry, for this raises the questions of why industries become oligopolistic and why they may remain so.

Contestable Markets

If there are no barriers to entry at all, the industry may approximate to perfect competition in its pricing and output policies. This situation, known as a contestable market, arises because incumbent firms realise that any large supernormal profits will easily attract entrants who would compete them away, hence supernormal profits may be kept to a minimum by the incumbents. New entrants must be free of sunk costs, such as initial advertising and investment in highly specific (i.e. immobile) plant, which are incurred on entry and cannot be recovered on exit. New entrants might divide the market so much that all firms make losses, in which case prospective entrants would themselves be deterred. Imperfect knowledge of the market, however, might still lead them to enter, so that the threat of their entry remains plausible, even if incumbents know that losses would result.

Entry Barriers

Perfectly contestable markets are rare. Entry barriers usually exist in various forms. One case, closely related to the question of natural monopolies, is that of large economies of scale.

DIAGRAM 23

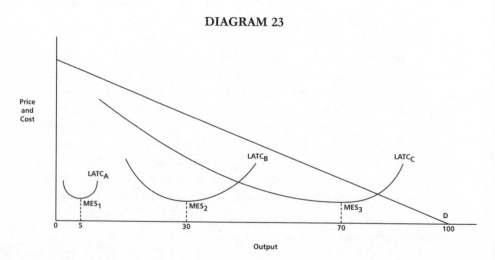

In Diagram 23, provided that economies of scale are exhausted at a low level of output relative to the size of the market, there may be a large number of firms in the industry (Minimum efficient scale – MES1). At the other extreme, very great economies of scale may determine a minimum efficient scale at an output level close to that of the whole market (MES3). In between, MES may divide into market size just a few times, which is very likely to create an oligopolistic market structure. In the diagram MES2 suggests an oligopoly of three dominant firms.

Any firm operating short of MES2 in that particular industry (B) would not be able to compete, and equally any one firm expanding beyond MES2 would experience losses as LATC(B) rose above market price. Industries like car manufacture, where economies of scale are considerable (at least for the type of mass produced car now prevalent) are almost bound to become oligopolistic.[4]

The argument from economies of scale, however, is often used inappropriately to justify oligopolistic or monopolistic markets, even when real economies of this type on a plant level are exhausted at relatively low outputs. In particular, economies of scale are sometimes invoked, when in fact economies of scope are operating. These latter are reductions in average or unit cost derived from the greater size of the firm as opposed to the plant. They include selling and advertising costs, bulk purchase, management and financial economies, and research and development costs. For single site firms such economies, if they genuinely exist, become external to the firm. Indeed they are externalised in cases like co-operative or government organised marketing boards, management and financial services by industry specialists, and research and development financed by government, universities or a collective levy on the industry. Whether they should be internal, and thus a reason for the growth of very large firms which become oligopolistic, is a contentious issue. Very large firms may rationalise their market power by appealing to economies of scope which would be more efficient for society if externalised.

Another form of entry barrier is indeed the deliberate creation by incumbent firms of obstacles to entry. Advertising can be used in this way. It may, of course, merely inform customers of products, prices etc., and enable firms to compete amongst themselves within

4 This gives rise to the problem of determining market boundaries. Within a national economy the conditions of LATC(B) etc. may be present, but in a world market the same cost structures may appear very different and lead to a more competitive many-firm industry. The incentive to produce a 'world car' arises from this consideration. New technology might greatly extend MES to enable a few firms to dominate a world market, which raises serious issues of standardisation and globalisation.

a market.[5] Often, however, advertising is used by large firms to attach customers to themselves at the expense of newcomers. New entrants are then forced to advertise heavily in order to break into the market. A similar and related device is the multiplication of brands within the industry, so that any customer changing brands is much more likely to switch to an existing brand than to change to the brand of a new entrant. If there are twenty brands of cigarettes produced by three firms, a new entrant brand will only attract about 5% of those customers changing brands. Hence the new entrant must incur heavy costs of advertising and/or heavy costs of multi-brand entry.

Another deliberate move by incumbent firms to deter entry is to make it clear that they will adopt a policy of predatory pricing. By selling at a price below unit cost for a certain period they may bankrupt the newcomer. Incumbents may also build excess capacity, which is held out of use until new entrants appear. Such capacity enables them to expand output at a low market price, ruining the entrant without depleting their own profits seriously. Of course, maintaining such capacity before new entrants appear is an additional cost, as is deterrent advertising and brand proliferation; but all such extra costs are justified for the oligopolist who wishes to maintain a price above LMC, especially if the threat of aggressive action succeeds as a deterrent.

Barriers of any type generally create sunk costs for the entrant firm, thus preventing a contestable market. The prospective competitor has to jump the barrier by incurring heavy investment in specialised plant, competitive advertising, brand proliferation *ab initio*, or in the case of real economies of scale or scope, heavy expenditure on capital or services which might leave him in an industry where his market share is insufficient to recover his fixed costs. If he exits from the industry, the sunk costs are by definition lost; the specialised advertising, plant, brands etc. cannot be used in another industry, nor are they likely to be bought by incumbents or other new entrants from a loss-making firm.

Land in Oligopoly
This whole analysis, however, accurate though it might be in logic, and even empirically recognisable in the practice of firms, suffers from the usual overriding defect of dealing with a more or less spaceless economy. Again we note Begg's claim that 'in the long run all firms or

5 Perfect competition excludes advertising, because such expenditure by one firm makes no difference to its perfectly elastic demand curve.

potential entrants to an industry essentially have access to the same cost curves' (Begg, p.147). This is profoundly untrue. It completely ignores, not only cost differentials arising from location, but also those arising from the nature of the land tenure of the firm. For oligopolists, like all firms, occupy land. The cost of holding a site cannot be merged vaguely in total costs without creating analytic confusion, for rent of land obeys its own laws. There are many cases of how this differential operates for oligopoly, as for the other kinds of market structure. A few critical ones are analysed here, using the kinked demand curve.[6]

Firstly, an oligopolist might be paying a full rent and also be making supernormal profits. This is likely if demand is inelastic, as in the case of a supermarket with little competition. A rise in the firm's LMC would reduce its supernormal profits, but leave it in equilibrium at the same price and output. A rise in industry LMC might move the kinked price point upwards and reduce output and profits.

DIAGRAM 24

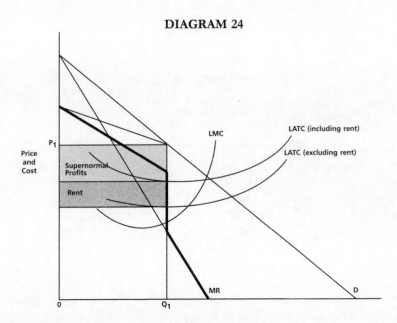

Secondly, an oligopolist might be paying a full rent and just break even with zero supernormal profits. There is clearly no incentive for new entrants in this case (see Diagram 25).

6 There remain theoretical problems associated with this, such as whether it implies a collusive price or whether the industry and the individual firm's LMCs can be clearly related, but these are unlikely to invalidate what follows.

DIAGRAM 25

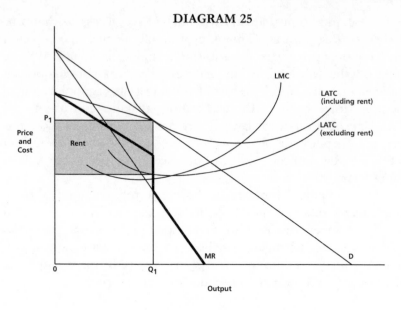

DIAGRAM 26

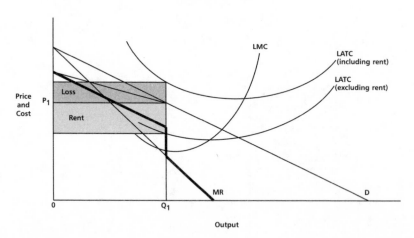

Thirdly, an oligopolist may be making a loss after paying a full rent. This firm would exit from the industry in the long run, except perhaps where it held a freehold or long lease at less than the current market ground rent (Diagram 26).

This latter exception is in fact critical to any effective analysis in all three (and all other) cases. Land tenure is the most important determinant of most oligopolists' behaviour. In all three cases the firm is shown as paying a full rent to a landlord. But suppose it has a freehold! Then it receives factor incomes both *qua* producer (super-normal profits, if any) and *qua* landlord. The latter income enables the freeholder to act differently from the tenant paying a full rent. Not only can the first case oligopolist cut his price and absorb the consequent fall in net receipts out of profits, he may absorb them out of rent also. The zero supernormal profits (Case 2) firm also can absorb a cut out of his freeholder's exemption from paying rent. Even the loss maker (Case 3) can absorb his losses in the rent and find a margin to make price cuts, if he is a freeholder. Hence such freeholder oligopolists have the best barrier of all: a shock-absorbing income enabling them to undercut all potential entrants, either because the latter will have to set a price yielding the rent payable to a landlord, or because the entrant has to purchase a freehold initially.[7] Only the strictly marginal oligopolist on a nil rent site would fail to have such an advantage if he held a freehold. No rent would be payable, but nor would it be received by him *qua* landlord.

DIAGRAM 27

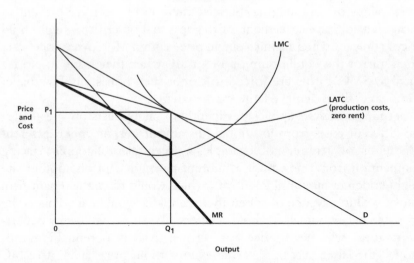

As Diagram 27 suggests, such a marginal oligopolist might find the market price too low if his own costs rise independently of the industry, forcing him to raise price along the elastic part of his demand curve and face losses.

7 Of course, if the freehold maintains its value he may sell it without loss on exit, in which case it would not be a sunk cost; but exit implies loss-making and hence a fall in freehold value for that site. Moreover, there are legal costs, stamp duty etc. to pay.

Cost structures vary with location, and marginal producers may be forced to close down when the collusive price is determined by price leaders within the industry on the best sites. In an oligopolistic industry, like oil, however, marginal producers may be in collusion with low cost producers on better sites, so that the collusive price may keep some producers in the industry who would exit at a non-collusive (lower) price.

Analysis taking into account land tenure and rent offers a new dimension also to the mathematical theory of oligopoly stated by another French mathematician, Bertrand. On the assumption that competitors would leave prices unchanged if one oligopolist's price varied, Bertrand deduced a (Nash) equilibrium whereby industry price would fall to equal LMC. Each oligopolist would seek to undercut existing prices and take the whole market, until the lower limit of LMC was reached. This seems very unrealistic, especially in view of the apparently more realistic assumptions of the kinked curve, for example. But Bertrand can be understood as describing an end state equilibrium regardless of how firms get there. Prices above LMC create states of disequilibria, because there is an incentive present to cheat on a collusive agreement, or to guess that other firms might hold prices constant when facing a single price cutter. Moreover, price wars often mirror this equilibrium of $P = LMC$ when they result in a price equal to SMC. Firms are forced to exit at such prices, until a smaller number of firms achieve large market shares.

Bertrand's analysis applies pertinently to oligopolists on sites offering different costs from locational (dis)advantages, or under different conditions of tenure. For example, a freeholder oligopolist facing competition from one who is a full rent-paying tenant on another site might undercut him until $P = LMC$, which would force the tenant firm to exit well in advance of when the freeholder would exit. This is the probable behaviour of freehold retailers, like supermarkets or department stores, who begin price wars against rivals or potential entrants, though the latter may be deterred even without price falling to LMC or even to LATC (net of rent) by the threat of this strategy. The recent tendency for supermarkets to accumulate land banks on a large scale is additional confirmation of this analysis.

Goodwill

The nebulous term 'goodwill', denoting the value attached to a particular firm's place in the market, under a trade name for example, is better understood as often attaching to the actual site(s) where production or services are carried on. Such advantages can be sold as the right to step into that market place, which usually means to occupy physically that site(s). To that extent, goodwill is a capitalisation of rent. Its power in an oligopolistic industry may derive from a Bertrand type advantage in undercutting rivals. Similarly the presence of 'goodwill' operates as a barrier to potential entrants without it.

Takeovers by oligopolist firms demonstrate this. Usually they preserve the business on site, but change the name, thus proving that the goodwill attaches to the place rather than to the name. Recent supermarket takeovers exhibit this fact about 'goodwill'. In other cases they sell off the assets and realize the land value, which proves the point even more clearly!

Control of Land as Cause of Oligopoly

Of the conventional barriers discussed above, several are probably consequences of the more fundamental barrier of privileged access to better sites. Economies of scope grow when oligopolistic (or monopolist) market structure is already in place, and accentuate it. So-called financial economies, for example, merely represent the greater credit-worthiness of firms with exceptional and perhaps collusive market power. Advertising against competitors and potential entrants often assumes a degree of prior oligopoly. Likewise, the deliberate creation of barriers, by brand proliferation, excess capacity or other means pre-supposes some departure from perfect or monopolistic competition, for single brand firms with their non-deliberate excess capacity are too weak for these intentional features of oligopoly. Differentials arising from locational variations are ubiquitous and unavoidable; they are rooted in the nature of a spatial economy, which is where we all live and work. If individual firms are allowed to take unrestrained advantage of them, they become the root of most forms of oligopoly, with the exception of those involving genuine economies of scale.

Whether an oligopolistic firm is a freeholder (or holds a lease at less than the market ground rent) is thus the critical condition which usually underlies the industry market structure of a few firms with entry barriers. As in the case of monopolistic competition, the advantage of the privileged land-holding firm can be attributed to the cost side or the demand side, or indeed, for some firms, both at once. For oil companies, for example, the advantage may lie in control of the best oilfields – a huge cost advantage. For supermarkets, on the other hand, the advantage lies primarily in location in relation to a market, say on the outskirts of a city. Yet both such industries are leading examples of oligopolistic structure. Their supernormal profits and rent are mainly consequences of the land tenure system. Analytically these surpluses arise from power to set a high price and/or from low cost curves, but the cause of each of these often lies in freehold land tenure, which creates a rent denied to competitors or potential competitors devoid of a privileged site(s). As with all market structures, access to land remains the hidden, and often deliberately obscure, determinant. Whoever or whatever distributes land – law, custom, government – manipulates the puppet show of a 'free' market economy.

PART THREE

Factor Incomes

CHAPTER 8

The Law of Rent

I F WE CALL wages the value of whatever a worker produces in goods and services as a result of his labour (including under the term labour all productive activity, however skillful), then every society produces a surplus over and above total wages. This surplus may fall into the hands of landlords, employers or the government, as rent, profits, interest or tax revenue and be put to multifarious uses, but it remains a surplus mainly attributable to society as a collective entity. It is not derived from the efforts of anyone *qua* individual, but from the actions, or simply from the existence, of the collective body of citizens. Who receives this surplus initially and who receives the benefit of it – two separate issues – depend upon the laws and customs of particular societies. Economic History is largely concerned with these latter questions. It is encumbent upon economists, however, to analyse the implications for a modern economy of the origin, distribution and use of this surplus; a task singularly neglected by economists, at least since the late nineteenth century. This failure stems from their setting aside the concept of economic rent.

John Stuart Mill called the law of rent:

> A theorem which may be called the *pons asinorum* of political economy, for there are ... few persons who have refused their assent to it except from not having thoroughly understood it
>
> J.S. Mill, *Principles of Political Economy*, Book II, Chapter xvi, s.5

Yet failure to understand the law of rent has made modern economics almost literally a 'flat earth' science.

David Ricardo had been the first to formulate and develop the consequences of the law of rent. His definition of it, however, was unfortunately limited:

> Rent is that portion of the produce of the earth which is paid to the landlord for the use of the original and indestructible powers of the soil.
>
> *The Principles of Political Economy and Taxation*, p.33, New York, 1962, Dent

By citing the natural fertility of land as the prime example of such powers, Ricardo's definition drew attention away from the many other 'powers' attached to land, especially those that fall under the general heading of location. The American economist, Henry George, and the German Johann von Thunen, were well aware that location was considerably more important than fertility in giving rise to rent, but George has been intellectually ostracised by the academic establishment, and von Thunen has generated a narrow specialist school of land economists, who have become diverted by issues of optimum location for town planning and the siting of businesses.[1]

Ricardo, however, saw two chief analytical features of the law of rent, both of which have also been largely forgotten, except by a few economists like Blaug.[2] Before discussing these we may formulate the law of rent as:

> Rent arises as the potential excess of production on a particular piece of land over and above the potential production from the same effort on land of equal area, which is the least productive in use.

The word 'potential' is crucial in this definition, for rent is not whatever surplus happens to arise from a particular use of factors of production. It is the surplus under conditions of optimum efficiency in the use of factors, where they are allocated to their best use. Thus, if a piece of potentially productive land is held out of use, this does not diminish its rent; similarly, if labour or capital are withheld from their optimum use on a particular site. Were rent not regarded as a potential in this way, there would be difficulty in explaining the actual current price of land, say in a city centre, which is held out of use by the landlord. Clearly it is rational to relate its price to its potential annual value and to regard the latter as rent. (See footnote 6, p.180 for a key example of the importance of this point.)

The above definition is supported by that of Alfred Marshall, though he omits explicit reference to the potentiality of rent:

> [Rent] is the excess of the value of the total returns which capital and labour applied to land do obtain; over those which they would have obtained under circumstances as unfavourable as those on the margin of cultivation.
>
> A. Marshall, *Principles of Economics*, p.355, 8th edn, MacMillan, London, 1956

1 The present author has learnt a great deal from the writings of Henry George, but has refrained from explicit use of these for two reasons. Firstly, George uses little mainstream economic analysis, even by the standards of his own time; and secondly, the treatment of credit and capital in this book is significantly different from that of Georgist writers.
2 See Blaug's treatment of Ricardo in *Economic Theory in Retrospect*, CUP, 1999.

Rent is thus the differential productivity of labour and capital with respect to the particular land on which they are used. Labour, using capital, will produce more on one site than on another, other things being equal. Mines vary in output with differences of mineral seams, farms with fertility, shops with proximity to their customers, offices with proximity to commercial centres, residential property with local facilities for tenants, and so on. Every site is unique, and has unique qualities, which endow work on that site with special advantages and disadvantages. This is by no means a matter of purely natural aspects, like soil, minerals, topography or climate, though these are of great importance. The presence of a settled community, its population distribution, law and order, infrastructure – roads, railways, bridges and municipal facilities – existing economic development in industry, commerce and finance, public utilities like water, gas and electricity, social amenities for culture, entertainment and sport, the whole host of opportunities available in a developed society, all of these contribute to the relative advantages and disadvantages of every site. They all play a part in making the application of labour, with capital, more or less productive in one place than in another. Any businessman, or any house buyer deciding on a location, knows this without a doubt. Everyone knows it. Yet economists neglect it!

Ricardo's Analysis

What then are the two analytical features that Ricardo clearly identified? Firstly, he saw that the law of diminishing returns as stated by several contemporary economists was closely related to the law of rent, indeed that the two laws are logically interdependent. Secondly, he distinguished between an extensive margin of production and an intensive margin of production. Both these analytical features are vital to a full understanding of rent and its central status in economic theory.

That productivity of labour and capital vary systematically with the place at which they are applied in production can be represented by columns proportional in height to output (see Diagram 28).

This assumes an equal application of labour and capital on each site and also a constant capital/output ratio. But why should a worker produce on any site inferior to the best one, and what happens if labour and capital remain of the same quality and effort, but the amount used per site does not remain the same? Ricardo answers both these questions at once. On the best site, continued applications of units of labour and capital would eventually lead to a fall in output per unit, because of the law of diminishing returns. A fixed area site must

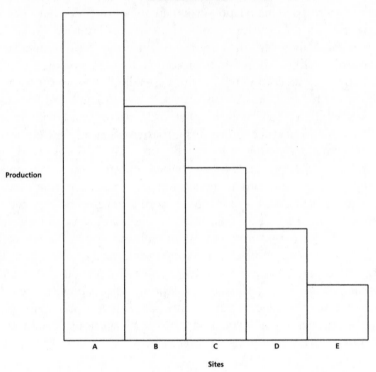

DIAGRAM 28

experience this fall as increasing variable units co-operate with it. At
the point at which diminishing returns set in, workers and capital would
begin to move to other sites where the returns to the first applications
of labour and capital were at least equal to the last return on the best
site. Such a process would continue on and between all sites, until
equilibrium were reached at the stage where the returns on the last
applications on all sites were equal.

There might be increasing returns to labour and capital initially on
each site as co-operation takes place, but sooner or later diminishing
returns set in. Thus the period of increasing returns does not affect
the eventual equilibrium condition of equality of returns to the final
units of labour and capital on all sites (Diagram 29).

This development of the original proposition about labour/capital
productivity thus leads into the second analytical feature emphasised
by Ricardo. In an economy where land is freely available at the
margin of production, labour might extend to site F, where the whole
product would be received by workers on that site. Their product

DIAGRAM 29

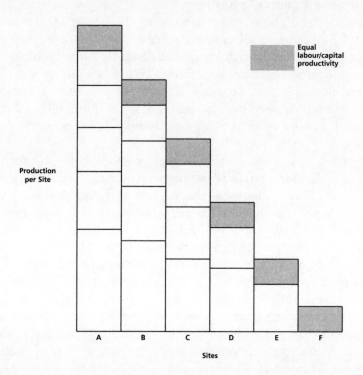

Equal
labour/capital
productivity

Production
per Site

A   B   C   D   E   F

Sites

would then be equal to the product of the final workers on each
of the other sites. F then represents Ricardo's extensive margin of
production. (The intensive margins on all the sites are represented by
the shaded areas i.e. the outputs of the final, or marginal, workers.)
The outputs of the extensive and the intensive margins must be equal,
if there is free movement of labour and capital between them.[3]
Production, however, may extend only to E because on any further
site labour productivity is too low. In practice this may mean that the
quality of the land has greatly deteriorated beyond E. Also, since
increasing returns operate usually at low levels of output, sites beyond
E may experience returns to small applications of labour and capital
which are too low compared with those on better sites where there is
greater co-operation.[4]

3 Blaug demonstrates this with a tabular example. Blaug, *ibid.*, p.78.
4 As a matter of theory, the quantity of land used could be varied, holding constant the labour/capital
input as a fixed factor. If so, the marginal product of land becomes equal to its rent. See Blaug, *ibid.*,
pp78-9.

Differential or Economic Rent

This basic model of how land is acted upon by labour and capital is universally applicable in all circumstances to any economy, since it arises from the natural immobility of land and the natural mobility of labour and capital. Modern economists say much about mobility of factors, including land, between different uses, but this is another matter, not to be confused with the inherent spatial immobility of land in relation to factors which are mobile. Mobility between uses is dealt with below (see pp.82-7 and 91-2).

How then does the law of rent emerge from all this? Obviously it is reflected in the differentials shown between sites A to E in Diagram 28. As Ricardo says, 'Rent is always the difference between the produce obtained by the employment of two equal quantities of capital and labour' (Ricardo, *ibid.*, p.36). But Ricardo goes on to say that 'Rent invariably proceeds from the employment of an additional quantity of labour with a proportionally less return' (Ricardo, *ibid.*, p.37). He perceived that this is true whether production is on one site only or on several. For if production is on one site which experiences, as it must, diminishing returns, a rent or surplus is created over the wages due to workers. The reason for this is that wages are determined in that case by the intensive margin, i.e. by the productivity of the last application of labour. If all workers are *ex hypothesi* the same in skill and effort, then their wages must be identical. Hence all earn an amount equal to the product at the intensive margin. (If an employer were introduced, he would in fact employ labour until the last worker made a net contribution to output equal to his wage.) Since 'earlier' workers produced more than this, the sum of the excesses over the marginal product is rent. Workers might share the whole product amongst themselves, thus appearing to make the total product wages with no residue, but strictly they would be sharing the rent equally, not receiving the whole product as wages.

The law of diminishing returns thus accounts for labour and capital moving to an inferior site, when their marginal product has fallen to less than the product from their first application on the inferior site. This process would continue through successive applications of labour and capital on sites, until equilibrium were reached at the point where the products of all intensive margins were equal and they equalled the product of the extensive margin, as in Diagram 29. The outcome is differential or economic rent i.e. a falling net output or value added on sites from A to F after deducting labour and capital costs. The rent is the excess on each site of the total value added on each site over total wages/capital costs, calculated as the marginal products of labour/ capital units times the number of units.

Before proceeding further, the confirmation in practice of the law of rent, and in particular of the equality of the intensive margins in equilibrium, may be demonstrated by a familiar case far removed from a Ricardian agricultural economy. The productivity of labour/capital in a small English town in the provinces is generally a great deal less than on a central site in the City of London. Dividing the total value of output on such a site, say, of a head office bank, by the number of workers would yield a much higher figure than the same calculation for, say, a small town branch bank. Yet the wages earned by an ordinary office worker in each are much the same (any London allowance compensates for higher expenses in London, giving a similar real wage). Why is this? The answer is clearly that the marginal product determines wages. The intensive margin on each site produces a nearly identical amount. If it did not, labour would be attracted to where it was higher. Rent on the City site is enormous; on the provincial site relatively low. For every worker, short of the marginal one, on the City site rent is accumulating equal to that worker's intra-marginal productivity less his/her wage. On the provincial site the same process occurs at a much reduced rate. But the intensive margins on both sites have the same value added.

Scarcity Rent

Examining the logical connection between diminishing returns and rent leads to a further important distinction; namely that rent can be analysed into differential or economic rent on one hand and scarcity rent on the other. The existence of rent even on a single site, owing to the eventual operation of diminishing returns as labour/capital is applied, is the feature that creates scarcity rent. If land were homogenous and freely available, diminishing returns would never appear, for labour would move freely to occupy sites the moment a potentially diminishing situation arose. In theory returns would remain constant on all sites. However, if sites are limited in relation to labour/capital to any finite number which makes labour work intensively on any sites, diminishing returns and hence scarcity rent appears. Thus if land is owned or enclosed by a part only of the population, leaving the rest landless, there is scarcity rent. Even were all sites equally good i.e. homogenous, but limited in this way, scarcity rent would appear, unless returns to labour were increasing on all sites in use. In practice, as has happened in modern economies, those who own land have kept large amounts out of use, making the remainder in use subject to very considerable diminishing returns. This, of course, greatly reduces the wage rate, which is equal to the intensive marginal product (see pp.104-6, Diagram 50).

Differential rent, on the other hand, is rent arising from non-homogenous land, as labour/capital moves on to inferior sites from the best one(s). This would occur even if land were not limited in quantity, provided that which was in use was not homogenous. The presence of even an infinite quantity of inferior land would not elim-inate differential rent, since the marginal return on the most inferior land in use would define the wage rate and give rise to a rent on superior sites. In short, differential rent is the result of the non-homogeneity of land, scarcity rent of finite land. In the American West until the mid-nineteenth century land was effectively infinite, but not homogenous, hence wages were high, but rent was also growing greatly. Once land was all enclosed by about 1890, scarcity rent began to appear more acutely alongside differential rent. Much could be learnt of American economic history from following through the results of these two fundamentally different situations. (In fact enclos-ure of land by speculators in advance of settlement complicated the situation long before 1890.) In all modern economies today both scarcity rent and differential rent are present on a very large scale.

Rent and Supply Curves

How then is this concept of rent related to rent in the theory of the firm, which was analysed above? (See Part 2.) On the assumption of a fair degree of competition, sites exhibiting different rents within the same industry can be shown in relation to the industry supply curve by superimposing on output columns the marginal and average costs for each firm, when these vary with location. Costs are assumed to be long-term (Diagram 30).

Each firm makes LMC = P, where P is common to the industry. The output of each firm is measured horizontally across its 'zone' i.e. A's output is 01-02, B's 02-03 etc. Outputs need not be equal; they are likely in practice to decrease from A to E. Total costs are LATC x output and rent is the surplus of total revenue (P x output) over total costs. This demonstrates that rent is a phenomenon which mathemat-ically arises from a difference between marginal and average cost. As LATC rises towards LMC from A to E rent decreases. On the marginal site LATC may equal LMC (see p.81). Hence, in the analysis

DIAGRAM 30

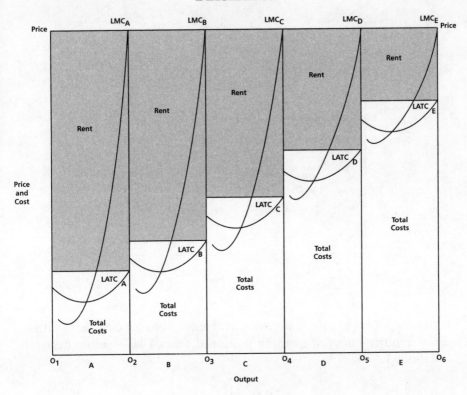

of perfect competition, supernormal profits remaining in the long run and attributable to site differentials are rent.

Alfred Marshall was aware of this long-run effect on costs of differentials between firms persisting even in perfect competition. His concept of the 'particular expenses curve' (PE) makes clearer the fact that a conventional supply curve, even when acknowledged to be rising in the long run, seriously understates the returns to land as the only fixed factor of production, if these returns are measured as the producers' surplus lying below the price line and above the curve.[5] (See Diagram 31.)

Since the long-run supply (LRS) consists of the summation of firms' LMCs, it shows at any particular output, say Q1, the sum of the outputs of all firms so far within the industry determined by the point on their LMC curves where price equals LMC. Since LMC is rising for each firm, unit or average cost at that point is below LMC for every

5 See *Principles of Economics*, Appendix H and elsewhere, 8th edn, MacMillan, 1956.

DIAGRAM 31

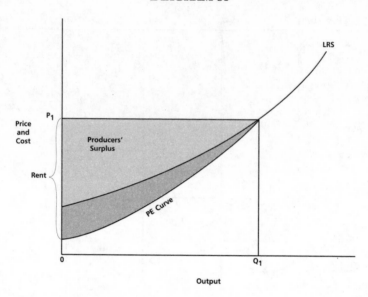

firm except perhaps the marginal one. Hence, rent is being received as the difference between quantity produced times LMC and that quantity times LATC.

DIAGRAM 32

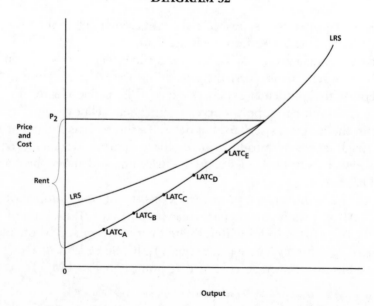

In Diagram 32 Marshall's PE curve for any one price, say P2, shows the LATCs for each firm in the industry at that price by drawing the locus of those LATCs for each successive firm at its equilibrium output (i.e. where its LMC = P). These points (LATC etc.) are equivalent to the points on Diagram 30, where LATC curves meet the final output of each firm (LATC [A] at O2 etc.)

What follows from this is that rent of land is the whole shaded area above the PE curve (Diagram 31) and not merely the so-called producers' surplus above LRS.[6] This point is made clear by comparing Diagrams 30 and 32. On the assumption of many firms in the industry, the line joining these average costs becomes continuous in Diagram 32.

The marginal firm requires a closer look. For simplicity it is shown in Diagram 30 as receiving a small rent, analogously to the intra-marginal firms. This is the case if land is limited by ownership or enclosure, so that workers are employed there beyond the point of greatest efficiency (minimum efficient scale) where LMC cuts LATC, thus giving rise to the usual rent derived from the excess of LMC over LATC at the maximising output of LMC = P. Were land not so limited, in other words if it were freely available at the margin, production would not expand beyond the point of MES on that site, for the reason that workers would be better off moving to the next best vacant site available where returns per worker would be higher than

DIAGRAM 33

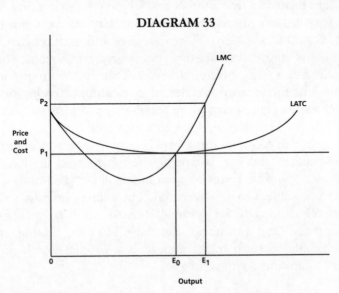

beyond MES. Their equal shares in the product of site E would take place at output E0 (Diagram 33). Price for the whole industry would now be set at P1, instead of P2. Only a price above P1 creates a rent on the marginal site.

In the absence of perfect competition there is, of course, no precise supply curve, although supply does in most cases expand in response to an upward shift in demand and contract for a downward shift. Nevertheless, rent varies with both cost differentials and with demand differentials arising from varying sites, as the discussion above indicates (Part 2). The natural and social factors that give rise to rent pay no respect to market structure. Monopoly, oligopoly and mono-polistic competition as market structures may give rise to supernormal profits, but the rent that firms operating within such structures receive arises from the same causes as in the case of perfect competition. Nor can any market structure make a substantial difference to the natural law that determines rent. The real question is not whether rent can be changed or eliminated by human laws or policies, but rather what laws or policies are just and rational in their treatment of rent. Or, in brief, who is to be allowed by law to claim rent?

Von Thunen's Analysis

Any general account of rent that draws upon the analysis of particular industries as in the theory of the firm, however, needs to explain how industries are related to one another and to the whole economy. Firms compete for sites not merely within an industry but between indus-tries, since almost all sites have alternative uses. Indeed it is often where sites have many alternative uses that rent is greatest. A framework for understanding this was offered by von Thunen, who provided a general model of concentric circles of agricultural development, or land use, around a central city. More recently economists such as Isard have applied von Thunen's analyses to urban land use.[7]

In a competitive economy firms will bid for sites according to what each firm believes the site is worth when employed in that firm's particular use. The final result of such bids will be to allocate sites to their best uses, subject to any overriding community interest reflected in planning regulations. If, for example, land use falls into broad groups like Commercial (and Financial), Retailing, Housing, Manufacturing and Farming, the pattern might appear as a profile, which in three dimensions is around a city centre O:

7 W. Isard, *Locations and Space-Economy*, Appendix to Ch. 8, MIT Press, Cambridge, Mass., 1956.

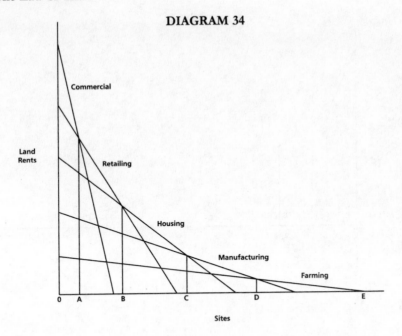

DIAGRAM 34

Land uses are OA Commercial, AB Retailing, BC Housing, CD Manufacturing, and DE Farming, where the relevant gradients show land rents offered for each use. In each zone (OA etc.) the highest bids succeed, so that, for example, housing outbids all the others in zone BC. By rotating the zones around an axis at O a three dimensional model is generated as indicated in Diagram 35.

Such a model shows immediately that zone DE is far more extensive than zone CD and so on inwards to the relatively very small zone OA. Thus there are a very large number of sites within DE and few within OA, although this is modified by the fact that DE zone activities, like farming, use land extensively, whilst inner zones tend to use it intensively. Land values per acre, of course, tend to increase with the intensity of labour/capital use and with the price of the product.

Analysis of the rent gradients begins with a firm considering where to be sited. It would take into account potential sales and costs at likely sites. Sales at a given price may be taken to be a function of distance from the city centre. Various expenditures on costs, including production, services, advertising etc., could be chosen by the business, each set of which would yield rather different sales profiles. Allowing for sub-centres within the city (e.g. suburban shopping centres) four such sales curves related to distance from O might be as shown in Diagram 36.

DIAGRAM 35

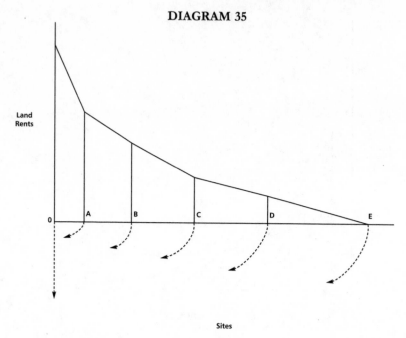

Land
Rents

0   A   B   C   D   E

Sites

DIAGRAM 36

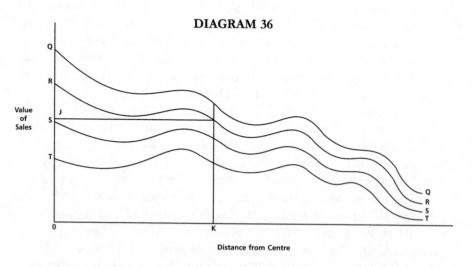

Value
of
Sales

Distance from Centre

At any point K a firm may make supernormal profits related to its sales as given by one particular sales curve i.e. after choosing some set from the cost variables associated with Q,R,S or T. Let us assume it chose R, giving sales of OJ. These may be shown horizontally on a conventional theory of the firm diagram, which then reveals supernormal profits of the shaded area (Rent, Diagram 37):

DIAGRAM 37

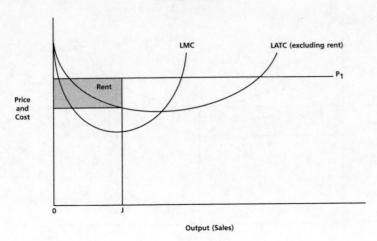

The LATC curve excludes any rent payment. On a rent review, provided other firms competed for the site, the rent would be taken by the landowner, leaving only normal profits for the firm (included in LATC). A diagram of the rent profile in this particular land use could then be established by plotting this rent and all others at each distance from the centre. The rent would be the highest obtainable out of the four (or more) possible cost combinations (Q, R, S, T) at each point. This might be on Q at one point, R on another (as for K), and so on. Each land use (Commercial, Retailing etc.) would have its own profile with the highest profile winning bids for sites each time.

This, however, cannot be the long-run equilibrium. The typical firm above could not remain in equilibrium with sales of OJ and rent as shown. Other firms in the same land use could undercut price P and offer a higher rent (i.e. make larger supernormal profits in the short run) by expanding sales until LMC = P. Equilibrium would occur when LATC, including rent, was tangential to P with LMC cutting LATC from below (see Diagram 38).

Although any firm might make greater supernormal profits (= rent) at a better location, if it were outbid by a firm with a different land use at that location it would have to settle for the inferior site. On that site it would then maximise supernormal profits by competitive adjustment of price and costs. This would be more or less so whatever the structure of the industries concerned. Where perfect competition did not operate, rent would be determined according to the analysis given above in the theory of the firm, and rent profiles would appear in a

DIAGRAM 38

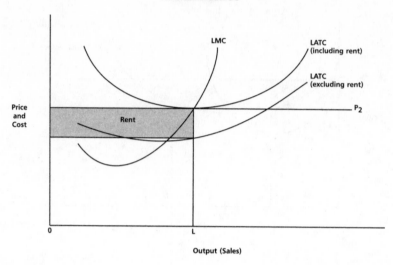

Output (Sales)

similar way. Whoever owned a site would receive the rent, whether landlord or freeholding firm, with rent shared between landlord and firm in the case of a lease with ground rent below market rent. Any element of permanent supernormal profits arising from monopoly power independent of location would remain in the hands of the firm. Such supernormal profits might appear as though excrescences on the rent profiles. Special cases where there were not competitive lessors of land on one hand and competitive lessees on the other would also affect the general profiles of rent.[8]

Subject to these exceptions, every site is allocated to the highest bidder and all supernormal profits paid or retained as land rent in the long run. The final outcome is a complex pattern of land use which corresponds to the real world. Concentric circles give way to a multiplicity of individual conditions related to the needs of firms and the precise conditions of each site in relation to such matters as transport facilities (which would make physical distance less important than time and cost of transport), accessibility of site, location of competitive and complementary products and so on.

The rent profiles would be complicated curves, which would cross each other perhaps more than once, as in Diagram 39:

8 See, for example, W.H. Carter and W.P. Snavely, *Intermediate Economic Analysis*, pp.322-5, McGraw-Hill, 1961, New York; and B. Curtis Eaton & R.G. Lipsey, *On the Foundations of Monopolistic Competition & Economic Geography*, pp.57-9, Edward Elgar, 1997.

DIAGRAM 39

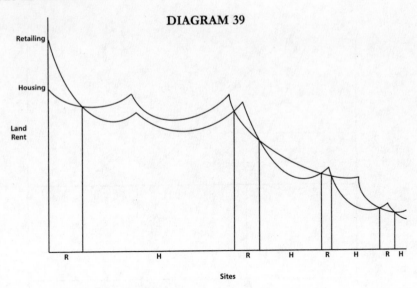

No planning regulations could emulate or improve upon such market allocation, which is undeniably a case of Adam Smith's 'invisible hand' achieving accuracy in efficient matching of needs to resources. Yet this does not rule out planning, if it were needed to prevent the market from ignoring social needs for public use. Parks, schools, hospitals, transport facilities and a host of other public uses require that the blindness of the invisible hand – to mix metaphors – be guided by a social conscience.

Inadequacy of Homogenous Land Model

Modern economic analysis is incomplete in its treatment of the allocation of land between uses. For example, Begg takes land to be homogenous and thus arrives at an unrealistic analysis of how land is allocated between such uses as housing and farming. Using two downward sloping demand curves, which are derived from declining marginal productivity schedules for land in each use, he finds an equilibrium price at which all the available land for these two uses would be divided (Diagram 40).

Total homogenous land available for farming and housing is fixed at T (SS). Demand for farming land is DF, demand for housing land DH. The equilibrium price is R1, where F1 plus H1, equal T. But does farming land and housing land change hands at this one price? The answer is only where the two uses cross on the Thunen rent profiles, for example, at point X in Diagram 41.

DIAGRAM 40

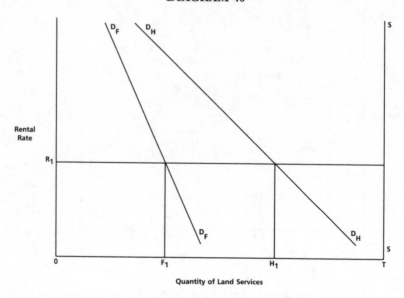

Quantity of Land Services

DIAGRAM 41

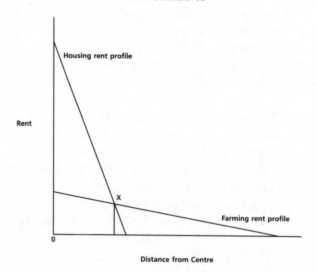

Distance from Centre

To the extent that some land is more or less homogenous and suitable for housing or farming in the region of X, Begg's analysis applies. Such an extremely limited range is quite inadequate as an analysis of land rents and land prices. Rent profiles show this. Empirical evidence of prices confirms that land varies greatly in farming use and enormously in housing use according to its quality and, above all, its location.

In south-east England agricultural land is worth £12,000 per hectare on average, while land designated for housing is worth £3.2m and land designated for general business use is worth £1.7m. In the case of housing the discrepancy is close to 300 to one.

Martin Wolf in *The Financial Times*, 7 July 2006

Hence simplistic demand curves based on homogeneity cannot be used to indicate the real relationship between rents of land in different uses.[9] Such an attempt to generalise so briefly and indeed to marginalise (in both senses!), the part played by land in an economy is typical of modern economic analysis and is symptomatic of a failure to understand the fundamental character of land and natural resources.

For the law of rent is indeed the *pons asinorum* of economics. It underlies all the major phenomena of a modern – or indeed any – economy, such as how wages are determined, returns on capital, interest, the level of unemployment, the housing market, public finance and government macro-economic policy. What follows will be an attempt to substantiate this claim, but a full justification must remain the work of many economists trained afresh to realise that what John Stuart Mill wrote is true – that he who has not seen the law of rent has not yet crossed the bridge of asses. In the past some have realised this: the French Physiocrats (especially Quesnay), Ricardo, Ogilvie, Walras, and George, amongst others, but their views of rent have been sidelined, perhaps deliberately, by 'orthodox' thinkers who have not wanted to draw rational conclusions about land ownership. The time has come, however, when the law can no longer be ignored.[10]

9 See Begg, *ibid.*, pp.212-13.
10 See Appendix on Rent and Landlord's Claim.

CHAPTER 9

Transfer Earnings of Factors

DESPITE MARSHALL'S contribution to the understanding of rent, other aspects of his work have led to ambiguity in its definition. Two quite different concepts of rent have been treated as though they were the same. Both are clear in themselves; one has a rather narrow application in relation to the allocation of resources between alternative uses; the other has a very wide application to the distribution of factor incomes in the economy as a whole. Previous analysis in this book has referred exclusively to the second broader concept, which is the traditional notion of rent in the early classical economists from Ricardo to Mill.

Transfer Earnings of Labour

What then is the former concept? It derives from Marshall's original idea of transfer earnings of a factor. In this sense rent is the payment to a unit factor of production in excess of what is needed to keep that unit in its present use. Everything else received by that factor unit is its transfer earnings, which are determined by the next best occupation available to it. This is applicable to any factor.[1] Labour in a particular use, say teaching, includes teachers who have other abilities they could use to earn a living and who differ one from another in their devotion to teaching. For both these reasons, even assuming one standard level of teacher e.g. with average qualifications and ability, there will be a gradient of transfer earnings in the whole profession (see Diagram 42).

Teacher 'a' is prepared to work for a very low wage, because he/she is very dedicated and/or incapable of much else. Teacher 'b' is only prepared to accept a high wage because he is not dedicated and/or could obtain highly paid work in a different occupation. Teachers

1 Since another related concept, that of quasi-rent, especially relates to the factor of capital, a discussion of the rent/transfer earnings of capital is deferred till later. See pp.115-16.

DIAGRAM 42

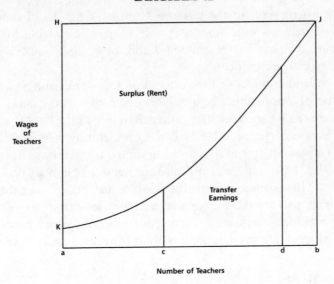

'c' and 'd' are intermediate in these respects. Therefore, if the demand for teachers is such that 'b' is required, wages paid to all teachers will be H and their total incomes the whole area abJH. This total consists of transfer earnings below the line KJ and a surplus or rent above KJ. If individual contracts were made with each teacher, regardless of any ideas of fairness or rivalry, then wages could follow the line KJ from a to b. This would not be a matter of different ability or skill within the profession, but merely of alternative work available for each teacher and his/her personal attitude to the profession of teaching.

Such an analysis applies to anyone, as a labour unit, in any occupation. If workers vary in ability then there will also be differentials paid for higher ability. Thus a star footballer may earn many times what an ordinary player may earn. The difference is not what the line KJ indicates. However, a star player, like everyone else, has transfer earnings, which depend on his alternative earnings, say as a football coach, and his dedication to football. Some star players may have very low transfer earnings and huge surpluses. Equally an ordinary player, who is also a trained bricklayer, for example, may have in theory higher transfer earnings than the star.

Transfer Earnings of Land

The same analysis applies to land as a factor of production. Land of a similar type and location may vary nevertheless in transferability to other uses, thus giving individual land units different transfer earnings and a surplus or rent (in the narrow sense of rent). Land unit 'a' in farming use may have no other use; unit 'b' may be suitable for buildings because it is, say, better drained. Land, of course, unlike workers, has no personal preferences.

For both land and labour the concept of transfer earnings gives rise also to that of opportunity cost, which is the cost to the economy of using a factor in a particular use, rather than in its next best alternative use. In the case of farming land 'b', the opportunity cost of its use in farming is what it could have 'earned' by transferring its use to building-land. Land unit 'a', on the other hand, has almost no opportunity cost. This is analogous to the labour case, except that the latter is influenced also by the personal aspect of dedication to particular work. An especially dedicated teacher, for example, may have transfer earnings which are considerably less than his opportunity cost.[2]

Ricardian Rent

This concept of surplus or rent is quite distinct from the broader concept of the classical economists. Rent in the Ricardian or classical sense is the excess of the returns to any factor unit over the returns to the unit of the same factor which receives the lowest returns in the economy i.e. the marginal factor unit. This also applies in theory to any kind of factor (see Diagram 43).

For labour the lowest returns are the wages of the lowest paid, such as general labourers. Any excess over this level of income, owing to greater natural ability, training or skill can be called a surplus. In the short run, of course, there are surpluses arising from shifts in demand and supply for particular kinds of labour as conditions in final goods markets and factor markets change. Wages of car workers may rise as demand for cars shifts upwards or as the price of car components varies. However, such disequilibrium differentials disappear in the long run, leaving permanent or equilibrium differentials that depend upon natural abilities, necessary training, effort required and ineradicable features like dangerous or unpleasant working conditions in some industries. Equilibrium differentials determine the surplus paid to each type of worker over the wages to the lowest paid. What determines the latter's wages, the basic wage throughout the economy, is dealt with later (Chapter 10).

---

2 This assumes that the wages of the teacher measure his contribution to the economy. In fact, his dedication may be a considerable unmeasured contribution.

DIAGRAM 43

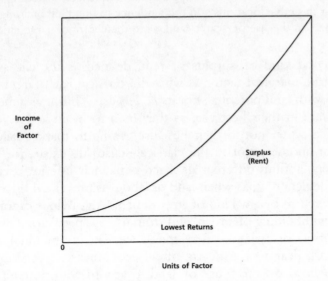

For land the lowest returns are the rent paid for land units of the least productive kind in use in the economy – marginal land. This may be zero in conditions which may be termed free land. In present conditions of land tenure and taxation in the UK and all similar economies – probably indeed throughout the world – marginal land does not have a zero rent, because no free land is available. Non-marginal land receives a surplus or rent which is determined by the nature and location of the land unit concerned. Type of soil, the presence of minerals or building-materials, proximity to populations, markets, transport facilities, public services, use of adjacent sites and so on create a surplus. The distinction between short-run and long-run differentials may not be clear-cut, but some will be permanent and others slow to change, such as transport facilities. Leases vary in length, or have rent revision clauses, partly owing to the likelihood of changed conditions.

Lipsey makes it clear that high mobility of land amongst alternative uses, (i.e. its low economic rent in the sense of excess over transfer earnings) in no way precludes its very high rent in the sense of excess over the product on marginal land when location is significant:

> Although land is highly mobile among alternative uses, it is completely immobile as far as location is concerned. There is only so much land within a given distance of the centre of any city, and no increase in the price paid can induce further land to be located within that distance.

> This locational immobility has important consequences, including high prices for desirable locations and the tendency to build tall buildings to economize on the use of scarce land, as in the centre of large cities.
>
> Lipsey and Chrystal, *Positive Economics*, 8th edn, p.340

This second kind of surplus or rent, defined as the excess over returns to the marginal factor, is what the classical law of rent refers to. It deals with land potential, not its *de facto* use. Thus it assumes that all factors are in their best use, as they tend to be in a free market system. If they are not in their best use, owing to market failure of one sort or another, rent in the classical sense still exists, for it is a result of equilibrium differentials. Factors in their inferior uses only appear to deplete rent, as when land or labour is prevented from finding its best return by any kind of impediment. An obvious example of this is the withholding of urban land from use by speculators, by planning authorities or by landowners' indolence. The optimum allocation of resources, dear to the hearts of all economists, is very much a matter of allowing *de facto* use of land to accord with potential best use of land as depicted by the law of rent.

Confusion of Rent Concepts

Modern economic analysis sometimes claims to have generalised the classical concept of rent by developing the concept of rent as excess over transfer earnings.[3] In fact, it has trivialised the classical concept by confusing it with the modern one. The outcome of such confusion has been a failure to explain major aspects of the economy as a system. The theory of the determination of wages has been, almost literally, undermined. Rent in the classical sense is no longer correctly identified and therefore can be safely ignored as a large part of national income available for taxation or other purposes. Since rent as a surplus over transfer earnings is only an incremental amount, it seems to be a fairly insignificant feature of a dynamic economy, best left in the hands of the recipients. Yet rent measured as the excess over marginal factor returns is huge and of compelling importance.

For example, the rent (in the narrow Marshallian sense) of a site in the City of London may be quite small, if its transfer earnings when used by a law firm are only slightly less than its earnings when used by a bank. Yet its rent (in the wider Ricardian sense) as the excess earnings over the least productive sites in the economy, say remote farms, is enormous. To assimilate the two kinds of rent is an astounding

---

3 See, for example, Lipsey & Chrystal, *Positive Economics*, 8th edn, p.343.

blunder, which plays into the hands of vested interests, i.e. landlords, who are unwilling to disclose their real 'earnings'.

If one sets aside questions of the motivation of property interests, there remains a further answer to why such confusion has arisen. Modern economics is often defined as the study of the allocation of scarce resources that have alternative uses. How the price mechanism works in a free market system is, of course, largely concerned with this. Prices are inducements to consumers to maximise their satisfaction by making marginal utilities proportional to prices, or (if cardinal measurements of utility are eschewed) by making marginal rates of substitution of goods equal to slopes of budget lines (using indifference curves). Similarly prices are inducements to producers to make marginal costs equal to prices of final goods, thus achieving optimum efficiency in the use of resources. All such analysis in consumer and factor markets reveals how scarce resources are allocated to alternative uses, and has plentiful fruits in applied areas of economics, like government policy on price controls and direct taxes, and questions of market failure related to social costs and benefits that the market ignores. However, at worst, such analysis tells us things that common sense recognises, and at best deals only with the rather superficial question of the allocation of resources after the present distribution of factors of production between owners is taken for granted. As a consequence of great inequalities in the distribution of land and capital, the outcome of the final allocation of resources to consumers in a market system is far from optimal. Hence governments are forced to intervene widely at many points in the economy, notably by means of an increasingly elaborate welfare state and a complex tax system to support it.

Confusion about the meaning and extent of rent has arisen because economists have forgotten the original fundamental questions that Ricardo, especially, was asking. What determines the level of wages? What determines returns to landowners? Why are unearned incomes and their capitalised values so large? Why is economic progress accompanied by endemic poverty? Above all, what is economic justice? Such questions drive economists back to root concepts, like rent in the classical sense.

CHAPTER 10

Wages

S INCE WAGES are the reward for work and most people obtain their income from work, the level of wages is undoubtedly the best measure of the material wellbeing of any society. This fact is surprisingly overlooked by those who attach more importance to Stock Exchange prices, and even regard rises in real wages as a cause for concern. The modern theory of wage determination enhances this attitude by failing to look at the basic conditions under which the laws determining wages operate. Lipsey and Chrystal, for example, regard the application of the general laws of supply and demand to the question of the incomes of factors of production (i.e. the principle of derived demand) as a 'great insight' (Lipsey and Chrystal, *ibid.*, pp.329-30). Yet they fail to note that these laws operate in the context of an economy where there are enormous inequalities in land ownership, which have a decisive influence on the level of wages. Nevertheless supply and demand analysis must play a part in wage determination, so we may use it as a starting point.

Equilibrium and Disequilibrium Differentials
In the short run, disequilibrium differentials in the labour market lead to workers receiving more or less than the equilibrium rate for the work they do. Such differentials include, especially, those arising from changes in demand and supply conditions in particular industries, as when demand for mobile telephones increases or cars are in short supply, so that workers in those industries receive short-term wage rises, until labour has moved from other industries which release labour. In principle, disequilibrium differentials disappear in the long run, leaving only equilibrium differentials due to permanent features of labour supply and demand, like rare natural ability, special training and gender. These may be associated with irrational views on inferiority of race or sex, for example, which nevertheless have a bearing on the wage rates determined by supply and demand.

Demand Curve for Labour

All such equilibrium differentials act to give workers higher or lower wages than what may be called the general level of wages. The real question is what determines this general level. According to the theory of derived demand firms will equate the marginal physical product (MPP) of labour, multiplied by the price of the product (which gives marginal revenue product MRP), to the wage rate WR (MPP x P = MRP = WR). Owing to diminishing returns MPP curves are downward sloping. If the firm has a downward sloping demand curve for its product due to a degree of monopoly power, then it will replace price with marginal revenue (MR), making MPP x MR = MRP = WR. If it has monopsony power in the labour market, because it employs a large proportion of the local workforce or dominates a particular industry, for example, then it will make MPP x P (or MR) equal to the marginal cost of labour (MCL), which is then above the WR. The firm is employing less labour than it would if it were not the sole buyer of labour, so leaving MRP above the wage rate.

DIAGRAM 44

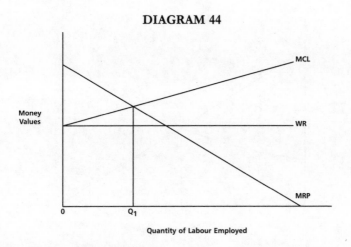

Quantity of Labour Employed

Cases where the labour market is not fully competitive are however divergencies from the general case where MRP = WR. Most firms will employ labour to the point where this equation holds, as part of the profit maximising strategy of achieving the equation of marginal cost and marginal revenue. The firm's MRP curve becomes its demand curve for labour, since whatever the wage rate it will move to an MRP equal to it. For the industry, however, the demand curve for labour will generally be steeper than the sum of the individual firms' MRP curves, as industry demand for the product slopes downwards, thus making the price of the product fall as the whole industry employs more labour.

Supply Curve for Labour

Supply of labour to a competitive firm will be very elastic, as labour can move from similar firms if any one firm raises its wage rate. For the industry, supply will be less elastic, to a degree determined by the mobility of labour to and from other industries, though it may be fairly high for unskilled workers and for skilled workers of the same kind. For example, carpenters may move easily from building to furniture industries. Mobility is likely to be much less between occupations than between industries. The elasticity of labour supply curves therefore varies considerably, though in the long term it is always greater, because new workers enter the labour force and others can retrain. For any industry then supply and demand analysis applies, with these and other qualifications, to the labour market, giving a determinate wage rate and number employed:

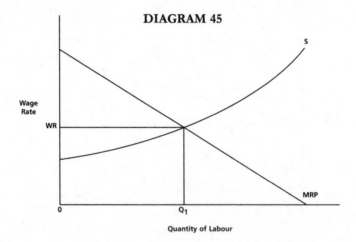

DIAGRAM 45

The General Level of Wages

For the whole economy, however, and therefore for the general level of wages, the analysis cannot be derived from a summation of all firms' MRP and labour supply curves. If all MRP curves are horizontally added, the resulting downward sloping curve cannot be a total demand curve for labour. The demand for, and prices of, final goods and services are themselves a function of the level of total wages.

Hence the derived demand for labour based upon MRP is not an independent variable; it is largely determined by the wage rate itself and by the quantity of labour employed. Hence there is no MRP curve for the whole economy.

There may still be a labour supply curve for the whole economy. Again we cannot simply add together firm (or industry) labour supply curves, for these are not independent of each other. However, labour supply in general consists of the total work force, made up of all people seeking work and actually in work. The number of hours worked and the number of people entering the work force – the participation rate – are both influenced by the wage rate, so some functional relationship can be established. Recent evidence suggests that the elasticity of supply of labour, at least for Western economies, is very low when measured as hours worked by the existing labour force in response to changes in the wage rate, though this is thought to be higher for women than for men. The income and substitution effects roughly cancel out.[1] The participation rate, on the other hand, shows a rather greater degree of elasticity of supply.

If unemployment benefits are taken into account, there is a minimum rate of pay below which workers prefer to remain unemployed.

DIAGRAM 46

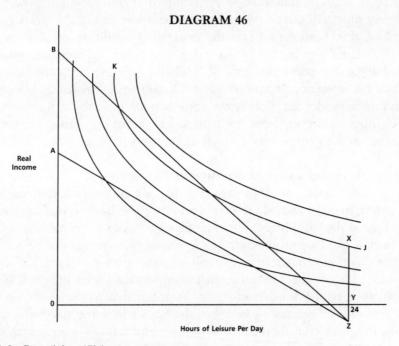

1 See Begg, *ibid.*, pp.170-1.

Indifference curves in Diagram 46 reflect choices between hours of leisure and real income.

If XY represents unemployment benefit and YZ the costs associated with working, such as fares to work, a rate of pay per hour shown by the slope of the line AZ is insufficient to induce a worker to get a job, since his real income does not enable him to reach the indifference curve KJ on which X is situated i.e. where he is if unemployed. Only a rate of pay like BZ, which cuts KJ, improves on his unemployed state. Unemployment benefit therefore sets a minimum below which wages will not fall. Yet since the actual wage rate usually exceeds this – indeed the government deliberately sets benefits below what would be regarded as an acceptable minimum in order to offer an incentive to take a job – the question of what determines the general level of wages remains.

Trade unions and minimum wage legislation influence the wage rate in some industries and occupations, but only at the expense of the level of employment. Unions can, of course, restrict entry into an occupation, which is what professional associations are also adept at achieving by means of a mixture of beneficial standards of training and detrimental artificial barriers. When firms have monopsony power both unions and minimum wage legislation offer countervailing power, and may support both the wage rate and employment in the industry. None of this, however, affects the underlying condition of workers, for differentials created in these ways, like other differentials, take as their starting point the general level of wages set by conditions outside the influence of unions and minimum wage legislators. Let us therefore consider an alternative approach to the whole question, which does, however, leave us with a labour supply curve for the economy and a general wage rate at a determinate point on it.

Self-employment as an Alternative to Employment
Every party to an exchange makes a bargain under one dominant condition, namely what alternative does he or she have to making the exchange at the price offered by the other party. For someone with no alternative, the bargain is made at the lowest price acceptable to him or her. Without an alternative no bargaining power is available. If workers have no alternative except unemployment, then they will be forced to take the lowest wage that is acceptable to them. Unions and minimum wage laws can only raise wages in some occupations above this, and even then much depends upon union funds available for unemployed workers during a strike. This apparent lack of an

alternative for workers when offered employment has become so much
a universal condition of modern economies that it is no longer noticed.
Yet even now there is an alternative in the form of self-employment.
In theory a worker who does not like to work for a preferred wage
rate can become self-employed rather than unemployed. A few do so,
but most workers do not even consider it. Why is this?

Habitual attitudes to work are part of the answer. Workers lack the
initiative to be self-employed. They literally do no know how to set up
their own business. They are deterred by bureaucratic demands, like
becoming a registered company or completing tax forms. But there are
two predominant obstacles which deter them far more than these.
Habitual attitudes might change were these two greater hurdles to be
removed. The first is the rent required, either as an annual charge or
as a premium in the form of purchasing a freehold or lease for the use
of a site; in short, the need for suitable and usually expensive land.
The second is the capital equipment required in most occupations to
make the business competitive.

Rent of land can be seen as a serious obstacle by adapting the
participation rate diagram:

DIAGRAM 47

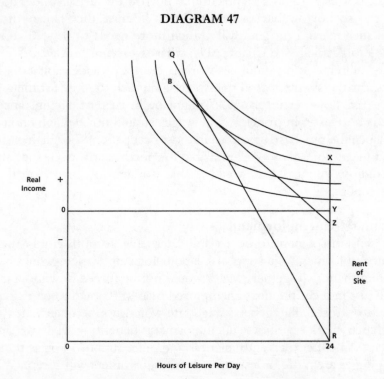

Real Income

Hours of Leisure Per Day

To make it worthwhile for an unemployed worker to rent a site for YR and become self-employed, his rate of earnings whilst self-employed must be at least equal to the slope of QR, with probably a working day in excess of eight hours also. For most workers this is unattainable, even without other costs of self-employment. How can a self-employed craftsman, for example, compete with firms which employ similar workers at the rate of BZ with a mark-up for overheads and profits?

Secondly, to be self-employed requires capital, in the sense of real goods used in the production of further goods, i.e. machinery, tools, vehicles and so on, and indeed buildings, which are capital and not land. Except for minor items, these are usually beyond the power of workers to purchase out of wages. Unemployed workers may set themselves up as window cleaners with a ladder and a bucket, as car mechanics in their own backyard with a set of wrenches etc., or as gardeners with a lawn-mower and spade, but they do not usually set up as a manufacturing business, a bus company, or a department store. Such capital intensive firms often depend upon borrowing in the form of shares, bonds or bank loans, of course, but workers whose sole income is wages are not in a position to borrow on such a scale. Those who can so borrow have access to loans because they already hold assets such as land or 'goodwill'. Much more needs to be said about the role of capital (see Chapter 11); what is certain, however, is that in general in modern economies workers do not provide capital out of wages, for the simple reason that wages are much too low for them to do so. Yet, however difficult this might be in current circumstances, there is no reason in principle why wages should not be high enough to finance the purchase of capital in most occupations. For high wages would mean not only money available for purchase of assets, but also the credit-worthiness that would enable workers to borrow on their own account.

'Voluntary' Unemployment

Were self-employment to be a viable alternative to both employment and unemployment, the supply of labour for employment would be a different matter altogether. Wages would not be forced down to a rate which just induces the next unemployed man or woman to participate in the workforce. The general wage rate would not be determined by a minimal mark-up above unemployment benefit – whatever just induces someone to give up idleness and State support. For as things stand wages are more or less at the least that workers will accept. Why should firms pay more than this? When unemployed workers are available, who are prepared to work for the least they will accept, why should any other worker be paid anything more, except when he has greater qualifications, skill or other qualities worth a differential payment? Unemployment ensures that the wage is the least acceptable. It makes no difference if some workers are 'voluntarily unemployed' and others 'involuntarily unemployed', according to recent analysis. Indeed this distinction helps to show how the wage rate at present fluctuates around the least acceptable. (A putative labour demand curve LD is retained for the purpose of this analysis.)

DIAGRAM 48

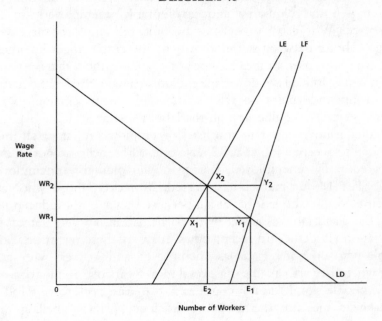

LF shows the labour force as a function of the wage rate, thus demonstrating that participation increases slowly as the wage rate rises. Yet employment may not be at E1, and the wage rate at WR1, because some members of the workforce, though induced into it, i.e. they are looking for a job, will not agree to work at a rate of WR1. This may well be because they have an above average degree of skill or wish to preserve some other kind of differential, but if not, then it represents those workers' view that WR1 is unacceptably low. They will only work for more. X1Y1 measures how many people take this view about WR1. At WR2, however, some of these are now prepared to work, but X2Y2

still hold out for a higher rate. Thus LE (labour employment) shows
that part of the workforce actually prepared to work at various wage
rates. The horizontal distances between LE and LF are said to
measure 'voluntary unemployment', which is a euphemism suggesting
that workers really choose to be unemployed. Part of this gap represents frictional unemployment as workers change jobs, but primarily
it means that some workers who intend to work find the going rate
unacceptable. Their 'choice' to be unemployed is like that of a man in
a prison, who 'chooses' not to eat the prison food because he finds it
unacceptable – he is 'voluntarily' hungry. But why is he in prison, or,
indeed, who put him there?

For the essential question is why is there a pool of unemployed
workers – both 'voluntarily' and 'involuntarily' unemployed – in the
first place? Why can workers not become self-employed or have a
genuine choice between self-employment and employment by others?
We have got so used to the existence of unemployment that we regard
it as normal. Indeed we now have the unfortunate phrase 'the natural
rate of unemployment' to refer to unemployment remaining when
there is so-called 'equilibrium' in the labour market. WR2 and E2 are
the 'equilibrium' wage rate and level of employment, since all those
prepared to accept a job at WR2 have one. Those who do not (X2Y2)
are 'voluntarily' unemployed, leaving no 'involuntarily unemployed'
at all. The labour market has cleared. Moreover, those who have
not entered the labour force at all, because they are not induced into
it by the wage rate associated with participation, are left out of the
calculation altogether. In recent times many of these might be young
people who do not register as unemployed and workers who retire
early when they are capable of several more years of productive work.
These people simply do not count as part of the work force. Modern
economists measure them out of existence, whilst labelling their
fellows who look for work but want a better wage as 'voluntarily
unemployed'.

Unemployment and Marginal Land

Why then has this condition of a pool of unemployed workers and a
wage rate set by the least that workers will accept become endemic in
modern economies? There is, of course, an historical answer associated with the gradual enclosure of land in European economies and
more rapid enclosure in America, where there was some unenclosed
land up to about 1890. Much historical debate centres on questions of
enclosure and its necessity or otherwise in relation to the industrial

revolution. What economists seem to ignore, however, is the present-day operation of land enclosure; the present economic system of an economy in which absolute private property in land fundamentally determines its character. In relation to the level of wages, such a system operates by effectively destroying the extensive margin as a natural regulator. The marginal revenue product of labour must be more or less equal on all sites in use in the economy – subject to equilibrium differentials and monopoly features of final goods and factor markets. On the least productive sites in use MRP must roughly equal MRP on all other sites i.e. the intensive margins are equal. If land were available free of payments to a private landlord on the extensive margin, then wages would be equal to the value of the net product there. Any worker choosing not to work for a firm elsewhere could open production, with other like-minded workers if they so chose, on an available rent free site. Since MRP on all other sites would then equal the MRP on the extensive margin and since the wage rate equals MRP, the wage rate would be set by the net product available on the rent-free site. This is the natural regulator of wages; the natural law which determines the wage rate. Karl Marx quoted E.G. Wakefield, who had seen at first hand the effect of free land in British colonies:

> Where land is very cheap and all men are free, where every one who so pleases can easily obtain a piece of land for himself, not only is labour

DIAGRAM 49

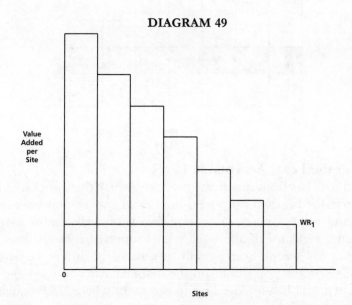

very dear, as respects the labourer's share of the produce, but the difficulty is to obtain labour at any price.

Karl Marx, *Capital*, Vol 2, p.852, Everyman edn, J.M. Dent, New York, 1957

With free land wages are set by the full product on the marginal site WR1 (Diagram 49) i.e. on the extensive margin. (NB height of columns is value added, or average product of labour, per site.) MRP equals WR1, on all sites.

On the other hand, with all land enclosed, the wage rate WR2 falls to the least that workers will accept and scarcity rent appears (Diagram 50, see also pp.77-8). With enclosed land MRPs on all sites are equal and also equal to the wage rate (WR2) now set by the least acceptable wage.

DIAGRAM 50

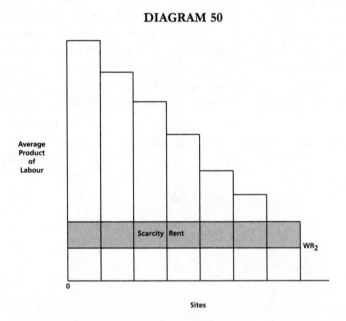

Wages at the Least Acceptable Level

When all land has become private property, which the owner may hold out of use for his own purposes, such as in expectation of a future rise in land values, there are no rent-free sites available for workers. The natural regulator of the wage rate is superseded by the least that the worker will accept. Scarcity rent appears as the difference between the average product of labour on the marginal site and the wage rate. Workers will still be employed up to the point where MRP equals the wage rate, as the preceding analysis confirms, but this point will generally be reached at a more labour intensive (and perhaps more capital intensive) style of production on most sites in use, because there are less sites in relation to the same labour force (even allowing for unemployed workers).

Land enclosure thus intensifies production on the sites remaining in use, a fact easily confirmed by observation of the highly intensive use of city centres and industrial complexes. The typical modern land use pattern of immense city populations, surrounded by relatively empty rural areas, to which we are now accustomed, is the fruit of land enclosure. A natural gradation of land use has been broken up by large areas either held out of use altogether, or under-utilised because workers are drawn into urban sites using what is literally cheap labour.

Rent is correspondingly inflated by the forced reduction in the wage rate. Rent differentials may be enhanced, and what appears on all sites left in use is a large element of scarcity rent attributable to the presence of a labour force seeking work on a limited number of sites. Free land effectively means an unlimited number of sites, for if a site is available free of rent it is irrelevant how many others remain (at least until a foreseeably small number only remain free). But if a land enclosed economy develops as population and/or technology grow, the intensification of land use makes scarcity rents rise continuously. As a share of total output wages fall and rent increases, greatly affecting both the functional distribution of income between factors and the personal distribution of income between individuals. Greater inequality of incomes is a clearly recorded feature of developing Western economies.

What then of the labour supply curve for the present-day economy? From the minimum wage rate just above the unemployment benefit level (N1M1 in Diagram 51), it rises slightly to induce more employment at N2. At the wage rate which is generally considered the least acceptable (N2M2), it becomes horizontal, until at low levels of unemployment it rises sharply (N3M3) and becomes in theory vertical at full employment (N4).

Obviously the actual wage rate may fluctuate slightly above or below N2M2 as real GDP varies in the short term, and in the long term the generally acceptable rate may rise or fall with changed conditions, such as workers' expectations of higher material living standards. What remains true, however, is that a wage rate so set is the mark to which all firms must approximate MRP. The latter is not the determinant of

DIAGRAM 51

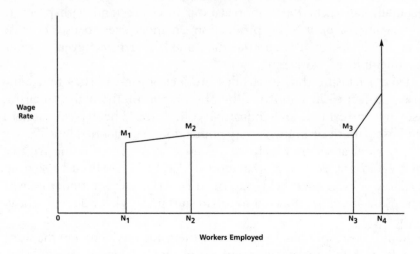

the wage rate. It is the marginal site in the economy that holds the key. Under what conditions do land and labour meet at that point? The answer to that question measures the material well-being of society, and also, it will be argued, the economic freedom available to its members.

CHAPTER 11

Capital

THE CONCEPT of capital in economic theory has been beset with difficulties. Not only have economists used various concepts, but many of them have failed to use their own concept unambiguously. From this confusion have arisen a host of problems concerning such closely related concepts as profit, interest, investment and saving. One source of these difficulties was Adam Smith's *Wealth of Nations*, where he asserts that:

> As the accumulation of stock must, in the nature of things, be previ-
> ous to the division of labour, so labour can be more and more sub-
> divided in proportion as stock is previously more and more accumulated.
>
> A. Smith, *Wealth of Nations*, Book II, Intro, p.241, Everyman, J.M. Dent, 1933

This assumes that a division of labour, where only some workers produce the means of subsistence, can only occur when these work-ers have accumulated subsistence goods sufficient to maintain them-selves and others, whilst the others go on to produce non-subsistence goods. Whatever the historical origins of economic society may have been – and Plato unequivocally begins with a division of labour when discussing origins in his *Republic* – Smith's view is certainly wrong as regards the operation of an existing economy. Subsistence goods are made alongside and contemporaneously with non-subsistence goods, and the process of exchange enables all workers to subsist. The fact that at any point in time there need to be stocks is of no more signif-icance than the fact that there need to be people working. Workers consume stocks, but equally stocks arise from work. Logically there can be no doubt that the application of labour precedes the accumu-lation of stocks. The dismal history of the wage-fund theory in the nineteenth century was a consequence of Smith's error; unfortunately wage-fund thinking still lurks in the minds of present day apologists for capitalism.

Further confusion has arisen and persists, especially in the field of applied economics and finance, over the distinction between capital and its ownership, or, more broadly, claims upon it. As Schumpeter said, you cannot ride upon a claim to a horse. Nor can you make textiles with a claim to a textile factory. Shares, debentures, mortgages, bills and other financial instruments are all claims, usually upon capital assets like buildings, machinery, vehicles and so on. They may loosely be called capital, but economics cannot advance by loose thinking. Of course, the distinction can be made between physical capital and financial capital, but to avoid ambiguity altogether it is preferable to distinguish systematically between capital, or actual means of production, and claims upon it.

Capital may then be defined as wealth used in the production of further wealth, where wealth is primarily a stock of produced goods. Individuals in their private capacity possess wealth, not capital, except in the sense of articles like a private car, washing machine, lawnmower and so on, which can be disregarded as only yielding future streams of private services. If all claims on capital, such as those of shareholders, were cancelled, the amount of capital in the economy would remain exactly the same. With the stroke of a pen the capital of firms could, in theory, be transferred to the workers in those firms, without any change in the capital actually available for production.

Is Land Capital?

Capital, so defined, includes neither money nor land. The former is a claim of a special kind; the latter is not produced and is therefore neither capital nor even wealth. (Claims on both money and land, of course, exist also.) Where economists treat land as capital, they are ignoring their own definitions and forgetting distinctions which are fundamental. Land is enormously more extensive than capital, both geographically and in its impact on an economy. It is the mother of production, whilst capital is the midwife. It is unmoving, indestructible, and the source of all raw materials. Both labour and capital work upon land always and everywhere. Since it is not produced it has no costs of production and therefore no supply price. To ignore these distinctions is to stand with the asses on the wrong side of the bridge. The fact that land, labour and capital can all be allocated to their best uses by a price system in no way obliterates the conceptual boundary between land and capital.

Contemporary opinion, including that of economists and politicians, often asserts that the distinction between land and capital is impossible to maintain, at least in any practical sense, since improvements to land are so widespread as to wipe out any identifiable component of 'pure' land as a gift of nature or God. Land and capital have 'merged' for so long, so the argument goes, that they are best treated as one for both theoretical and practical purposes. This question is discussed later (pp.329-30), but a short answer to it is that any time period can be chosen – say twenty-five years – within which improvements can be identified as capital expenditure and recorded as easily as any other capital expenditure (adjusted for inflation or deflation, if necessary). All earlier improvements can then be treated as land. Any further questions about who owns the improved land are about claims on it and not about capital as such. It is usually those making such claims who seem to find it very difficult to distinguish capital from land, for they suffer from the myopia of vested interest.

The Use of Capital

In the very long run, of course, there is no capital because it is all used up in production. With the exception of buildings and much social capital, like roads and port facilities, most capital has a life which amounts to only a few years and could be treated as current expenditure in a ten year accounting period. Dramatic historical proof of this was given by the recovery of West Germany after the Second World War, when almost all industrial capital there had been destroyed. Within a decade West Germany had recovered as an industrial power. Land, labour and credit had created new capital, which technologically was more advanced than that of competing industrial nations. Loss of national land by comparison is a calamity, as German politicians in the inter-war period were only too keen to dwell upon.

Strictly the use of capital is the use of services that capital offers. A machine is not consumed or cannibalised in production, though of course stocks of raw materials and work-in-progress are. Its services are used in the productive process. Hence capital costs to users are of the nature of a rental charge in a time period. Three equations therefore define the character of the production and use of capital. The producer of capital goods equates his selling price per unit to the marginal cost of production ($P = MC$). This is modified if he has monopoly or monopsony power in final or factor markets. The lessor of the capital good, who may in principle also be the producer or the user of the good, equates the price which he pays for the good with the present value of the future flow of rentals from hiring it out ($P = $ Discounted rentals or DR). Thirdly the lessee or hirer equates the annual rental with the annual value to him of the use of the goods (Rental R = Marginal Revenue Product of capital or MRP).

Many capital goods are sold directly to the user. Hence a simpler analysis might seem more appropriate, which does not take into account a lessor. There are, however, two major reasons for an analysis including producer, lessor and user. Firstly, capital includes buildings, many of which are leased for a rent payment. Secondly, the function of an interest rate in the analysis is more clearly identified, since the lessor is the recipient of the interest. If the user buys the capital goods outright, of course, he is the recipient of interest, but then he needs to be regarded in two roles, as user and as lessor. In view of the argument below concerning interest rates, it is crucial to identify at what point in the analysis interest rates appear.

The capital producer thus settles for an output of Q1 units in Diagram 52

DIAGRAM 52

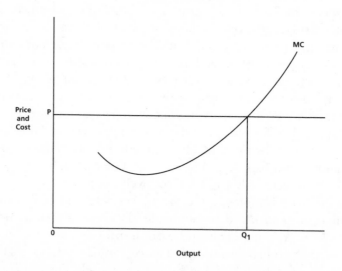

The lessor buys capital goods at the market price (P) and calculates the discounted rental flow (DR) by taking into account the market rate of interest and the life of the good. If the former is i, expressed as a fraction, and the latter is t, then an annual rent of R yields a present value of:

$$\frac{R}{i} \times \left(1 - \frac{1}{1+i}\right)^t$$

If the life were infinite, the formula reduces to R/i.

The user experiences a falling MRP of capital, if he increases capital by one unit holding other factors constant, assuming production is carried on under diminishing returns. Thus he employs K1 units of capital (Diagram 53).

DIAGRAM 53

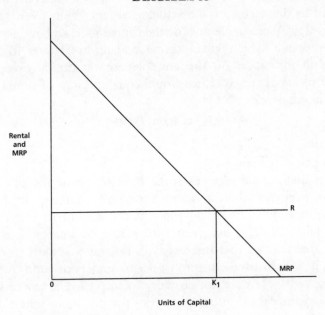

The firm's MRP curve thus becomes its demand curve for capital, in the same way as the MRP of labour curve is its demand curve for labour.

Thus we have three equations:

$$P = MC$$
$$P = \frac{R}{i} \times \left(1 - \frac{1}{1+i}\right)^t$$
$$R = MRP$$

It follows that for any given capital good price P, the rental required for it to be sold to a lessor must be higher the higher the rate of interest, since a higher rate of interest depresses the discounted flow of rentals. Therefore the higher must be MRP, which has to equal the rental. Hence, as the market interest rate goes up or down the amount of capital employed by the firm will be less or more respectively. This is, of course, a common sense conclusion, which any business man would endorse.

Interest and the Supply Price of Capital

What is perhaps less evident is that interest is not part of the supply price of capital. It is received, not by capital producers, but by lessors, or by those who lend funds to lessors if the latter are not self-financing. In the latter case the lessors pay over to lenders the interest represented by the excess of the actual total rental flow over the total discounted flow. Were the lessor (or the capital user) to have access to funds interest free (which will be discussed later in Chapter 13), there would be no inhibition on the employment of capital except the amount of its supply price.[1] Price would equal the sum of rental flows ($P = Rt$), in which case:

$$P = MC = Rt = (MRP)t$$

Such equations are the root of a labour theory of value to be developed below (Chapter 14).

The idea that capital receives some kind of economic reward or earnings is deep-seated in modern economic thinking. In fact, it receives nothing above its supply price. Without a rate of interest this would be fairly evident; but even with a rate of interest it is clear enough if one realises that interest is in no way a reward to capital producers, lessors or users. It simply goes to lenders of funds, who do nothing else *per se*. They are not providers of capital. The workers, land and capital in the capital goods industries provide it, and their capital is similarly so provided. Such a process – roundabout production using capital goods – needs credit (not 'stock' or a wages fund), but that is another matter (see Chapter 13).

In this very real sense capitalism does not exist. There are no capitalists, unless we call firms that make, lease or use capital goods by this name, which would be very confusing because they are just producers of particular types of goods and services, namely capital goods and, indirectly, capital services. In every society, especially industrial ones, capital is needed, regardless of who owns or lays claim to it. In that trivial sense only, societies are capitalist. We may designate societies that use very large amounts of capital per worker or head of population capitalist, but if we do then ancient Egypt with its irrigation systems and pyramids and the post-war USSR were perhaps as capitalist as any modern Western economy. Castigating a modern economic system as exploitation by capitalists is to blame an army of ghosts. Economic injustice has a more substantial source.

---

1 Lessors would need to make a charge for their services, quite distinct from interest.

Quasi-Rent

Yet since Alfred Marshall invented the term quasi-rent, economists have been aware of how capital may indeed receive a factor income in excess of supply price. This, however, is a short-term phenomenon, arising from the specificity of capital. Fresh capital cannot be rapidly introduced into an industry using specific capital, because it cannot be transferred from other industries. Nor can it be moved out for use elsewhere. Hence until the capital goods industries produce more on one hand, or until specific capital wears out on the other, specific capital will receive returns above or below its supply price.

DIAGRAM 54

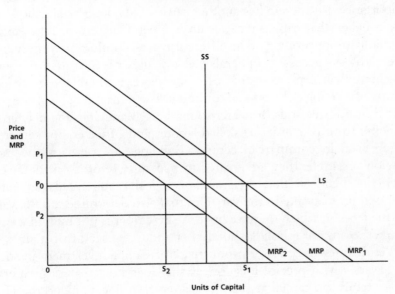

In Diagram 54 if MRP rises or falls to MRP1 or MRP2, with say a rise or fall in demand for the final product, price moves to P1 or P2 along the fixed short-run supply curve SS. When, in the long run, the supply of capital can expand or contract to S1 or S2 along the long-run supply curve LS, then MRP equals the long-run supply price which may be unaltered at P0 if LS is completely elastic. P1 creates a positive quasi-rent; P2 creates a negative quasi-rent. Whilst explaining how the price system enables capital supply to meet final goods demand via derived demand, this in no way implies that capital receives an income in its own right. Short-term market gains and losses are a feature of all free markets. Only if artificial barriers intervene, such as monopoly power of a capital goods producer, which enable it to keep prices permanently high, do quasi-rents appear to be a genuine return. In which case they are in reality monopoly profits.

In the case of the industry demand curve for capital, the summation of capital goods firms' MRP curves, as with the case for labour demand, must be modified to allow for the fall in the price of the final product as more is produced at higher levels of capital use. Thus the industry demand curve will be steeper than the summation curve to a degree determined by the elasticity of demand for the final product.

Capital and Rent

In the whole economy the question of land use again is of critical importance, for therein lies another cause of the long-established mistaken belief that capital receives an independent return. Like labour, capital is more productive in different places. Mining machinery on a site with easy access to minerals yields a higher return than the same machinery on a poor source of minerals, e.g. where there are coal seams of varying richness and/or depth. Farm machinery is more productive on fertile soils or nearer to markets. Manufacturing machinery benefits from proximity to skilled labour, and office equipment from being used in commercial centres. Buildings are perhaps the most obvious example: they are created to maximise returns on the investment in them, so that their size, technical requirements and style respond dramatically to the variables that also determine the site value of the land on which they are built. A skyscraper is not built in a small market town, nor a holiday hotel in an industrial sector of a city.

Yet the greater or lesser productivity of capital investment in so far as it varies with precise location or site does not create a greater or lesser return on capital as such. It is a return to location and therefore to land i.e. rent. For who captures this return? Not the firm producing the capital – the builders or the capital machinery manufacturers, for they only receive the supply price of capital (subject to the usual strictures about monopoly power, quasi-rents, etc.); nor the users of the capital (or their suppliers of rental services of capital), for if they are in a competitive industry they can only receive gross receipts which just cover their costs, including capital (services) and normal profits. The gain from this rent received for employing capital on better sites, i.e. compared with marginal sites, must be received by whoever owns the site, for the landowner can demand from the user all revenue which does not need to be paid for the supply of inputs on the site. The firm as a tenant of the site may be the initial recipient of all the revenue, but any residue above normal profits will be claimed by the landowner. Leases at fixed rents for a period of years, of course, may yield some rent to the tenant.

Rent arising thus from the employment of capital has led economists who underrate the importance and role of land to assign to capital a power to create a return or income of its own which it does not possess. Capital is inert. It is used by labour on land. Without labour capital is always useless. Human consciousness, and usually human mental and physical work, are required for capital of any form at all – from robots and computers to stone buildings – to be productive. The greater the capital investment on a site, other things being equal, the greater the return on the capital, but this return is only the supply price of that capital. If there is a further return, as there will be on all except marginal sites, then it goes to the landowner (or leaseholder, as the case may be). Of course, without capital investment the full rent of the site may not be realised; it remains in potential, but this is precisely so with the application of labour, without which no rent is realised also.

Returns on Capital Investment

Two other features of capital investment tend to reinforce the illusion of a special return to capital over and above its supply price. One is the frequency with which the landowner (or leaseholder) is often the very same individual or firm as the capital investor. Indeed many successful businesses ensure that they obtain a freehold before they invest on a site.

> Ironically, Ray Kroc, who founded and then expanded McDonald's as much by buying and renting property as by selling hamburgers, has left the group a gold mine to exploit. Peter Oakes, an analyst at Merrill Lynch, notes that the group owns 75% of the buildings and 40% of the land at its 30,000 locations. He calculates that the land alone, which has a book value of $4 billion, would fetch $12 billion (before tax) today. That value could be exploited through a sale-and-leaseback programme.
> *The Economist*, 12-18 April 2003, p.67

Conversely many unsuccessful businesses fail to obtain freeholds and find that they cannot pay the landlord's rent, particularly when it rises on the termination of a lease. If, however, the recipient of rent and the owner of capital are one and the same, it is easy to confuse the two streams of returns.

Secondly, the phenomenon of decreasing returns to capital also reinforces the illusion, since until the marginal unit of capital, which just produces its supply price, is reached the earlier units of capital appear to be receiving a special return of their own in excess of their supply price (the latter being the same for all units). Surely this means that capital does get an extra return?

But do non-marginal workers receive more than the marginal worker? Of course they do not, since all workers receive the same wage rate (subject to differentials). So too, all units of capital must receive the same return, equal to that received by the marginal unit. The businessman investing on a site would be surprised to be asked to pay more by the capital supplier for the 'earlier' units. He might hope to make greater profit per unit on the use of the earlier units, but the key question is, 'Is he able to?' Were he to do so then either the landlord is not demanding as much rent as he is capable of getting, or there is a lack of competition in the industry which prevents the landlord from leasing the site to another firm which would settle for a higher rent. For whenever an owner of capital receives a return above the supply price of capital, other entrepreneurs will buy and use capital to the point where excess returns are eliminated. Hence the capitalists' so-called return can only be a disguised rent of land or a monopoly profit (or in the short term a quasi-rent on capital).

A diagrammatic analysis of the application of capital to land follows closely that of labour to land. Identical units of capital applied on sites of varying potential output yield different returns initially. If a single unit is applied the returns may vary greatly, as in the case of retail shops built on sites at increasing distances from a city centre, or mining machinery employed on mines of decreasing richness or accessibility. As units of capital are increased on each site, diminishing returns operate until the last unit on each site produces only the supply price of capital (Diagram 55). (See also Diagram 29, p.75.) Since all units of capital receive the same supply price, the surpluses on non-marginal sites are rent of land. The differential return on capital with respect to location is as much rent as it is in the case of labour.

Such an analysis raises the question of why an entrepreneur who receives no rent, because he pays all the 'excess returns' on capital to a landowner, would take the trouble to remain in business. Must he not receive some return 'on his own account' i.e. *qua* entrepreneur? This issue is discussed below (Chapter 12).

The nullity of the concept of a return to capital can be understood also by showing capital expenditure as a 'below the line' payment on a diagram of differentiated sites (Diagram 56).

DIAGRAM 55

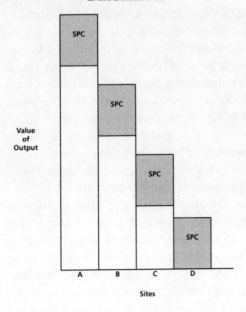

DIAGRAM 56

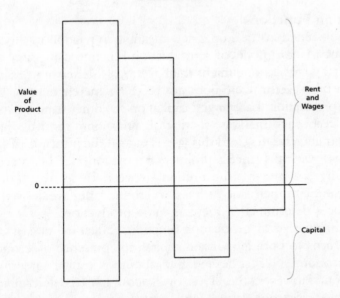

Capital need not vary systematically with output, since capital intensive industries are not necessarily high output ones. Rent and wages
can be interpreted as value added. Capital adds no value; it is simply a

cost recouped out of gross revenue. Labour and land, on the other hand, contribute to the value of production, except that land's contribution is zero on the marginal site if there is free land. By more or less ignoring rent, Karl Marx arrived by this route at the concept of labour as the sole source of value, derived from the ability of labour power to yield a return above the 'socially necessary' wage rate required to maintain it. His concept of exploitation of labour may be understood as a misreading of the effect on wages of scarcity rent.

The intensive use of capital in modern industry obscures this creation of value by land and labour exclusively. Yet if one considers a highly capital intensive industry, like car production, it is clear that all the capital on the site is 'bought in', just as are the materials, parts, power and so on. All that creates the value on the site is the application of labour in that particular place. Capital simply recoups its supply price, just as materials etc. do. If one imagines all inputs equally as a kind of inflow to the site, there is no reason at all why inputs of machinery should be taken to create value any more than inputs of steel or aluminium or glass. Machinery lasts longer in the productive process; that is all. Charging it to output as annual depreciation makes this even clearer.

Production Functions

Production functions take on a new meaning in relation to this analysis. The two-factor model of a production function using only labour and capital is not, as one might think, seriously deficient in excluding land as a third factor. Land does not receive a merely marginal increment of production. Labour and capital on the other hand are 'priced' by their respective markets, so that all units only receive what the marginal units receive. 'Unto this last' is indeed the principle of labour and capital pricing. Hence a production function may be interpreted as showing the rate of substitution between these two factors in conjunction with their isocost lines, where the latter are derived from factor prices determined at the margin of production.

The actual shape of production functions reflect the rate of diminishing returns to both labour and capital, the presence of economies and diseconomies of scale and the labour or capital intensities of production. However, the slope of isocost lines is determined by the relative prices of labour and capital as set at the margin of production.

The lines TC are total cost lines joining points of tangency of isoquants and isocost lines, where the condition that the marginal rate

DIAGRAM 57

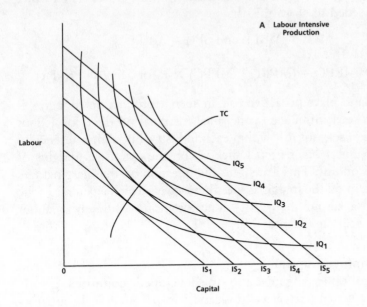

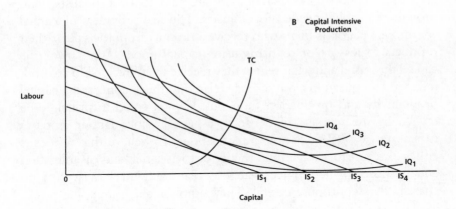

of substitution between labour and capital is equal to their relative prices is met. TC therefore represents the minimum cost of producing various outputs, given the shape of isoquants and the prices of labour and capital. The minimum cost equation is:

$$\frac{\text{Wage Rate}}{\text{Supply Price of Capital}} = \frac{\text{Marginal Physical Product of Labour}}{\text{Marginal Physical Product of Capital}}$$

or

$$\text{WR/SPC} = \text{MPPL/MPPC}$$

The firm maximises profits at some point on the TC line. The further condition needed to show this is:

$$WR = MRPL \text{ and } SPC = MRPC$$

where

$$MRPL + MRPC = (MPPL + MPPC) \times P \text{ (or MR) of Product}$$

Though land plays no active role in such a production function, it exerts an unseen influence on it, since marginal products of labour and capital are set, not just within each industry, but with reference to marginal products on marginal sites i.e. on the extensive margins of the whole economy. This leads into the question of the marginal rate of substitution on the marginal sites themselves, which again raises the question of a labour theory of value, or more accurately a labour theory of price (see Chapter 14).

Labour Employs Capital

Modern economic organisation in developed countries greatly obscures the actual part played by capital in production. Proprietors and, most confusingly, shareholders are said to be capitalists, who provide the capital needed for industry. The real providers of capital are the capital goods firms who receive a revenue from the sale of their products to lessors or to firms using capital goods. Who owns the capital thus used and what return they receive from ownership are both independent questions, not directly related to those concerning capital productivity and production functions. Capital could in principle be owned by the workers who use it, especially since labour employs capital. For capital does not employ labour. To believe that it does is either to revert to a wage fund theory or to assign a kind of animation and purpose to inert objects such as plant and machinery. Nor do shareholders contribute capital. They simply make purchasing power available to firms, which in present circumstances would not have sufficient. Such a function, if it is needed at all, could be performed perfectly well by banks, for what capital-using firms need is credit, and that is in the gift, not of shareholders or other *soi-disant* 'capitalists', but of banks (see Chapter 13). For while 'capitalists' are ghosts, credit is a real player in the economic drama, which has been largely ignored by apologists for the present system of ordering economic affairs.

CHAPTER 12

Profit

CAPITAL AS PRODUCED means of production receives its own supply price from future production and nothing more. Hence profit is not a return on capital. It makes no difference if profit is analysed into supernormal profits, risk premium and normal return by using the concept of opportunity cost. For the opportunity cost of capital is not how its money value could be re-invested elsewhere, but merely what next best alternative use could be made of the actual produced means of production, like a machine. Most machines would simply be re-allocated to an existing industry of the same type to 'earn' their supply price there.

Profits as Return on Capital

Yet there are some peculiarly persuasive arguments to the contrary. For example, does not the varying life of capital and, indeed, its life-span when compared with the almost nil life-span of variable expenses, like wages, that are written off the instant they are paid or incurred, necessitate a return for the capital owner? Take a machine lasting ten years in comparison with one lasting five years, of the same cost of £1m: surely the former must earn an extra return for the owner who has tied-up his 'capital' for twice as long? Without this return would only five year machines be used (and *a fortiori* not even five year machines compared with non-roundabout methods of production?) But what has the capital owner really done? He has bought a machine from a capital goods industry at its supply price, using £1m of money of his own or borrowed from others. Only the return on the money, which is interest, must be greater for a ten year machine, measured at compound interest, whether it is his money with an opportunity cost of the market rate, or money borrowed directly at the market rate. This return, however, is merely what the firm using the machine must include in its expected revenue in order to pay the provider of funds (which may be itself) for the use of his money. It is still in no way a return on capital.

A further argument is similar. Consider an investor deciding where to put his money in order to receive the best return. Will he buy a ten year machine if it 'earns' no more than a five year machine? Clearly not, but again what are the extra receipts so required to cover the investor's charge? Once more it is obviously interest on money invested or the opportunity cost of the money in an economy where the interest rate is positive. Capital receives nothing beyond its supply price. Its owners have to pay the excess 'earning' over to the investor. They cannot retain any claim on the excess *qua* capital owners or 'capitalists'. If they could retain any further excess it would be competed away as the industry found that the 'earnings' of capital exceeded its supply price. Indeed the firm itself would buy more capital until its marginal revenue product fell to make 'earnings' equal to supply price. (The excess on 'earlier' units of capital is received as rent by the landowner as explained above.)

What then of an investor who makes a choice between putting his money into interest-bearing bonds or into financing the purchase of machines by a firm? If the machines yield nothing above their supply price surely he will never choose to finance them, but will always buy bonds? Of course, but all this proves is that the firm must charge more for the products of the machines in order to finance them – not to pay for them, but to pay the financier the opportunity cost, perhaps plus a risk premium, of his money. This extra charge for the product is not a return on the machines.

But is there a risk premium return on capital, since the bonds do not receive one, but the machines seemingly do? No, there is not, because the risk attaches not to the machines, which can be independently insured against fire etc., but to the firm itself and the nature of its activities as a whole. Indeed no investor in a firm earmarks his funds for machines, any more than the firm ring-fences the funds under the heading 'finance for machines'. The risk really attaches to the people running the firm, for the investor is making a loan to people, however this may be disguised by legal covers like limited liability companies. How much does he trust these people to repay his loan and to pay him regular interest on it? That is the real question that he addresses when deciding upon the loan, as anyone lending money must recognise. Many conditions affect the answer – the type of business, the future prospects, competition etc., – but these are conditions surrounding the question of trust between lender and borrower. The degree of trust settles the risk premium. No return is attributable to the machines as factors of production.

Ambiguity of 'Capital'

Much of the confusion surrounding the so-called 'earnings' of capital arises from the simple ambiguity of the term as currently used. 'Capital' conventionally means both produced means of production and money or funds used to finance them. Hence whilst the former only receives its supply price, the latter receives interest. Economists make this distinction clearly in principle at the outset and then often forget it in the analysis that follows. Similarly, economists distinguish between rent of land, interest on financial 'capital' and earnings of labour, but some of them, and certainly most people untrained in the subject, fail to make these distinctions when examining company accounts, financial reports and so on. When the term 'profit' is also introduced confusion is twice confused.

In a small business the correct economic terms are easy to apply, and the firm's accountant may elucidate this. Proprietor's wages for time and skill measured as the opportunity cost of his or her next best employment may be deducted from 'profits'. So may rent of firm's premises owned by the proprietor and interest on the financial value of the 'capital' tied-up. Thus a residual profit satisfactory for an economist may be derived, though what this is a return on or for, if anything, remains somewhat obscure. However, in a large firm such refinements are easily lost. The full opportunity costs of management (i.e. as labour), rent for land of freehold property owned and interest on financial capital provided by owners are regularly left in the profits figure, making true assessment of the viability and competitiveness of the firm almost impossible. Economists who believe that capital itself (machinery etc.) receives a return *sui generis* make matters worse.

Returns for Risk

Correcting abuses of language, like inconsistencies in usage of terms, helps, but it does not answer the question of what profits really are. One strong candidate as an answer is a return for risk. In present conditions business enterprise is undoubtedly risky. Firms can be thrown off course by innumerable events endogenous or exogenous to the firm, such as natural disasters, collapse of markets, unexpected competition, rapid technological change, terrorism or war. Almost by definition a firm is an organisation which charges fairly predictable future costs against rather less predictable future income, thus in the nature of things taking a risk. Yet who takes the risk? The fact that a major part of the risk is borne by workers is often overlooked. Not only are workers' jobs at risk to the degree that an enterprise is risky, and may reduce its activities or close down, but their ability to earn wages at all is at risk when they choose an occupation, for it may turn out to be in low demand or even useless in the future. Hence a major part of the risk inherent in modern industry is borne by workers who receive little if any risk premium, beyond some redundancy payments and bonuses for dangerous work.

On the other hand, capital is usually regarded as receiving a risk premium in the form of a return above the average rate. This is a mistake. The means of production may be insured at its supply price for the risk of damage or destruction. A machine can be fully insured, perhaps at its replacement cost, and has no returns *sui generis* to be insured also. Investing in capital in the sense of firms buying capital goods to produce future final goods has no more claim to a risk premium for possible loss arising out of general uncertainty than does offering one's services as a worker or, indeed, just staying around in an uncertain world! Of course, if capital goods are very scarce for any reason, they will attract an extra receipt, but this belongs to the seller of capital goods as much as the owner. Highly specialized scarce labour attracts a similar reward.

Interest on financial 'capital', on the other hand, is 'insured' by its particular interest rate, which varies from the general market rate on loans according to the risk involved in the loan. This risk is a personal one, for the loan is a debt incurred by the proprietor of a firm to a creditor, the lender. The interest rate is a direct measure of the degree of trust between them. Modern industry obscures this also, largely owing to the legal device of the limited liability company standing between the people who manage the business and their creditors. Since the proprietors are liable for the higher interest payable if their firm's future production is risky – since they are to that extent less trustworthy – they must plan for a rate of 'profit' high enough to cover this charge. Once more, the extra returns are not profits, but interest on loans.

Returns to Entrepreneurs
Perhaps the most plausible answer to the profits puzzle is that they are a return to entrepreneurs, where the latter are taken to be an additional factor of production. The lack of focus in identifying who the entrepreneur really is stems partly from the complexity of modern industry, in which limited companies, their shareholders, directors and

managers all seem to carry some qualities of entrepreneurship and receipt of profits. Part of the problem is a tendency to circularity in the argument: entrepreneurs receive profits and profits are what entrepreneurs receive! We can only break into the circle by identifying each independently. Joseph Schumpeter made a valiant attempt to identify both, to which we return below. Meanwhile we may consider much of the so-called entrepreneurial function as a special kind of labour, which has become peculiarly conspicuous in modern conditions of industry. As firms have become larger and more complex the need for people highly skilled in organisation and management has grown. Since a pyramid structure is necessary for unified decision-making to take place, the growth in size of firms does not involve a proportional growth in the number of 'directors', but a less than proportional one. The chairman is the chairman is the chairman, even if the underlings multiply. Hence such 'directors' become increasingly powerful, prestigious and, no doubt, wealthy. It is not easy to see them as workers or labour. Yet their particular ability is intrinsically no more worthy of praise or reward than that of a scientist, technologist, lawyer or craftsman. Historical and economic circumstance since the enclosure of land and the industrial revolution has elevated organisational talents to unprecedented heights. Much more could be said about this, not least about the huge responsibility undertaken by such captains of industry and the pressures to which they are submitted, but the fact remains that they are simply workers of currently singular importance and hence earn wages, albeit exceptionally high ones. They are not as such entrepreneurs, meaning receivers of profits.

Profits of Tenants of Land

Schumpeter is certain that the entrepreneur is not the risk bearer:

> Risk obviously always falls on the owner of the means of production or of the money-capital which was paid for them, hence never on the entrepreneur as such.
>
> J.A. Schumpeter, *The Theory of Economic Development*, p.75, n.1, trans. R. Opie, OUP, New York, 1961

Schumpeter, however, like most economists, does not pay much attention to the legal relationship on a productive site of landlord and tenant (the tenant, of course, may also be the freeholder). Generally it is the tenant who carries on the business. Usually he has borrowed money to pay for the capital on the site. As tenant he receives all revenues from the enterprise and is responsible for all debts, including current expenses – wages and inputs – and long-term commitments,

like loan interest and, critically, landlord's rent. Long-term commitments are of fixed annual amounts under the terms of loan and
tenancy agreements, such as payments under bonds and leases. Even
current expenses have some element of fixed expenditure about them,
if there are legal contracts with employees and if the wage rate is
inflexible downwards, as it usually is. Revenue,
however, is entirely subject to the whims of   **DIAGRAM 58**
the market. Consumers' demand is fickle.
Retail expenditure is unpredictable and capital
goods are subject to even greater cycles than
are consumer goods. In short the tenant/pro-
ducer is faced with a steady stream of certain
outgoings and an unsteady stream of uncertain revenues. Is that not in the nature of
businesses in a competitive economy? In conditions of a genuinely free economy where
labour, land and credit are not beset by the
extraneous claims of non-producers, this
predicament of asymmetric uncertainty would
be no more than a stimulus to initiative and
foresight. Unfortunately in modern conditions of so-called 'capitalism' it has become
an almost intolerable burden.

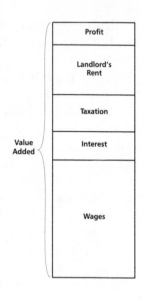

The position of the tenant/producer can
be shown diagrammatically (see Diagram 58).

Out of value added on the site (capital expenditure or depreciation
is treated as an input 'below the line'), the tenant has to pay the charges
shown. His profit is the residue. The effect of taxation is considered
at length below (Chapter 15). Most significant is the landlord's claim
for rent, which will usually absorb in the long run any rise in profits
above the minimum that the tenant regards as sufficient to stay in business. Frequency of rent reviews and length of leases determine how
quickly the landlord catches up with increasing profits. If profits fall,
the landlord's claim remains unaltered, as of course do all other claims,
except to some extent taxation, and the tenant's situation immediately
becomes precarious. He is like the man on the end of a bench full of
people, who will fall off if anyone else sits down, or even if a little
jostling takes place! Yet he is the entrepreneur upon whom the under-
taking literally depends. However large and well-established a firm may
be, if it operates as a tenant paying a full rent to a landlord its
position is always precarious.

Comparison between three conditions of tenants makes this clear.[1] The first is a firm with a long-standing freehold on its site; the second a firm which has just recently bought out the freeholder by means of a loan on which it pays interest; and the third a firm paying a full annual rent under a short lease:

DIAGRAM 59

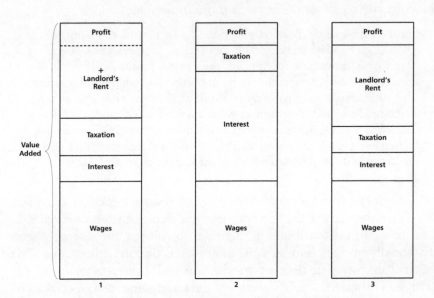

The actual rate of profits is the same in all three cases, but Firm 1 receives the landlord's rent, which in its financial accounts is probably not distinguished from profits, or may be charged as a nominal amount based on historical cost of the freehold. Firm 2 pays additional interest charges more or less equivalent to its landlord's charge prior to the recent acquisition of the freehold. It may in the course of time benefit from the fact that its interest charge remains constant in money terms, whereas its new freehold may appreciate in value, both as an asset and in its productivity. Meanwhile, it suffers from being 'highly-geared'. Firm 3 has its profits permanently subject to a landlord's claim, which can be regularly reviewed. Can these three firms be said to be competing in a free market? Yet modern economies are completely subject to these unequal conditions of producer tenancy. Such an analysis does no more than confirm by

1 See L. MacLaren, *The Nature of Society*, pp.236-7, School of Economic Science, London.

a different approach what Part 2 above demonstrates in the theory of the firm.

Schumpeter's Theory of Profits

Schumpeter gives an example of how a landlord may capture a stream of income originating as profits from promotion of a 'new combination'. A planter of sugar cane switches over to cotton production when he correctly sees that the latter is more profitable:

> For the time-being rent of land appears in the lists of costs only at the amount appropriate to sugar cane cultivation.... competition sooner or later forces down the receipts of the cotton producer. If a surplus remains, however, how is that to be explained and what is it economically? Neglecting friction, it can only result because the land either is differentially suited to cotton-growing or the rent of land has risen in general as a result of the new employments – in principle it is always a consequence of both elements. This at once characterises that part of the increase in total return which is permanent as rent of land.
>
> J. Schumpeter, *ibid.*, p.152

Schumpeter thus recognizes the place of rent, but goes on to explain how profits arise for the entrepreneur. He denies entrepreneurial risk, but nevertheless attributes a permanent role to the entrepreneur. Essentially he sees him as a promoter of economic enterprises. The normal undisturbed flow of production and consumption proceeds without entrepreneurs. Organisation and management are special kinds of labour, their reward wages. But all economies change, if only because circumstances change. Demographic, cultural, scientific and technological developments, and mere changes of taste by consumers, as well as other exogenous forces like foreign competition or war, all require that an economy adapts to circumstances. Who recognises the need to change and translates the need into action? The entrepreneur. He alters the flow of production by intervening with the aid of credit:

> What have the individuals under consideration contributed to this? Only the will and the action: not concrete goods, for they bought these – either from others or from themselves; not the purchase power with which they bought, for they borrowed this – from others or, if we also take account of acquisition in earlier periods, from themselves. And what have they done? They have not accumulated any kind of goods, they have created no original means of production, but they have employed existing means of production differently, more appropriately, more advantageously. They have 'carried out new combinations'. They

are entrepreneurs. And their profit, the surplus, to which no liability corresponds, is an entrepreneurial profit.   J. Schumpeter, *ibid.*, p.132

Indeed Schumpeter assigns an even more important role to the entrepreneur than that of responding to changes; the entrepreneur initiates advantageous changes through a kind of creative act. He envisages new combinations which will enable the economy to develop, to produce new types of goods, to meet new needs or wants, to enable new possibilities to be realised. Without the entrepreneur the economy is a repetitive process, making the same products in the same way to meet the same desires. With the entrepreneur it makes new products, by new methods, for new desires. This kind of genius of the entrepreneur marks him out from ordinary labour, however knowledgeable or skilled the latter may be. In relation to the economy even an entrepreneur who successfully develops and markets a new style of hat is a creative individual compared with the non-creative work of, say, a nuclear physicist managing an existing atomic power station. The function itself of entrepreneurship is creative:

> In the breast of one who wishes to do something new, the forces of habit rise up and bear witness against the embryonic project. A new and another kind of effort of will is therefore necessary in order to wrest, amidst the work and care of the daily round, scope and time for conceiving and working out the new combination and to bring oneself to look upon it as a real possibility and not merely as a day-dream. This mental freedom presupposes a great surplus force over the everyday demand and is something peculiar and by nature rare.
>   J. Schumpeter, *ibid.*, p.86

Profits in Modern Economic Conditions

One may, however, question Schumpeter's assumption that the rarity of such a talent is a natural fact about human nature. Modern industry enforces upon so many workers a life of routine and even drudgery, that much creative talent, initiative and foresight, i.e. entrepreneurial ability, is probably stultified. How many 'mute, inglorious Miltons' of the twenty-first century might be valuable entrepreneurs, if not poets, in radically different economic conditions? Why indeed is a 'great surplus force' required – only perhaps because the present system places in the way of creative individuals obstacles that only a few can summon the force to overcome? How can a modern farm labourer develop a farm? How can a modern department store employee create a new shop? How can a modern factory hand set up an original manufacturing enterprise? How does he or she obtain access to the land required? How is the necessary capital to be purchased?

The structure of modern industry reduces the entrepreneurial function to the province of a handful of individuals who succeed against the odds in setting up small businesses or in becoming directors of large ones. In both cases the need to set fluctuating revenues against regularly accumulating costs in order to 'earn' a precarious profit, except where rent of land comes to the rescue of freeholders or beneficial leaseholders, makes profit into a reward for risk. Tenant firms are so insecure that the limited liability company has become the standard form of business enterprise. Historically the rise of limited liability has been a consequence of the growth of land enclosure. Tenants have increasingly been forced by the ratchet effect of land-lord's rent, interest and taxation to defend themselves against their creditors by the legal device of restricting their liability for debts to the amount of financial capital already invested in the firm. Thus the limited liability company, a fictitious person, stands between the actual tenants of a site and their creditors. Without it they would be unable to raise the finance necessary to initiate and carry on production. The unprotected risk of losses is too great. Profits become a reward for risk-taking, even with the risk so reduced. The tenant-firm must receive a profit both for this and as a reward for its entrepreneurship. Yet such a profit is minimal. The claims of landowners, loan creditors and taxation ensure this. Competition between tenants reinforces it. Where profits do not appear to be minimal, then there is monopoly power, or the beneficial occupation of land obscures the issue by confusing rent and profits.

As a short-run phenomenon, however, profits fulfil a function in any economy operating with free markets. For they act as a signal to firms to change their behaviour in a favourable direction. Large profits may signal that more resources should flow towards the existing mode of production; small profits or losses the opposite. Firms expand or contract, new firms enter or leave the industry. The allocation of resources is optimised. Factors of production move to eliminate excessive variations above or below their opportunity costs. The best use of land, labour and capital can be approximated. Producers respond to the effective demand of consumers. The market system drives towards its goals through the green lights of profits and stops at the red lights of losses.

Not all firms seek to maximise profits all the time. Some minimise losses or operate with a minimum profit constraint; some may maximise revenue, especially where managers are paid for the scale of their organisation. Present conditions of land tenure, borrowings and taxation, however, certainly enforce tight profit maximisation on all firms that are marginal in the extensive or intensive sense, i.e. that occupy marginal sites or are squeezed by landlords' rent to employ factors of production to the point where all final units just 'earn' their factor price. Subject to the important proviso that firms owning freeholds or beneficial leases can afford to be less careful, Lipsey's conclusion about profits surely holds true:

> Even if no firm starts out with the intention of maximising profits, in the long run, the firms that survive in the market place will tend to be those that come closest to profit maximisation. Lipsey, *ibid.*, p.322

Function of Profits

In conclusion, profits are not a return on capital, for the produced means of production generally receives only its supply price, and returns on financial 'capital' are interest. Nor are they a return to those who organise and take responsibility for a firm, since that is a special kind of wage. Correctly identified, i.e. when rent of land and interest have been separately considered, they are a return for the tenant's risk, for the entrepreneur's promoting of new combinations of factors of production, and in the short run for correctly responding to changing conditions of the market. Often two or all three forms of the profit stream coalesce in the same firm. When the tenant is content to continue in 'traditional' fashion he only receives a risk premium; when he becomes a creative innovator he attracts what may be very substantial profits; when he responds to the market he makes short-term gains. In an economy where the availability of free land gave tenants greater security, the first of these might disappear, leaving profits as the due reward for firms that are genuine innovators and for those who merely respond effectively to ever-changing market conditions. Men and women whose natural talents meet these entrepreneurial requirements would become the proper leaders of such an economy, displacing the experts in organization, finance and net-working who tend to dominate modern 'capitalism'.

PART FOUR

Money and Value

CHAPTER 13

Money, Credit and Interest

MONEY IS WHATEVER is generally accepted in payment of a debt. Although historically many things from courie shells to cigarettes have been so acceptable, in modern economies money as legal tender consists of coins authenticated by government and notes bearing a promise to pay by the central banker. Coins stamped by the government are acceptable wherever the government is trusted to have the power of taxation and therefore to possess the actual means to pay debts, if necessary in goods and services. Notes also are effectively backed by the power of taxation, since the central bank is usually either nationalised or fully supported by the government. Hence money is generally accepted because people trust the government. Legal tender, however, is a narrow definition of money, since bank deposits are also generally accepted as a means of payment.

Means of Exchange

The reason why money is needed at all is because all modern economies are built upon the division of labour and therefore upon the need to exchange products. Barter requires 'a double coincidence of wants': A must find B, who not only wants A's product but also has something that A wants; a grossly inefficient form of exchange. A wants to exchange with X, Y and Z and to receive back goods from P, Q and R. Hence a generally accepted means of exchange is essential. Now in theory A could accept in payment a promissory note from X or Y or Z and exchange it later for the goods of P, Q or R. He cannot, of course, because P, Q and R will not accept promissory notes from strangers. If trust throughout society were very great this might be possible. If it were even greater, society would be like a family, where the internal division of labour within the household operates perfectly well without promissory notes. Money, therefore, arises from a certain level of trust (or distrust). Without any trust there would be no money; with complete trust there would also be no money.

Credit

Every exchange without exception requires some degree of trust. If I sell my watch for twenty pounds either I hand over the watch first to the buyer before he pays me, or vice versa. In other words, one of us gives credit to the other. The underlying condition is that exchange is not instantaneous; it takes time. Whoever gives first, gives credit. This is true even for barter, but also for work done and land rented. A worker who is paid at the end of the week or month gives credit to his employer. A tenant who pays a landlord in advance gives credit. A milkman who leaves milk on the doorstep before payment gives credit (or his firm does). A football supporter who pays at the turnstile gives credit; so does the footballer on a monthly salary and bonus. Workers paid in advance, like lawyers with a retaining fee or footballers on a signing-on contract, receive credit, but in general it is labour that gives credit by working in advance of wages in the trust that it will, in fact, be paid. This simple point refutes the old nineteenth century belief in the wage fund theory that 'capital' advances wages to workers – a belief originating probably with Adam Smith, who wrote at the beginning of his great treatise that:

> The number of useful and productive labourers ... is everywhere in proportion to the quantity of capital stock which is employed in setting them to work.   A. Smith, Introduction, *ibid.*, p.2

and which still holds sway in the idea that 'capital' employs labour rather than the truth that labour employs capital.

Credit is the belief that the other party to an exchange will complete the bargain. In effect a promise is given by him or her, so that the giver of credit receives a promise in exchange. Since most people's promises are only accepted within a narrow circle of personal acquaintances and business associates, as in the important case of trade credit, a generally accepted promise must be found in order to make general exchange possible. Bankers are the makers of generally accepted promises. A reputable banker is trusted by everyone, hence a banker's promissory notes are money. Anyone will take a bank note simply because they believe that anyone else will also take it. The notes need not be those of a central banker, though in modern conditions economic uncertainty has led to the demise of bank notes not issued by a government backed central bank.

Bank Deposits

Money then is itself no more than a kind of formalised aspect of credit, necessitated by a modicum of trust. It is, as Keynes said, 'a subtle device for linking the present to the future' (Keynes, *ibid.*, p.294). Money is built upon credit; credit is not built upon money. Indeed without credit money is clearly useless. Division of labour requires exchange; exchange requires credit; credit without great trust requires money. Money thus becomes the principal means of exchange. However, since bankers' promises are what money essentially is, it follows that its particular embodiment in bank notes is only a convenience arising from the making of many small transactions. Of course, the presence of legal tender underpins the whole system, as would soon be experienced in an acute crisis of confidence, when only government authenticated tokens would become acceptable. Yet in normal conditions a banker's promises are the most voluminous means of exchange. This means that bank deposits are the most extensively used money. Cheques are accepted, not as money, but as claims on bank accounts in the name of the signer of the cheque. The account may be in overdraft, but the recipient of the cheque believes that the bank will honour it. As Schumpeter wrote, you cannot ride on a claim to a horse, but a claim on money serves almost equally well as money itself. Hence effectively bank deposits are money, because they represent bankers' promises to pay in legal tender, if asked.

Advances Create Deposits

The principle of the money multiplier, whereby banks create money from a base of cash plus balances held at the central bank, rests upon this fact.[1] Every advance creates a deposit. When a banker gives an advance or overdraft facility to a customer, the customer's drawing upon this by cheque results in a deposit elsewhere in the banking system when the recipient of the cheque banks it. What is often ignored – indeed by recent textbooks – is that the great bulk of deposits originate in this way. With the small exception of deposits created by the public's paying of notes and coins into bank accounts, all the rest – the great majority – of deposits are created by bank advances. Depositors do not create money and 'should not be invested with the insignia of a role which they do not play' (J. Schumpeter, *History of Economic Analysis*' p.1114, Routledge, 1994). For banks are

---

1 See, for example, Begg, *ibid*, p376-7.

not just relending deposits when they give advances; they are creating money. Once more Schumpeter puts it pithily when he says that banks create purchasing power out of nothing.[2] The overlooking of this crucial point cripples economists' ability to see the real potential of a banking system.

Production Time Requires Credit

Although in principle all exchange takes time and therefore requires credit, some exchanges take much longer than others. Much production is roundabout, in the nature of an exchange economy. This is often associated with both the production and the use of capital goods, but that is not the essential point. For example, slow growing crops require much time; rubber plantations take years to mature; good wine requires years of storage; services may involve long periods of training. Capital, of course, by definition is used up in future time periods and hence time passes during its complete use. Capital goods, like buildings and heavy equipment, take time to produce. In so far as time is expended in the full production process, i.e. until the final expiry of the use of the factors of production engaged, then so far is credit required. Those who exchange the product of a lengthy time of production need credit to enable them to survive that time. They need consumer goods while they are producing. Even the farmer cannot eat only last year's crop while he grows this year's. Producers of and users of capital goods need access to the current output of consumer goods. Everyone needs credit, but producers of a roundabout product need more than average. Schumpeter emphasises this with great clarity:

> By credit, entrepreneurs are given access to the social stream of goods before they have acquired the normal claim to it. It temporarily substitutes, as it were, a fiction of this claim for the claim itself. Granting credit in this sense operates as an order on the economic system to accommodate itself to the purposes of the entrepreneur, as an order on the goods which he needs: it means entrusting him with productive forces. J. Schumpeter, *The Theory of Economic Development*, p.107

Example of Bridge Building

Every society answers the question of how this credit is to be provided rather differently in detail, but all answer it in the same way essentially. Consider the building of a bridge. Whether it is a publicly or privately built bridge or a publicly or privately owned bridge makes

2 A.J. Schumpeter, *The Theory of Economic Development*, p73.

no essential difference. The bridge builders, i.e. the construction workers and the suppliers of inputs to them – brick, cement or equipment makers etc. – all need consumer goods during the whole process. Society supports them in advance of receiving the benefits of the use of the bridge. Users of the bridge and others extend credit to producers of the bridge. Bridge workers could in principle issue promissory notes of their own which they could use to buy consumer goods, but their credit would usually be inadequate. Therefore they need a bank to give them credit. Provided the bank trusts that they will produce a satisfactory bridge for which payment will be made in the future, it will allow them to draw cheques for wages etc. against an overdraft facility (double-entry book-keeping may lead the bank to debit their overdraft account and credit a deposit account with the amount granted). As work on the bridge proceeds the facility might be extended *pro rata*. The bridge is being exchanged, as it were, *pro rata* with consumption goods. When completed, the bridge is bought by a public authority or perhaps by a private firm. For this credit must also be extended by a bank. The authority or the firm then repay the bank out of future receipts from the use of the bridge, which are received from toll payers or from tax/rate payers if the bridge is free.

Credit and Entrepreneurs

The bridge case demonstrates the fact that credit not only involves the trust by someone, usually a banker, that someone else intends to repay a debt and has the future ability to do so, but also an even more comprehensive trust in the power of nature. Those who grant credit for new enterprises require confidence that, in a sense, out of nothing will spring forth something of value. The means of production, land, labour and capital (not that to be produced, but that to be used in the production) are perceivable, perhaps in the hands of the entrepreneur, perhaps about to be gathered together, but their product is not. It lies in the unknown future; it will be a creation, something that only exists in potential, only discernible perhaps in the mind of the entrepreneur. The best evidence that the credit provider may have probably lies merely in the words of the entrepreneur. Is what he says plausible, is it rational, is it indeed creative? And what does the entrepreneur himself perceive that may make him credible? He must see, and convey to his creditor, the creative potential of nature embodied in the particular land, labour and capital that he intends to employ. He must envisage things of value hidden in the earth, in labour power, in machinery: tangible things like minerals and manufactured products, intangible things like the power to cure illness or spread information. He must see the social benefits of a new bridge inherent in the land forms, the pattern of human settlement, the desires of people. Thus may the staid, conservative figure of the banker become 'the ephor of the exchange economy' (J. Schumpeter, *The Theory of Economic Development*, p.74), when he finances such visions.

Non-productive Bank Credit

Provided banks advance money against future production, this whole process of facilitating exchange through time is unproblematic. It lies at the heart of every economy, except one without division of labour or one with a general degree of trust equivalent to that within a family. The former would not really be a human society at all, and the second would be the economy of a golden age. Yet bank credit in modern economies has become problematic, for it is given not just for future production but for a variety of other purposes. Two of these are particularly destructive. Firstly, credit is regularly offered by banks (and by building societies) for the purchase of land, and secondly it is granted for the purchase of consumer goods.

The ultimate supply price of land is zero, for it is not produced. A price may be needed to bring it to the market, but that is not a genuine supply price. To the dealers and buyers it may appear to be a supply price, but for the whole economy the supply is fixed and unresponsive to price, except for very small amounts of reclaimed land. A particular price for particular land may induce some owners to sell it. All this means is that someone (producers and ultimately consumers) is paying an owner of land to release it for use, not to produce it. Hence credit provided for land purchase is merely being used to pay landowners to release land. Any land price above zero is such a payment. This price enters into what the user of the land calls his cost of production and may therefore persuade both him and his bank that credit is being given against future production. This is a mistake. Were the land available free of payment to a landowner, the same production could take place; whereas if bricks or cement were free none would be supplied, for they have a genuine supply price, namely the marginal costs of bricks and cement. Whilst absolute private property in land holds sway, of course, the landowner holds out for his price to release the land, much as slave owners hold out for a price for labour. Human institutions may erect barriers that raise the illusion of natural conditions. What is natural is that goods and services, including capital, require a supply price, whereas land does not.

In practice the granting of credit for land purchase is a major cause of inflation. Land prices are demand determined. As more credit is given for land purchase, land prices rise and generate a round of inflation. Moreover the investment multiplier effect is nullified to the extent that the investment funds are used for land purchase.[3]

Recent experience in the sub-prime mortgage market in the USA shows clearly the fragile nature of bank credit given on the security of land values. The fault is not so much that sub-prime mortgages are particularly vulnerable; it is rather that the whole system of lending against land values is ultimately destructive, for the simple reason that land values are merely the capitalisation of privately collected rents. Since rent is created by the community, its capitalisation in private hands is sure to create fundamental problems.

Secondly, bank credit for the purchase of consumer goods introduces purchasing power, i.e. money, into the economy against which no corresponding production takes place. It is not to enable exchange of present goods and services against future ones, as in the case of credit for capital goods, but simply to stimulate artificially present demand for present goods. Inflation is clearly the outcome. In a depressed, underemployed economy, of course, credit for consumption goods may play a part in reviving employment in the short term. Thus it may prove an expedient for an underemployed economy. But the real question then becomes: 'Why are such expedients needed, or why is the economy underemployed?' (See Part 6.) There can be little doubt that any economy which relies on increasing volumes of bank credit to finance consumer purchases is digging a grave for itself.

Yet credit cards have given a massive boost to the creation of money for the purchase of consumer goods. Since the credit card owner buys things some weeks in advance of settling the debts incurred against his bank deposit (which may be in overdraft!), the credit card effectively increases the bank deposits, i.e. money, available at any one time. If the amount of credit extended on credit cards were to remain constant, this would not be inflationary, but, in fact, it usually continues to increase steadily over time. Any increase not matched by a corresponding increase in output must be inflationary.

Why is there an Interest Rate?
Were credit granted only to facilitate exchange by enabling production which takes time to be exchanged against current production,

3 See Chapter 22

there might be no need for a rate of interest on bank advances above the marginal cost of money. The insight of Aristotle would be vindicated:

> Interest is a yield arising out of money itself, not a product of that for which money is provided. Money was intended to be a means of exchange, interest represents an increase in the money itself ... Hence of all ways of getting wealth this is the most contrary to nature.
>
> Aristotle, *The Politics*, trans. T.A. Sinclair, p.46, Penguin, 1964

Consumers' desires, however, for consumer goods in excess of those which their current purchasing power would buy leads them to ask for bank credit. This implies a preference for current consumption goods over future ones, since future goods would in fact be forthcoming when future purchasing power were available to buy them. Such an idea of time-preference is the root of the influential theory of interest created by the Austrian economist, Bohm-Bawerk, who argued that people naturally prefer a good now to the same good in the future, and therefore will pay a premium for the right to consume now. The premium is the interest rate, for they value future purchasing power less than present and therefore discount future sums of money. If £100 today is equally valued with, say, £105 in a year's time, the interest rate is 5%, because the present holder of £100 would have to be paid £5 to compensate him for deferring the use of £100 for one year. In other words, the lender of £100 for one year will expect £5 interest.

This is a very plausible theory, based as it is upon what appears to be a psychological truth. Yet is this 'truth' really the case about human nature? For the choice between a good now and the same future good ignores the question, 'Has the good been earned, or alternatively has value been given in exchange for it?' Future goods result from future production, involving human work. Present goods are the result of past production, involving work. Someone has a claim to a good if he has contributed usefully to production or otherwise given value. Offering work, or capital which is the result of previous work, or goods which have been received in exchange for either of these, establishes a claim. Merely wanting a good does not establish a claim to it, any more than does theft or greed. That someone wants the good is beside the point. The real question is 'does he or she have a claim to it?' Does one have a claim to present goods in preference to future goods? Only in so far as one has helped to produce present goods.

If there is indeed a natural time preference, then it causes both a rate of interest and inflation. For production gives rise only to claims of an equivalent value. If these are supplemented by credit given for current consumption goods, prices must rise. Hence whether it is natural or not, should such a time preference be allowed to generate superfluous credit and the consequent interest rate and inflation? Of course, to borrow money from someone willing to lend it is a different matter, since that only involves a transfer of purchasing power. It is the creation of money by the banking system which is at issue. An economy based upon the 'fact' of a natural time preference is bound to run into difficulties, since it is assuming that people can lay claim to goods before they have produced them.

An alternative view of the origin of interest was put forward by Alfred Marshall, who supported the theory that interest is the reward for waiting. The owner of money who could purchase consumption goods with it defers his consumption to a later date, and in return for this sacrifice – for waiting – receives interest on his money. What underlies this theory is the assumption that investment – the purchase of capital goods – is financed entirely by savings, a view rendered implausible by Keynes' theory of income determination (see Chapter 20). For the argument depends upon the money which is temporarily not spent being lent to a producer, who makes use of it to finance his enterprise, thereby enabling him to charge his customers with a 'return on capital' with which to reimburse the lender with interest. There is no such return on capital; but, even if there were, why does the lender need to be paid more than the amount of his loan? Did he only choose to 'wait' in order to get interest? This implies that the reason for holding any money balances is to spend them immediately on consumption goods, so that an inducement is needed to prevent this happening. Common sense says this is not so. Keynes, more elegantly, cited the transactions and precautionary motives as good reasons for holding interest free money balances. More significantly, however, the theory is wrong because capital is not financed by a kind of scooping up of casual money balances. It is financed mainly by bank credit created 'from nothing'. Indeed that is what the money balances themselves really were in origin.

The Speculative Motive
Keynes claimed that there is a third motive for holding money, namely the speculative motive. If there is a market in bonds, which pay fixed or variable interest (bonds are defined by Keynes to include shares and bank deposit accounts), then holders of money choose between retaining their money or buying bonds. However, since the bond price

DIAGRAM 60

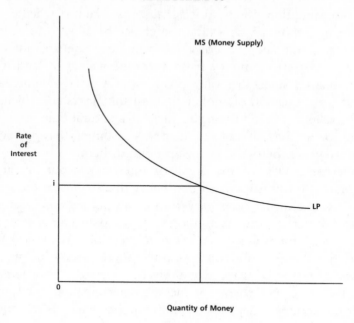

varies, owing to market supply and demand for bonds, the motive for
holding money may be to delay buying bonds in expectation of their
price falling. Hence the money holder is speculating on a future fall in
the bond market.

This gives rise, Keynes argued, to a liquidity trap. 'Investors' remain
liquid, i.e. hold money, when the bond price rises very high, because
they have a strong belief in a future fall. Since the interest rate moves
inversely to the bond price, because the yield on bonds (i.e. interest
paid divided by bond price) is the market rate of interest, this means
that at low interest rates the demand for money to hold becomes very
elastic. Diagram 60 shows this levelling out of the liquidity preference
curve. If interest rates rise, potential capital loss far exceeds any gain
from the higher interest rate itself, and if the rise in rates exceeds the
square of itself, the capital loss wipes out the whole of the interest.[4]

Keynes assumed, like most economists at the time and since, that
the money supply was a total sum fixed by the authorities, and hence
represented by a vertical line. The interest rate is thus set by supply
and demand for money (excluding liquidity for transactions and

4 For example, a rise in rates of 0.04% from 2.00% (i.e. 2.00% squared) will give a capital loss of 2.00%,
whereas a rise of 0.1% from 10% gives a capital loss of only 1.00%.

precautionary motives which can be treated as an additional quantity at any given level of income), namely the supply determined by the authorities and the demand determined by 'speculators' (see pp.239-40).

Assumptions of Keynes' Theory

What, however, are the assumptions of this theory? Firstly, Keynes assumed that the supply of money is fixed. He was aware that a government might be prepared to produce unlimited supplies of money (though he knew, of course, the inflationary implications of this), but he believed that the liquidity trap would prevent this from reducing the interest rate to near zero. This belief, however, relies on his second assumption, namely that there is an organized bond market based upon a market rate of interest. What he seems to have ignored is that the existence of such a market rate depends upon a fixed money supply in the first place. For if bank credit were freely available for production (especially for investment) there would be no need for a bond market based upon a market rate. There might still be loans, with interest, for non-productive purposes, but what drives the existing bond market (including shares) is demand for credit by producers.

Keynes theory of interest, indeed, is dangerously close to being circular, since the demand and supply curves are not really independent of each other. It is because bonds carry interest that holding money has an opportunity cost, both in lost interest and in lost capital gains. Were there no interest rate on bonds at all, no one would hold money in order to avoid a capital loss. There would be no 'bears' waiting to buy bonds at a future lower price when interest rates rose in the future. In short, if the interest rate were close to zero, all money would be held solely for the transactions and precautionary motives. Since they are what money is designed for, i.e. its natural function to facilitate exchange, this would be a healthy state of affairs.

Keynes, of course, made these two assumptions because they are how things are now ordered in modern economies. Yet he was perceptive enough to see that a zero rate of interest was in principle possible in the future, and would be greatly beneficial:

> For a little reflection will show what enormous social changes would result from a gradual disappearance of a rate of return on accumulated wealth. A man would still be free to accumulate his earned income with a view to spending it at a later date. But his accumulation would not grow. He would simply be in the position of Pope's father, who, when

he retired from business, carried a chest of guineas with him to his villa
at Twickenham and met his household expenses from it as required.

J.M. Keynes, *General Theory of Employment, Interest and Money*, MacMillan, 1957, p.221

Money as Stock or Flow

Textbook economics regards money unequivocally as a stock:

> Money is a stock. It is the quantity of circulating currency and deposits
> held at any given time.   Begg, *ibid.*, p.386

Yet, as the word 'circulating' implies, money can also be viewed as
a flow. Just as a river can be seen as a stock of water at an instant in
time, but also as a flow over a period of time, so money can be understood as either. As a stock it is obviously strictly limited; it has a totally
inelastic supply, as does any good or service in an infinitely short time
period. However, in a finite time period money flows; it has a supply,
the source of which is bankers' decisions to give advances. When these
are later repaid, the flow returns to source. This movement may be
impeded by government authority or by bankers' monopoly power,
which if excessive reduce the flow to make it appear merely as a stock.
Nevertheless, in principle, a free, competitive banking system could
contribute a flow of money which might make the money supply
almost perfectly elastic at a very low interest rate.

Supply Price of Money

Indeed, the interest rate would then be no more than a genuine
supply price for money, in the sense that money would be produced
at its marginal cost. This would consist of the production costs of
notes and coins, which amount to a tiny fraction of their face value
as money, the costs of banking services i.e. wages, rent etc. in the
banking industry, and a risk premium related to the average rate of bad
debts on bank advances. Only the last might be a significant percentage of money face value, but even this is entirely dependent upon the
conditions under which production generally takes place. The precarious situation of modern entrepreneurs' reliance upon residual
profits – leaving out of account, of course, any ownership of freehold
sites and any monopoly power – greatly enhances the risk premium.
In radically different conditions of production, the premium would be
no more than a kind of insurance premium on normal risks of trade
and integrity.

Marginal banking costs of money production, banker's services and
a low risk premium need not rise significantly with a greater volume

of bank advances. Hence the MS curve would be almost horizontal at a very low level of interest rates. Such a money supply, however, would be highly inflationary were bankers to persist in their present policies of giving advances. If money is created for the purchase of land and consumer goods, its purchasing power simply generates higher prices, since both land and consumer goods in excess of those currently produced have no supply price. On the other hand, if bankers followed rational policies of creating money only by advances for the employment of factors of production, whose future output would finance the repayment of the advances, then an elastic money supply at a very low interest rate would be highly beneficial. Such an interest rate is itself no more than a genuine supply price of money.

What then of the demand curve for money, or the liquidity preference curve? Transactions and precautionary motives are indifferent to interest rates (except at high levels) as they are a function of the level of income. What then becomes of Keynes' speculative motive, or the asset motive as it is now called? This is entirely a creature of interest rates. At a zero interest rate, there is no opportunity cost of holding money (beyond any possible carrying cost). Equally there is no conceivable capital gain from a future rise in rates; the bears who were responsible for the liquidity trap would disappear, since their gains from 'hoarding' were contingent upon such a future rise in rates on bonds. But could there be an absence of interest-bearing bonds? Surely this is a highly unrealistic state of affairs? We have become completely accustomed to a bond market, as a sophisticated range of interest-bearing assets available for purchase and sale. Yet such a market is dependent upon a rate of interest above the marginal cost of bank advances.

Origins of Modern Interest Rates

So once more we return to the central question. What is the root of such an interest rate? Time-preference, waiting, return on capital and liquidity preference are inadequate explanations. As a historical fact, the existence of a pervasive interest rate permeating the whole economic system is a phenomenon only of the past few hundred years, or roughly the modern period. In the Middle Ages, for example, interest was morally reprehensible and charged only on especially risky, or personal, loans. Profound changes of attitude have turned 'usurers' into eminently respectable financial institutions of all types, so that even bankers, whose vital creative function in the economy is thus obscured, are judged nowadays on their ability to extract interest from borrowers.

Whilst this huge growth of the charging of interest is categorised by economists as a step forward into a highly productive world of 'capital growth', 'mobile capital', 'efficient capital resource allocation' and similar rationalisations, in reality it is no more than an unfortunate, though inevitable, consequence of injustice and ignorance. The injustice lies in a failure to see that land, as a natural resource, is not a proper object of unrestricted private ownership, whilst the ignorance lies in the misconceptions about money and credit outlined above.

Historically, land enclosure since the sixteenth century gradually destroyed communal rights over land, replacing them with private rights to buy, sell, collect rent, restrict access, or even despoil, regardless of the rights of others. A full account and explanation of this process is a matter for economic historians, but the present operation of these rights (or, more pertinently, the failure of duties regarding land) is a matter for economists. This is not in itself a moral issue, but a question of natural law. What is undeniably the case is that in present conditions most productive enterprises are not owned by those who work in them. Workers occupying a site, i.e. land, are dependent upon others – the freeholder or legal tenant – for access, for employment and for a strictly limited share of the produce as wages. In addition, they must rely on borrowing money from shareholders and creditors to finance their capital.

So deeply rooted are these conditions that we take for granted the separation of 'capital' and labour. 'Capital' is seen to employ labour. 'Capital' is provided by shareholders, companies, bankers or perhaps the government. The enterprise may legally be a fictitious person, usually a limited liability company, whose shareholders, scattered throughout the economy as individuals and financial institutions, are providing 'capital', for which they are duly rewarded with interest (in the guise of dividends or capital appreciation). Were someone totally unfamiliar with this complex set-up to observe the actual productive enterprise, they would naturally, and correctly, conclude that it is in fact constituted by the workers and the (real) capital which they use, rather than the mere claims made upon it by external creditors.

Why then do the real producers – the workers, including managers, technicians and so on – not provide their own capital? Why must they be dependent upon others for their buildings, machines, plant and tools? The answer is obvious: they are not worthy of credit to that degree. They cannot issue their own promissory notes against the future value of their productive work; nor can they obtain credit from banks which could give them spending power to buy capital and maintain production. Their claim for wages, at a general level set by the least that an unemployed worker will accept, cannot possibly induce banks to grant overdraft facilities on a scale sufficient to finance modern industry. The few workers who tire of the monotonous and dependent nature of much employment and strive to set up independently as firms face powerful competition from existing larger firms, usually on superior sites, as well as the same difficulty of finding credit. They have little to offer in the way of security for bank loans, and may endanger their family's standard of life by mortgaging a house and risking personal bankruptcy.

Who then is worthy of credit? Again the answer is obvious: those whose claim on production is not wages, but rent of land or interest on bonds (in the Keynesian sense of all interest-bearing assets, including shares in companies). They have both the assured levels of income and the security to obtain bank credit. They can borrow to finance the purchase of sites and capital. Today such credit-worthy 'people' are often institutions, especially limited liability companies with control of valuable sites, increasingly those which are multinational. The complexity of modern economies masks this basic fact that credit goes, not to workers, but to those who control rent and interest. A company may itself be owned by institutions which are the ultimate beneficiaries of bank credit, or even be owned by a banking institution.

The pattern is immensely complicated, but the underlying root of the separation of productive work from credit is the inadequate level of the actual producers' wages. They cannot buy the very capital they use in their work. They may be worthy of their hire, but they are not worthy to own their own tools. No wonder that such concepts as Marxist alienation and exploitation have beguiled workers into seeing entrepreneurs as oppressors, when the real oppressors are the system of land tenure and the artificial restriction of credit. Making credit available to those who control the land on which production takes place compounds the confusion, for credit for land purchase, including credit for long leases, is a major secondary defect of the present system, as has been explained. It is not credit for future production, which is the natural function of credit.

Interest and Resource Allocation

A further argument remains to be dealt with, which seeks to establish that a positive rate of interest above the supply price of money is rational for any society. This runs as follows. An economy needs to allocate scarce resources of land, labour and capital amongst alternative uses. The price mechanism, or a command system, may do this to a certain extent, but the allocation of resources through time requires an extra price being placed upon the use of resources according to the time absorbed in the production process. Projects taking a long time should be charged more than projects using the same resources for a short time. The interest rate is such an extra price. Western economists were fond of using this argument in relation to the inefficiency of full socialist economies, like the Soviet Union, and indeed the latter did introduce a notional rate of interest so to allocate resources.

This argument raises yet again questions about underlying time preference and about whether capital yields anything above its supply price. It also bears out the point that restricting the money supply makes money artificially scarce, for the Soviet government certainly did not have a free banking system. However, the argument is best met by quoting a brilliantly succinct reply to it from Keynes:

> If the rate of interest were zero, there would be an optimum interval for any given article between the average date of input and the date of consumption, for which labour cost would be a minimum – a shorter process of production would be less efficient technically, whilst a longer process would also be less efficient by reason of storage costs and deterioration. If, however, the rate of interest exceeds zero, a new element of cost is introduced which increases with the length of the process, so that the optimum interval will be shortened, and the current input to provide for the eventual delivery of the article will have to be curtailed until the prospective price has increased sufficiently to cover the increased cost – a cost which will be increased both by the interest charges and also by the diminished efficiency of the shorter method of production.
>
> Keynes, ibid., p.216

Keynes' reasoning is entirely supported by the obvious difficulties encountered by economies, like the UK in the 1980s, which have suffered from the effects of high interest rates putting a premium on short-term projects. Very long-term projects, of which the construction of the Channel Tunnel was an outstanding example, were charged enormous 'extra' prices in the form of interest on borrowed funds. 'Short-termism' became the order of the day. The present movement towards financing public investment by means of private 'capital' – the Private Finance Initiative – is sure to create similar distortions, for the cost of private borrowing is greater than the cost of public borrowing. In the 1980s this contraction of investment of all kinds towards the short-term end was largely dictated by the government's desire to maintain a high sterling exchange rate by means of a high interest rate, with a view to keeping import prices down. Since this policy was taken to be the best way of dealing with inflation – the real cause of which is mainly a failure to provide credit to productive industry rather than to buy land and consumption goods – the circle of misguided policies was complete. If a high interest rate distorts production compared with a low interest rate, then *a fortiori* a low one distorts it compared with a zero rate.

Conclusion

In short, interest arises from a combination of a fixed money supply and the onerous position of debtors in relation to creditors. Were bankers to create credit by the advancing of money only to genuine producers of future goods and services, who would repay out of the proceeds of future production, rather than to lend for the purchase of land and of consumption goods, the supply side of the 'market' for money would be elastic, with a 'price' at the very low marginal cost of money. Were the actual producers of goods and services, meaning workers of all kinds of skill and status, to be relieved of their onerous position so that they became truly credit worthy, the demand side of the 'market' would be freed from the need to borrow from those whose access to funds arises from control of land and credit. Supply side reform would require a really competitive free banking system or, perhaps, a State administered one. Demand side reform requires a fundamental change in the system of land tenure and taxation. Both are necessary, for they are complementary. Meanwhile, we are locked into a system which cannot be ameliorated by tinkering with monetary, fiscal or so-called supply side measures.

CHAPTER 14

Value and Price

Q UESTIONS ABOUT value and price have always beguiled economists and yet bedevilled the subject. Perhaps the reason is that prices, which are precise and measurable, are dependent upon values, which are imprecise and not obviously measurable at all. As a result, economists since Adam Smith have created concepts like exchange value, value in use, labour power and others in attempts to solve the problem of how value and price are related.

A solution is important, for not only do the answers to many questions, like 'What determines the relative prices of goods and services?', depend upon it, but so too do far-reaching attitudes to the economy, especially those that concern distribution of the product. Marx' concept of labour power, for example, giving rise to the conclusion that all workers in a capitalist society are exploited by the appropriation of surplus value created by them, lies at the root of most socialist movements to disappropriate capitalists. Similarly, normative economics, making use of explicit value judgements, must take a stand on where value arises, in order to decide who ought to receive what. But even without making value judgements, economists concerned with efficiency may question whether 'factor returns' should be paid to those who contribute no value to output.

How Far can Values be Measured?

Two statements about values would be accepted today by most economists without dispute. Firstly, values cannot be measured interpersonally i.e. A's values cannot be said to be greater or less than B's. Secondly, even for one person, his or her values cannot be given cardinal measurements of how much they are worth. Fortunately, a third statement of general accord may be added: that, for one person, values can be given ordinal measurement. Each person can decide and make evident his ranking of values, at least within particular fields of activity, one of which could be loosely called economic i.e. for goods and services. Thus A prefers X to Y and Y to Z, but he cannot say quantitively by how much, nor can anyone directly compare his valuations with those of another person.

Exchange, Values and Price

A great deal flows from this minimal fact about values. It explains how exchanges take place. A possesses good X; B possesses good Y. If A values X more than Y, or if B values Y more than X, no exchange will take place. However, if A prefers Y to X and B prefers X to Y, they will exchange. Two ordinal judgements only are required. Nothing needs to be known about inter-personal or cardinal measurements of values. When the exchange takes place, the price of X is Y and the price of Y is X, for price is whatever is actually given, done, or promised, in exchange for something. Thus whilst values are based on subjective judgements, influenced by desires, beliefs, feelings and so on of the individual, prices are actual objective and measurable things, like precise quantities of goods and services. Obviously, values and prices cannot be measured against one another, although prices are, in some sense, an effect of various valuations.

Indifference Curves and Valuations

This raises the obvious question, however, that if X and Y are quantifiable, how much of X is exchanged against how much of Y? Again, ordinal valuations provide at least part of the answer. A and B both have upper and lower limits on their valuations. A will sell X for a price in terms of Y somewhere above a minimum measure of Y. B will buy X for a price in terms of Y somewhere below a maximum measure of Y. The price has to be agreed somewhere between these limits. Indifference curves demonstrate this (see Diagram 61).

A has Q1 tea; B has Q6 sugar. At a price of tea in terms of sugar of Q2/ Q1 A will not sell any tea, since his marginal rate of substitution of sugar for tea as shown by indifference curve IC1 is higher. Similarly B will not buy tea for sugar at a price of tea of Q6/ Q5 since IC2 is steeper at Q6. There are nevertheless precise prices at which A will begin to sell tea and B will begin to buy it. These are Q3Q1 and Q6Q4, which are tangential to IC1 and IC2 respectively at Q1 and Q6 i.e. marginal rate of substitutions equal prices. The actual price agreed upon must be somewhere between these two prices, say Q1P1 and Q6P2, which have the same slope and length. Transactions along these put both A and B on to higher indifference curves than IC1 and IC2.

DIAGRAM 61

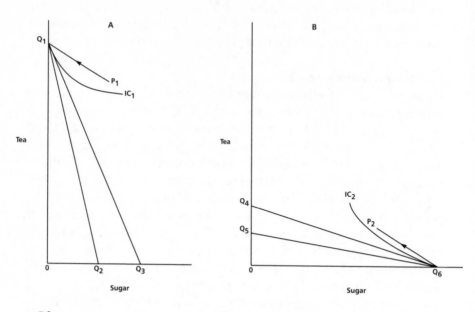

If we now replace sugar with money, the same analysis applies, giving money prices for tea above which it will not be bought and below which it will not be sold. This is the actual situation for almost every transaction in a modern economy. An exchange is an individual matter of buyer, seller and four valuations giving a high and low price for each. The final agreed price depends on the relative bargaining strength of each party. This is very evident in many cases: tendering for contracts, selling a used car, dealing at an auction (where reserve prices are used), buying a Wimbledon ticket off a tout or agreeing on a house price. It is less evident in cases like retail shopping where prices are marked. However, these are not legally prices, but invitations for offers from buyers, and sometimes – in Italian shops, for example – genuine bargaining takes place. Moreover, the buyer is always aware of some kind of upper limit on price. The seller may appear to operate with a fixed price, but either he is already at his minimum or may be preparing to change the 'invitation' price later, as in the case of fresh food shops near closing time.

Supply and Demand

Despite all this, are not prices in fact set by supply and demand? From the point of view of the individual, supply and demand operate to affect greatly the bargaining position. For each buyer and seller has in mind the alternative market, comprising other possible sellers and buyers respectively. Someone who buys a new suit has in mind the other suits on offer and, in particular, their prices. Someone selling a suit does the same. Other factors influence their bargaining position – trust or suspicion, personal likes and dislikes towards the other party, time available, character traits and so on – but the greatest influence in general is the available alternatives, constituting the supply and demand, and therefore the market, for similar goods or services to the particular one at issue. For this reason, the knowledge available to buyers and sellers becomes a key condition for a perfect market. Anyone selling his car to a dealer is only too aware of his weak bargaining position arising from the dealer's superior knowledge of the alternative buyers and sellers.

How then can the basic principle of a highest and lowest price and an agreed price between, for an individual exchange, be represented using supply and demand analysis?

DIAGRAM 62

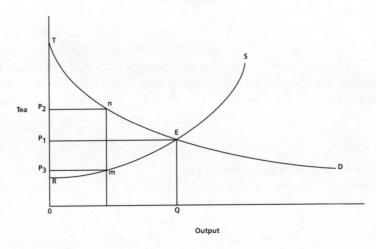

S and D are normal supply and demand curves for tea. The vertical line at nm represents the nth buyer B and the mth seller A in the tea market, such that B will only buy at a price at or below P2 and A will only sell at a price at or above P3. Thus P2 corresponds to the slope of Q6Q4 (Diagram 61) and P3 to the slope of Q3Q1. The actual price for their individual transaction must fall between P2 and P3. Clearly in a well-developed market, assuming good knowledge possessed by all buyers and sellers, the actual price will turn out to be

P1, the market price, subject to any minor influence, such as friendship between individual dealers. Such an analysis applies to all points along S and D from O to Q. Of course, A and B may enter the market more than once, so that prior or subsequent transactions may take place at higher and lower valuations, but with the same final price of P1.

At E the marginal buyer confronts the marginal seller at price P1, which is exactly equal to the former's top price and to the latter's bottom price. All buyers and sellers finally trade at P1, which means that they may each choose a quantity of tea just sufficient to make their individual marginal rates of substitution between tea and money exactly equal to P, which is the general rate of exchange in the market. All then stop exchanging at points of tangency between price lines and indifference curves. The adjustment to differences of taste on the side of buyers or consumers and to differences of productive conditions on the side of sellers or producers is then brought about by both adjusting the quantity taken from and brought to the market respectively to a level which meets this requirement of tangency. That is the beauty of the market. Every pair of buyers and sellers are on their contract curve, provided they carry on making transactions beyond points like n and m where they may first have entered the market.[1] Of course, if in any given time period discrete units are exchanged, which exhaust the buyer's or seller's desire to continue transacting, as when a consumer buys a car or a producer sells a large capital good, exchange may be limited to nm. Perfect markets do not like indivisibilities.

Consumer and Producer Surplus

In Diagram 62 the area P1TE is consumers' surplus, measured as the sum of all the differences between individual top buying prices and market price, whilst the area P1RE is producers' surplus, the sum of differences between individual bottom selling prices and market price.[2] Consumers' surplus is wholly dependent upon consumers' valuations and the level of P1, but producers' surplus is a matter of costs. In modern conditions, costs include wages, interest, profits and taxation. Exactly how much of each enters into price at E is a very complex matter, much disputed amongst economists – though perhaps more easily identified by businessmen – but the real issue is which of these would be costs in conditions of economic freedom.

---

1 See T. Scitovsky, *Welfare and Competition*, Ch. 4, especially Fig. 4.1, Allen & Unwin.
2 Producers' surplus in the long run is part, but not all, of rent – see pp.78-82.

What Costs Enter into Price?

Interest is a result of the restriction of credit. Were credit freely available for productive purposes only and denied to purchasers of land and consumers claiming goods in advance of contributing to production, bankers would charge merely the cost of their services, which would include providing against occasional bad debts. Since interest is thus a claim derived from the artificial scarcity of credit for production, it would not exist in conditions of abundant credit (see Chapter 13). At present, of course, interest is a major feature of all economies, but this no more makes it a genuine cost of production than does protection money in a mafia-ridden society. In short, all claims are not costs. Failure to make this clear leads to highly complex and contentious theories of how prices are determined.

Profits, as currently measured, are similarly a mixture of claims and costs. A large element in them may be rent, which is considered below. The remainder consists firstly of interest on money lent by shareholders, disguised under the title of dividends, because it is distinguished from interest paid to bond-holders and others who have no equity, and secondly a return to entrepreneurs for their work in creating the business, managing it and shouldering the risk and responsibility. This entrepreneur's return is a genuine cost, which would be paid in conditions of economic freedom, and like the banker's charge, could be regarded as wages (see Chapter 12).

Capital receives no return denoted as profits, nor as interest, for it is merely a particular labour input that arrives at a firm in large discrete amounts of stored-up labour. Amortised as depreciation it can be treated as regular short-term payments in any case. Of course, in modern conditions, capital inputs are bought by firms at prices that also include 'stored-up' interest payments, but that is no reason to include them under a separate category called capital with a special return called profits. In the long term, capital is no more than just another input of labour, to which labour on the site concerned adds value (see Chapter 11).[3]

Taxation is a claim on production that amounts to an appropriation by government and is in no sense a real cost. It enters into price, like all the above claims (except rent), since the producer tries to recoup it from customers, but that is no real measure of cost. It clearly has no

---

3 Monopoly elements in the price of capital inputs are dealt with below.

part in any theory of pricing, except perhaps in so far as various forms of taxation have different incidences.

Is Rent a Cost?

What then of rent? Surely all firms must include in their prices a major mark-up to cover their rent charges, which are either directly payable to landlords, or nominal if they themselves are landowners? This is a classic conundrum raised by Ricardo, who answered it categorically in the negative:

> If the high price of corn were the effect, and not the cause of rent, price would be proportionally influenced as rents were high or low, and rent would be a component part of price. But that corn which is produced by the greatest quantity of labour is the regulator of the price of corn; and rent does not and cannot enter in the least degree as a component part of its price.*
>
> * The clearly understanding this principle is, I am persuaded, of the utmost importance to the science of political economy.
>
> Ricardo, *ibid.*, pp.40-1

Firms must receive in their total revenue a stream of income required to pay rent, and total revenue divided by output equals price, but this does not make rent a component of price, since everything depends, as Ricardo states, upon the direction of causality. The reason why price determines rent is, as he shows, that price must cover the labour costs of the firm whose labour productivity is least, which means, not the least efficient firm, but the firm with the worst location. Were these labour costs not covered, that firm would close down and the next worst located firm would become the marginal one, whose labour costs would just be covered by the price. Ricardo's principle lives on in the marginal cost theories of modern Economics. In so far as marginal cost (MC) is labour cost, price equals MC. If a firm tried to pass rent on in the price of products, it would be undercut by producers on similar land and also by those on better and worse land, since all are competing with each other in a market where the price rises to the cost of production on the marginal site, a price which enables the non-marginal producer to pay his full rent in the first place. In other words, such a firm would be charging a premium which was not actually needed to enable it to pay rent; in a sense it would be passing the rent on twice over. Rent is indeed a surplus and not a cost, a fact which confirms that the landowner is not providing anything, but rather levies a charge for releasing for production a service which in the nature of things exists regardless of his intervention (see Chapter 8).

In cases like the purchase of homogenous goods which are easily transportable, the exclusion of rent from price is confirmed in everyday experience. A consumer who buys a bag of apples from a greengrocer on a High Street prime site does not pay more than if he bought them from a back street shop. The price of a raw material, like timber, is much the same within the UK wherever you buy it. Provided there is a competitive market, prices generally do not vary with rent. There are, however, notable exceptions which appear to refute this. Most obviously, houses vary greatly in price according to their location. Yet what a 'house' buyer acquires is a house and a piece of land on which it is situated. Land prices vary very greatly with location. House prices, strictly defined, do not. A house of similar construction to another has much the same building costs wherever it is built. Rent enters into land prices, not as a cost – for land has no cost – but as what is capitalised in the land price. Rent does not enter into the house price, either as a cost, or as capitalisation. At the other end of the scale of apparent counterexamples are cases like buying a cup of coffee at a cafe with a view of the Eiffel Tower, at a price perhaps double that of a cup in a side street. Does location enter into the price? Clearly it does, in so far as the consumer is buying a product identified as coffee consumed in that special location. Perhaps it is pedantry to argue that the price paid has two components: one for the coffee and one for the seat with a view, yet that is probably the best way of analysing cases of this kind, especially if the cafe-owner could hire out the seats without coffee for roughly the second component!

Monopoly Elements in Price

At this point in the argument the only genuine constituent in price appears to be wages. We have not, however, quite reached this conclusion, for what may remain, even if interest, profits, taxation and rent are eliminated, is an increment arising from monopoly. Price may not equal marginal cost, because the firm may have monopoly power, giving it the incentive and ability to produce where $MR > P$ and $MR = MC$. In such cases, of course, price does contain a premium above marginal labour costs. The above analysis of an equilibrium price P1 and E (Diagram 62) uses a supply curve, derived as the sum of firms' MC curves, as in the case of perfect competition. Most industries do not conform to this model, owing to monopolistic features giving various degrees of downward sloping demand curves.

In so far as a monopoly element in price arises from a branded product, giving a falling demand curve but zero supernormal profits in the long run, wage costs per unit of output are above what they would be at the perfect competition output i.e. where MC cuts LTAC at minimum efficient scale (see Chapter 5). Workers are not receiving the excess in wages, for it is simply a cost of inefficiency or excess capacity. Price does not include a mark-up for monopoly profits; it simply measures labour costs at the level of output where long-run profits are zero (i.e. point of tangency of LTAC and demand curve). The situation may be compared to a group of protected inefficient workers whom society deems worthy of a 'living wage', but whose wage costs per unit are high. In the branded product, however, consumers are offered a choice of similar branded goods, each of which has its adherents who are prepared to pay a little 'above the odds' for their favoured product. Standardisation would bring costs down; hence consumers may be said to choose variety instead of a cheaper homogeneity. Whether present day brands sold with expensive advertising campaigns constitute genuine variety is questionable. 'Brands' that vary owing to skilled individual craftsmanship, for example, might be a more significant case of real consumer choice with an element of monopoly price perhaps analysable as wages or rent of ability.

In so far as a monopoly price is attributable to complete control of a raw material or site of unique locational advantage, like a port or airport, rent does enter into price (see Chapter 6). For in this exceptional case there are no competitors at all on worse sites whose marginal costs determine the price of all goods in the same market. Indeed, there is no market, only a single seller who extracts the highest price possible from his control of the source of the product. Even so the rent of the monopolist does not determine price, though it enters into it; rather the monopoly price determines the rent, so that rent remains a surplus. If the site were put up for auction, its price would represent the capitalisation of the surplus. The monopoly power cannot be separated from the power to extract a rental income from the land.

When, however, monopoly power is so separated, as in the case of a landlord leasing a site to a monopolist, rent paid to the landlord will be very little above, or equal to, whatever rent the landlord could obtain in another use. If that use is not controlled by a monopoly, then this alternative rent would not enter into the price of the first product. Hence, indirectly, one may argue that if the monopolist pays a 'competitive' rent of this kind, then that does not enter into the monopolistic price that he charges. His price would then contain only wages costs – though not those at an output where $P = MC$ – and a monopoly mark-up.

The third case of natural monopolies, where LATC falls over a large range of output, making competition impossible in a market not much greater than that range, may also show price falling to equal marginal wage costs, but at that point losses would be made. Either such a monopoly is allowed to operate without restriction in the private sector, enabling it to charge a large monopoly mark-up, or, if it is regulated or State-owned, price may be set at marginal wage cost by means, if necessary, of a subsidy. In neither case, however, is there a market equilibrium price that only covers that cost. This indicates that some form of State intervention is necessary, as indeed for all cases of monopoly (see Chapter 18). Arguments in support of monopoly pricing, originating with Schumpeter, to the effect that research and innovation are encouraged, are a separate issue. Much of their validity rests upon the lack of available finance for smaller and more competitive firms, and upon the absence of leadership and initiative in many sectors of industry. Both these features inherent in modern economies would be greatly reduced, if not eliminated, in conditions of economic freedom.

It is difficult, nevertheless, to lay the monopoly problem to rest in the context of a theory of price. If there are monopolies in the economy of any kind, then unless they are controlled in the public interest, so that price does not include a charge levied by monopoly power, then that charge will permeate into other prices, like a dye fed into a river system. Producers' prices will pass on monopoly elements from the price they pay a monopoly supplier. Monopoly, like interest, is pervasive in its effects. Yet since the root of most monopolies lies in unrestricted private ownership of land, there always remains the opportunity to extirpate them by modifying the system of land tenure.

A Labour Theory of Price
Let us make the visionary, but not illusory, assumption then that an economy might be freed from the shackles of interest payments, profits, taxation and monopoly, if not of rent itself. In such a case the famously discredited labour theory of value would flourish once more. However, it would need the more accurate title of the labour theory of price. Prices would be determined by the marginal cost of labour on all sites. Labour costs on marginal sites equal marginal labour costs on all other sites (i.e. at the extensive and intensive margins. See pp.73-5), and both equal price. Keynes himself, when discussing the merits of a zero rate of interest, saw this implication.

For the only reason why an asset offers a prospect of yielding during its life services having an aggregate value greater than its initial supply price is because it is *scarce*; and it is kept scarce because of the competition of the rate of interest on money. If capital becomes less scarce, the excess yield will diminish, without its having become less productive – at least in the physical sense.

I sympathise, therefore, with the pre-classical doctrine that everything is *produced* by *labour*, aided by what used to be called art and is now called technique, by natural resources which are free or cost a rent according to their scarcity or abundance, and by the results of past labour, embodied in assets, which also command a price according to their scarcity or abundance. It is preferable to regard labour, including, of course, the personal services of the entrepreneur and his assistants, as the sole factor of production, operating in a given environment of technique, natural resources, capital equipment and effective demand.

Keynes, ibid., pp.213-14 (his italics)

All this is not to re-establish the traditional labour theory of value, least of all the Marxian version. Firstly, it is profoundly wrong to think that value, an entirely subjective, individual notion related to, but in no way to be identified with, price, can be measured against labour. It is price itself, what is given, done or promised in exchange for something else given, done or promised, that can be measured against labour. Secondly, labour is a measure of price only at the margin of production. Hence price is in no way equal to labour costs at intra-marginal outputs, either on marginal or other sites. Only the marginal labour cost on all sites, which ultimately is set by that cost on marginal sites themselves, is equal to price. Thirdly, even this is only true after analysis of what is to count as a cost. It might be said that the argument, therefore, is circular i.e. only labour is counted as a cost, thus only labour costs enter into price. Such a criticism, however, ignores all the reasons given above for the elimination of interest, profits, taxation, rent and monopoly as real costs. Of course, contemporary analysis, looking at the obvious mark-up of price by businessmen, who count at least interest and taxation as costs, and by economists who count normal profits (and perhaps rent) as a cost – few go so far as to count monopoly! – seems to refute a labour theory of price. Thereby the possibility of clearly distinguishing between the present state of affairs and an underlying natural and permanent condition is ignored. Or, to put it differently, such ignorance precludes the possibility of improving the future by reforming the present.

That marginal labour costs measure prices conforms to the common sense idea that goods and services more or less exchange against each other according to the labour embodied in them. If a good takes twice as much labour to produce as another made by similar labour, we expect it to be worth about twice as much. If more skilled labour is used, we expect a mark-up commensurate with the skill. Since skills are acquired over time, there must be a rough correlation between time spent acquiring the skill and the mark-up. Of course, people vary in natural ability; yet even here marginal analysis applies, for those who are capable of switching their labour easily between occupations provide again a rough means of equating prices to labour times. Large rent of ability is only received by non-marginal workers. If the wages of bus drivers rise, workers move out of other industries and relative wages and prices change to new equilibria. Needless to say, interest, profits and the rest complicate the outcome, but the underlying trend keeps prices in some conformity to labour costs.

Optimum Resource Allocation

The existence, even in principle if not in present practice, of an equi-librium free market price, such that goods and services exchange at prices equal to marginal labour costs, opens up many questions about the allocation of resources and products. Do such prices meet the Pareto optimum, under which no change can be made in allocations of final goods and services, nor in factors of production, without making someone worse off, and its converse, whereby non-optimum situations can be improved for someone without making anyone worse off? A free market for consumers enables them to buy in the market whatever quantities bring relative prices of goods into exact pro-portion to their individual marginal rates of substitution between those goods i.e. all price lines are tangential to indifference curves. Hence no consumer can benefit by buying more or less of a good, and any exchange not at the market rate would make someone worse off.

At the same time, on the supply side, if all final prices are equal to labour costs per marginal unit of output, no producer can benefit by producing more or less. No shift of labour between firms can benefit both firms, because the general wage rate is the same throughout the economy, so that any movement of labour at a different wage rate would benefit one firm at the expense of the other. Since capital is stored labour, its price equals the marginal labour cost of its pro-duction, again at the same general wage rate. Firms deciding on a capital/labour ratio are simply deciding upon the relative proportions of stored and current labour, and minimise their costs at any chosen output by making the marginal cost of capital equal to the marginal cost of current labour. In other words, the marginal rate of substitution between capital and labour in each firm equals the relative price of a unit of capital and a unit of labour. Both capital and labour are employed in quantities which make their marginal revenue products equal to their respective prices, capital and labour prices both being measurable in terms of wage rates. For the moment externalities are left out of the argument as they are dealt with later (Chapter 17).

In consequence the price system is enabling the marginal rate of substitution between goods for consumers to equal the marginal rate of substitution between the quantities of labour embodied in those goods. Labour is perfectly allocated to the choices of consumers. The whole argument assumes that other apparent elements in cost, notably interest, profits, taxation, rent and monopoly premiums, are excluded. This is an heroic assumption in modern conditions, but it at least reveals those aspects which prevent such a perfect free market solution. At zero interest, with entrepreneurial ability and effort the only measure of profits, with no taxation, and no monopoly element in price, the ideal would be achieved.

Who Receives Rent?

Yet this allocation of resources says nothing about the effect of land rent on the distribution of income. For such rent does not enter into price and thus plays no part at all in the process that leads to a Pareto optimum. Income distribution will be heavily skewed towards rent receivers, if land is in the hands of private landlords whose power to receive rent is set simply by factor markets. Every one of the outcomes described above in terms of prices and marginal rates of substitution is consistent with claims on output by landlords based upon their receipts of rent. They appear as consumers in the perfect final markets, but not as factors in the perfect factor market. For the latter is a market only in the variable factor of labour (including stored-up labour in capital). Whilst labour receives a wage rate equal to its marginal revenue product, landlords receive rents equal to the natural surplus attributable to land, which is not an element in final prices. In short, landlords receive a free ride. Their legal claim is recognised by the system. They are paid for releasing what they claim, not for producing it. They are a consequence of history, not of economic rationality. The economy needs land, but not landlords. Payments to them could be diverted elsewhere with no consequence to the perfect price system, beyond any effect from the new pattern of consumer expenditure out of the diverted rents.

It follows that the free market system is only one aspect of the whole question of equity or justice in the economy. A labour theory of price highlights this by throwing into relief the limitations of a free market, even when stripped of the complicating accretions of interest, profit, taxation and monopoly. Rent of land remains as the great enigma. What are its implications; how is society to deal with it in justice? To fail to understand the law of rent is to fail to cross the bridge of asses. To understand it, and to make no reasoned provision for it, is to step blindly upon the further side.

PART FIVE

Public Revenue

CHAPTER 15

Taxation

T HE MODEL of an economy from which profits, interest and the toll levied by monopoly have been stripped away, brings into relief the place of taxation. This is not an unrealistic approach for two reasons. One is that a model of rent and wages only is a reflection of the natural division of production between the two primary factors of land and labour, of which profits and the rest are subdivisions. The other is that many of these subdivisions, if not all of them, are in fact largely the very long-term consequences of the way in which taxation has been levied. The latter reason may seem to overemphasise the role of taxation, but the formative influence of government upon the economy is exerted primarily through types and rates of taxes. Moreover taxation is intimately related to another principal determinant of the economy, the system of land tenure.

The Fundamental Division of Production

Modern analysis of taxation at the micro level deals with questions like incidence and welfare effects. At the macro level taxation features in models of national income determination as a leakage or withdrawal (see Chapter 20). There is, however, an important aspect of incidence at the macro level which is ignored. Once more the omission of land from the analysis leads to the oversight. When the fundamental division of production (and therefore national income) between land and labour is recognised, the impact of taxation has a macro dimension obscured by the theory of income determination.

In its simplest outline the profile of sites i.e. firms in an economy in which rent and wages are the only streams of income, shows a constant level of wages and a level of rent diminishing towards the margin of production.

Labour productivity rises from the margin at M to the center at O.[1]

1 The analysis of Chapter 8, especially Diagram 30, shows that this is average labour productivity.

DIAGRAM 63

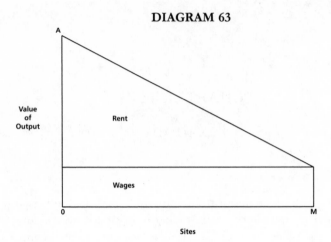

DIAGRAM 64

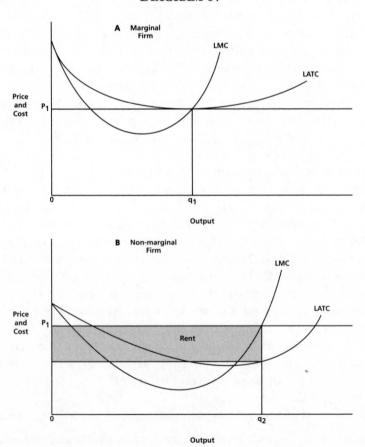

Obviously in practice there are many subsidiary 'centres'. Also the model is really three dimensional, formed by rotating it on the axis OA, so that there are an increasing number of firms towards the margin. For the individual firm, its equilibrium position differs crucially if it is marginal rather than non-marginal (Diagram 64A and B).

As has been shown, firms with monopoly power may receive a return over costs in addition to rent, but these monopoly profits do not alter the fundamental profile of marginal and non-marginal firms. Monopolies are likely to be concentrated towards central, i.e. high rent, sites. Fortunately the analysis of the incidence of taxation focuses upon marginal sites, where little monopoly exists, as this is where significant tax effects occur. The marginal firm breaks even (after paying scarcity rent); the non-marginal firm makes a permanent rent, payable to a landlord if there is one. Central firms' rent may be very great. Indeed, the real profile of the division between rent and wages is likely to be a shape difficult to show diagrammatically (Diagram 65).

DIAGRAM 65

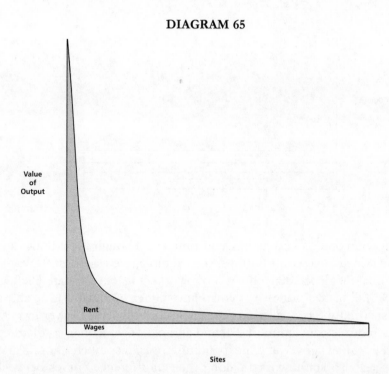

In the UK, for example, farmland in lowland areas costs about £2,000 per acre in 2006. (With development rights the same land can become worth £500,000 per acre.) In the City of London, planning permission enables land to be sold for £15m per acre.[2] Since the price of land measures the expected yield from it as rent, the current rent profile must be a reflection of these prices. Hence the 'central' end of the profile is perhaps 7-8,000 times the height of the marginal end, a scale which has important implications for what follows.

Three Bases of Taxation

a) Tax on Wages

Given this analysis, taxation may be assessed on three bases only: upon wages, total output or rent. The impact of each basis is profoundly different. Assessment upon wages is the easiest to consider. If it succeeds in its intention, it reduces the wage level by the tax rate, leaving rent and output unchanged (Diagram 66).

DIAGRAM 66

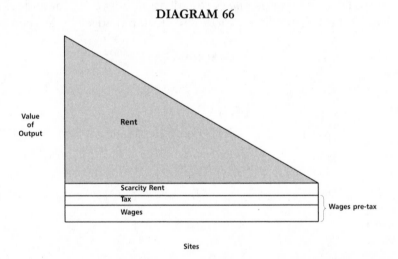

This outcome is very unlikely in practice. Though income tax and national insurance contributions, for example, are assessed on wages, their final incidence depends on how workers react. They are likely to resist a fall in real wages by demanding higher nominal wages, and if they succeed the tax will affect rent. Even if they fail, a lower level of wages reduces consumption demand and national income, so that rent also falls (unless government expenditure rises in compensation). A tax on wages also shifts workers along their indifference curves between work and leisure, affecting the amount of work forthcoming.[3]

2 See G. Monbiot, *The Captive State*, p.98, Pan, London, 2001.
3 See Lipsey, *ibid.*, p.430.

With land not freely available at the margin, scarcity rent forces down wages to a level below the natural wage on the margin, even before taxes have been levied, so that a tax on wages is acting upon an already diminished wage rate. Workers are usually receiving the least that they are prepared to accept. A tax is therefore almost certainly strongly resisted, with the result that it is shifted on to rent in the form of a higher wage claim. Scarcity rent may absorb the tax. In the short run the impact would vary according to whether firms are freeholders or leaseholders, but in the long run the tax may be borne by landlords. However, if marginal firms are subject to interest charges as well as a landlord's claim, the tax may render them sub-marginal, leading to closures and unemployment.

b) Tax on Total Output

Taxes on total output take the form mainly of excise duties and sales taxes, like VAT. If the overall rate of taxes on output is uniform, then the effect is felt primarily by marginal firms (Diagram 67).

DIAGRAM 67

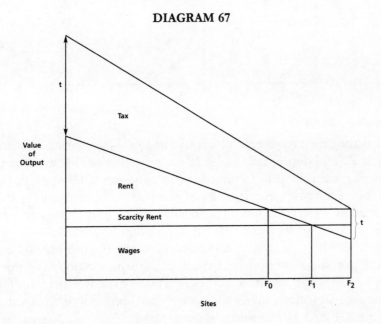

A tax of t per unit closes down firms between F1 and F2, whose costs, including t, rise above revenue. Firms from F0 to F1 may also close down, if scarcity rent is already being absorbed by interest charges. This is similar to a tax on wages which has been successfully resisted, except in so far as more labour intensive firms would be hit harder by the former.

Output taxes, of course, have other incidence effects on consumers and producers. A tax rise of t may be shown as an addition to the supply curve or as a deduction from the demand curve, with effect on prices, output and costs (Diagram 68).

DIAGRAM 68

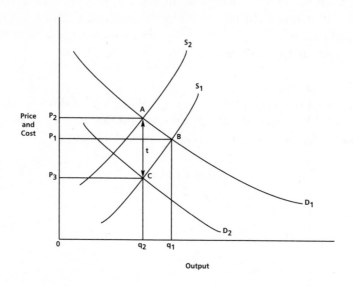

P1 is the original price. If t is treated as a cost, the consumer's price rises to P2 and output falls to q2. If t is treated as paid directly by the consumer, then the price received by the producer is P3 at output q2. The consumer has borne P2 – P1 of the tax, the producer P1 – P3, a distribution determined by the relative elasticities of supply and demand. Such an incidence affects the optimum achieved by a free market. The triangle ABC is a dead-weight loss, the top half of consumers' surplus, the bottom of producers' surplus. Since the latter in the long run is rent, the loss accrues to whoever receives the rent. (The rent in fact is greater than the area above the supply curve, as explained above pp.78-83.) Furthermore the tax prevents marginal costs from being equal to price and price in turn from being equal to each consumer's marginal valuation of the good. In short, it upsets the Pareto optimum (see pp.165-6).[4]

4 See Begg, *ibid.*, pp.310-13.

Not only is there distortion through the separation of marginal costs and prices in the taxed industry, but also in two extended ways. Firstly, substitute and complement goods face shifts in their demand curves up and down respectively, and secondly there is the 'second best' effect on all other goods. The latter means that the distortion away from a Pareto optimum, owing to the direct effect on the taxed good alone, cannot be seen as the second best alternative to the optimum, because the distorted quantities demanded and supplied of that good lead to a mismatch with the marginal benefits and costs of other goods. For example, if a sales tax is levied on clothes, labour will move into other industries and consumers of clothes will buy less, a gap having opened up between the marginal benefit of clothes and their marginal cost. In the food industry, for example, labour will be employed until marginal costs are equal to marginal benefits at an untaxed price P3 (Diagram 69). However, the opportunity cost of labour in the food industry in relation to the clothes industry is greater than its marginal cost producing food, since consumers of the marginal output of clothes would be prepared to buy more at a price above their post-tax marginal cost. Hence the social marginal cost (SMC) of labour in the food industry is above its private marginal cost (PMC). A tax on the food industry would redress the balance by making marginal benefit equal to social marginal cost at price P4.

DIAGRAM 69

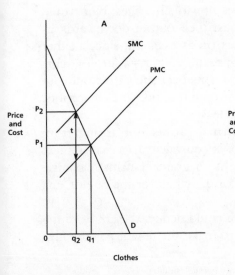

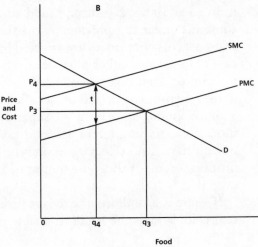

This does not imply that all industries should bear a tax equal to that on the first one taxed, which would raise far more tax than was intended. It does mean, however, that any indirect tax should be distributed amongst as many industries as possible to raise the required amount, if a Pareto optimum is the aim. There will be administrative costs associated with this, of course. Current tax policy in the UK, to judge by the myriad of taxes from a wide-ranging VAT to such oddities as taxes on insurance premiums and on airport departures, takes the second best theorem very seriously.[5]

Output taxes, therefore, have at least two further disadvantages. They create deadweight losses and they upset the Pareto optimum. But more significant is the fact that both taxes assessed on wages and those assessed on sales or output – practically all taxes in modern economies – act indiscriminately against the margin of production, for the simple reason that they disregard rent. Their impact, assumed to be upon a 'flat earth' economy, in fact strikes against the profile of a real economy, which is not flat but composed of firms with differential rents. The inevitable result is that marginal sites are relatively much harder hit. Where there is rent it can cushion the impact of taxation. Firms with no rent have no recourse. Any tax whose incidence is not proportional to rent must have such an effect.

c) Tax on Rent

The third broad method of taxing, however, is to assess taxes on economic rent. In principle this has no impact upon wages (Diagram 70). A tax on rent of 30%, ATM, does not touch wages. Nor would it do so at 100%. No firms would adjust their output downwards, as some do under the previous two bases of assessment, since neither marginal costs nor prices are affected by taxing rent. As a surplus, rents cannot enter into either price or costs. Firms bear such a tax only out of rent, or what may be recorded for accounting purposes as profits, if they own freehold land or beneficial leases.

Since in the long term all supernormal profits not arising from monopoly are rent, a rent assessed tax is equivalent to a tax on such profits, having no effect upon output. In Diagram 71 firms maximise profits (= rent) at the same output q1 or q2, whatever the rate of tax, even if it is 100%.

If there is a landlord, the tenant firm could deduct the tax from the rent paid. Why is the landlord unable to make the tenant pay the tax?

---

5 This gives a rather weak rationale to the current tendency towards 'stealth taxes'.

DIAGRAM 70

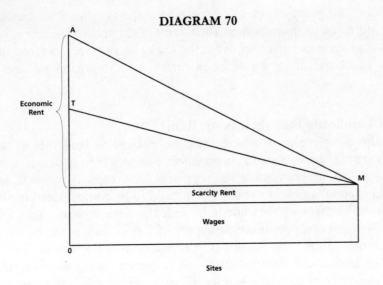

DIAGRAM 71

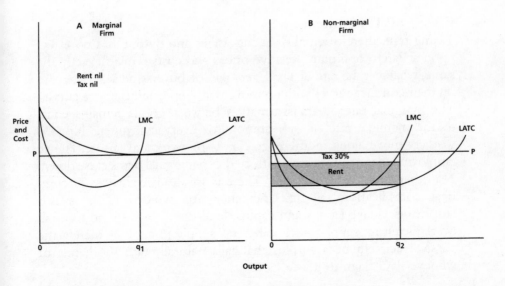

If he is letting the site for the maximum free market rent, when he tries to add the tax to the tenant's bill, he finds that it pays the tenant to move elsewhere, since the differential of the rent above rents of sites which would be the tenant's second choice just measures the extra benefits of the landlord's site. If it did not, tenants would move until it did.

Hence no premium can be charged for the tax. Since all sites are bearing taxes proportional to their rents, their relative benefits, and drawbacks, are not affected. Were the tax to be assessed on some sites only, of course, there would be distortions in the pricing and use of land.

Can Landlords Pass on Tax on Rent?

Another simple way of appreciating the inability of landlords to pass a tax on rent on to tenants or productive factors is to imagine, firstly, taxes levied proportionally on wages and on capital. In each case workers and owners of capital would need to be compensated for the tax in order that they continue to provide the same services in the long run. Without compensation the supply of labour and of capital would diminish. On the other hand a tax proportional to the annual value or rent of land does not enable landlords to demand compensation, since the land remains the same – other things being equal – in the long run, even if they paid a 100% tax.[6]

Effects of Tax on Rent

Taxing rent, therefore, unlike taxing wages and output, has no effect upon a Pareto optimum. Relative prices and costs remain exactly the same, whatever the rate of tax. Every pair of buyers and sellers remain on their contract curves with no movements along indifference curves. The marginal rate of transformation between goods remains equal to the marginal rate of substitution for every consumer.[7] Nor do workers move along indifference curves of work and leisure. Hence employment and output are unaffected. No marginal firms close down. No other firms reduce output. There is no deadweight loss. Second best complications of tax incidence are avoided. This is not surprising. Unlike labour and capital, land does not respond to a tax by reducing its supply, since it has no supply price. It is merely the passive recipient of a surplus that falls naturally into the hands of whoever lays claim to it.[8]

---

6 If they withdrew the land from use, they would still be liable for the tax, provided it is assessed on potential income and not income from existing use. The latter point is crucial, since a so-called land tax assessed on the value of current income from land fails to improve resource allocation by encouraging the best use of sites, or even to encourage vacant sites to be used. This is a significant example of the need to use precise terms in Economics: rent is defined as the *potential* yield of land. See p.72.

7 See Lipsey and Chrystal, *ibid.*, pp.404-7.

8 A tax on the capital value of land, even if assessed as the capitalized value of its economic rent (i.e. potential annual value), may be ineffective in so far as it diminishes the capital value and ultimately becomes

It might appear that a tax assessed upon rent, by falling more heavily upon firms with higher outputs and by nil assessments on marginal (no rent) firms, would penalise the efficient and protect the inefficient. This is definitely not the case. Such a tax has no effect whatsoever upon firms' decisions as to what to produce and how to produce it. Productive factors are employed in the very same proportions after as before the tax, since it is only borne by the surplus accruing to land. As every site remains where it is, unchanged, whatever tax is assessed upon it, its rent remains the same. Entrepreneurs' efforts towards efficiency are unaffected. Only if an entrepreneur is also the landholder of his enterprise may the tax influence his efficiency by denying him the power to subsidise his firm out of rent. In those circumstances a tax on rent would raise efficiency in the long run by eliminating such *ad hoc* subsidies. It does so, also, if it brings sites into use which are lying vacant, a frequent condition in modern cities. Hence the tax may raise productive efficiency, but would never reduce it.

If a tax on rent were assessed upon the current use of land the effects would be different. Rent is the potential annual income of land, not its actual income in current use. Taxing current uses of any factor, including land, deters those uses and distorts the pattern of use, causing some factors to fall out of use altogether.

> The real estate tax on building thus always favours old over new; gas stations over apartments; junk yards over factories; parking lots over parking structures; high income residences over low (higher income residencies are usually less intensive …); billboards over offices; unused over improved land; waiting over acting. This bias has half-destroyed the market as an arbiter among competing land uses, and as an agency promoting urban synergism. *The Losses of Nations*, ed. F. Harrison, p.193, Othila, 1998

Tax assessed on rent, however, in no way affects the potential output of land. That is determined independently by many influences, such as climate, topography and location, public expenditure, population and transport systems.

self-stultifying. This would happen if the capital value were calculated on the post-tax rent. Furthermore, a land development tax assessed on capital values has the effect of withdrawing land from the market, since it taxes only land which landowners make available for sale. The present Government's Planning Gain Supplement will deter development in this way, as a recent report on the UK Olympic project makes clear:

> A number of agreements allow the parties to walk away if PGS goes ahead. Many of the landowners have sat on this land for years and are in no rush to sell it now. They can wait for a better environment.
> *Sunday Telegraph*, 4 March 2007

The issue of land use, however, does raise the question of whether
the actual rents received from current use of land are to be assessed
for tax on rent? If all sites were utilised to the full in the best possible
land use, which means that their full potential were realised, this would
not be a problem, since rent as potential surplus output over costs and
rent as actual realised surplus would be the same. Indeed in the pure
model of land and labour, with all prices equal to marginal labour costs,
this would be so, at least in the long run, when all profits and losses
had served their purpose of indicating the optimum allocation of all
resources, including land. But what of the present world of imperfect
allocation: non-optimum land use with rents received below potential
rents, and labour and capital applied in measures determined, not just
by the natural division between land and labour (including capital as
stored labour with zero interest), but by monopoly profits, interest
payments and taxes assessed on output? For it is these subdivisions, or
additional claims upon output, that prevent recorded rents (including
rents retained by a freeholder) from being equal to potential rents.
They do this by taking large shares of the rent, reducing what is left
for the landholder, but also by distorting the use of land, so that it
falls below its optimum use (see Diagram 72).

DIAGRAM 72

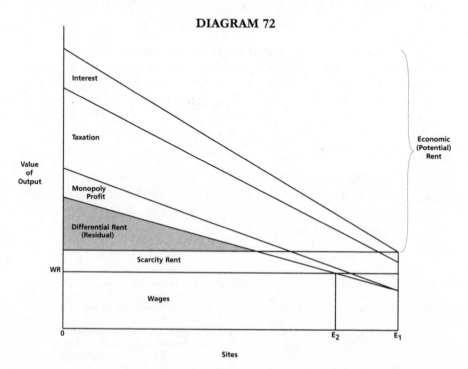

Rent under Non-optimum Land Use

Compared with the underlying division of rent and wages, there is now superimposed upon it the additional claims of interest, taxation and monopoly profits, all of which are in effect paid out of rent, including scarcity rent created by landless workers being forced to accept the least acceptable wage rate. Diagram 72 once again represents value added by firms, with all costs, including capital but excluding wages, charged 'below the line' against gross revenue. Above the line claims thus consist of wages, rent, profits extracted by monopoly power,[9] taxation more or less proportional to output, and interest, which tends to be higher for firms on better sites with above average use of capital. The overall effect is to reduce employment towards E2, since the combined impact of these claims on the margin is to close down firms employing workers between E1 and E2.

Taxing Rent in Present Conditions

It is evident that a high tax rate on the full (potential) rent would have an abrupt effect, given the present day structure of industry. The impact on monopoly profits might not cause difficulties for anyone except monopolists, but many firms would be unable to meet interest payments, leading to closures, especially of highly geared firms. In view, however, of the remarkable and unique zero impact on free market resource allocation of a tax on rent – quite apart from moral and other considerations (see Chapter 27) – it is worth analysing the effect of assessing a tax on the residual differential rent (including rent retained by freeholders). Were such a tax to be substituted gradually for a wage or output based tax, there would be correspondingly gradual relief on the margin of production, enabling employment and output to expand. On a three-dimensional diagram it would be clearer that most firms are towards the outer rim (or right-hand end), enabling substantial growth of firms and employment (Diagram 73).

Employment expands to E3, as tax on the margin is reduced and monopoly profits are largely eliminated.[10] Were this process to

---

9 Profits from monopoly are treated as proportional to rent, since part is for rent arising from monopolisation of minerals etc. and the rest is more or less concentrated on better sites.

10 A vital condition for this beneficial process to occur is that the residual rent upon which tax is assessed is itself the best rent obtainable for the site and not necessarily the actual rent charged by a landlord or collected by a freeholder. If not, an inefficient use of a site would not be penalised by a tax based upon the most efficient use. Such an assessable value of rent must not be confused, however, with the full potential rent.

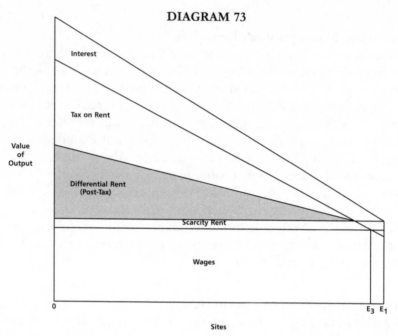

DIAGRAM 73

continue until all tax was assessed on rent, the outcome would be dramatically different.

As employment expands, workers' bargaining position is strengthened and wages rise, perhaps to the point where it is only interest on marginal firms that maintains scarcity rent. Higher wages make workers more independent, not only of landlords but also of entrepreneurs, for credit may be extended directly to workers to finance capital. In principle this transformation of industry could develop until capital was bought entirely by workers and not by absentee owners. Interest as a claim on industry would fall to zero and the fundamental division of output between labour and land could be established with all rent available for taxation (Diagram 74).

During this process residual rent itself is likely to increase as workers' enterprise and effort grows with their autonomy and direct control over capital. The rent profile, however, would probably be flatter as more sites came into use and monopoly profits were eliminated. Any reduction in credit restrictions, particularly by switching credit from land purchase to productive investment in capital would hasten the move towards higher employment and output.[11]

11 Multiplier and other effects implied by income determination theory are dealt with later in Part 6, though these are relatively short term in any case.

DIAGRAM 74

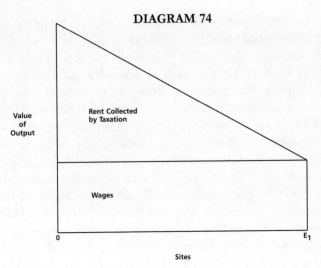

Landlords as Free Riders

Assessing taxation upon rent has at least one further economic justification. Wages as a claim upon production derive from the work done
by workers. Apart from any moral claim, wages are the return to work,
without which it would not be forthcoming, at least in sufficient
quantity and in places and forms which a wage structure makes
evident. Wages indeed are a direct effect of work, as when partners
share in the joint net product of a partnership. To whom then is rent
attributable? Is it a return for effort and skill? Landholders merely
release land, to which they lay claim, for production to take place
on it. But what is the economic basis of their claim? Inheritance or
purchase do not constitute such a claim, even if the previous claim
were well based. In fact, the previous landholder contributed no more
to production than his predecessor or successor. Claims to the rent of
land are purely historic and in no way economic, in the sense of being
a return for any effort made or service rendered. They are merely
claims on a surplus, which accrues naturally to land from its passive
role in production. Such claims are akin to those of free riders,
who can partake in benefits which they have no part in creating. Thus
landholders as such serve no economic function. A system of private
property in land which leaves rent in the hands of private landholders
may serve to allocate land to users in so far as it has to be allocated in
some way, but there might be many more efficient ways of doing this,
and in any case such a function certainly does not require returns to

landholders commensurate with rents. To allocate a marginal site to a suitable firm may be as judicious a task as to allocate a central site. If landholders were asked to give up their rents and receive *in lieu* a wage appropriate to their effort and skill in allocating land to productive uses, what would be the response? Both the owners of vast grouse-shooting tracts and Mayfair office sites might be reluctant to reply.

By withholding access to land services and then charging for the access, landowners are extracting a penalty, not offering services themselves. A story familiar to followers of Henry George illustrates this. A man was thinking of buying a site to build a house and was rather surprised at the price demanded. Whereupon the landowner said that the high price arose from the excellent facilities afforded by the site – drainage, roads, refuse collection, access to water etc. – so the price was paid. Shortly afterwards a large bill for rates arrived from the local authority – for drainage, roads, refuse collection, access to water etc.

Community Creation of Rent

Who or what then does create rent and thereby establish an economic claim to it? Natural conditions play an important role, which perhaps justifies a kind of green tax on rent whereby nature is repaid. Yet human agency must be involved, especially as nature unaided creates not rent but a wilderness. No individual, however, or even groups of individuals, creates rent. It is a product of communities. Remove the surrounding community from a site and its rent diminishes, probably to nothing. Remove public services like roads or drains and sites become unproductive. Remove government and organised economic activity breaks down. For rent is created primarily by three things: nature, population and public authorities. Hence it is the natural return to the whole community that occupies the land concerned.

By this argument individual landholders have no valid claim on rent in the first place, however they may have acquired it. Economics concerns the present, not the past, as so many economic arguments make clear. Rent arises from day to day; claims upon it are made as it arises. Are claims justified now? Of course, claims to occupy land are another matter and may need to rely on past agreement, custom and law in order to give continuity and security to individuals, firms and the community itself. But such claims are separable from the claim to the rent of the land occupied. Rent *ab initio* is the property of the community that creates it. Even to tax it is not strictly logical, for a tax is a compulsory contribution paid out of someone's property. It is really a matter of landholders simply giving back to the community its own property.

Arguments about property have many strands. Ideally, as in a perfect family, individuals might claim nothing as their own, and indeed claims may be inwardly renounced whilst conforming outwardly to the practice of the community in which one lives. In the present state of human society, however, rules of property are evidently necessary. On what principles are they to be based? To create something by one's own efforts surely gives rise to a legitimate claim upon it. To be given or to buy something from a person having himself such a claim must create a valid claim, if exchange is to be possible. But no one person ever created the rent of land. The natural division of production between wages and rent is at the same time a natural division between the claims on production of individuals and those of the whole community.

Despite his reservations about the imposition of a tax on land values, Alfred Marshall was very clear about this underlying principle:

> ... a far seeing statesman will feel a greater responsibility to future generations when legislating as to land than as to other forms of wealth; ... from the economic and from the ethical point of view land must everywhere and always be classed as a thing by itself. If from the first the state had retained true rents in its own hands, the vigour of industry and accumulation need not have been impaired ... Nothing at all like this can be said of the incomes derived from property made by man.
> A. Marshall, *Principles of Economics*, p.661, 8th edn, MacMillan, London, 1956

CHAPTER 16

Historical Analysis

C OLLECTION OR non-collection of economic rent by the community which creates it is an aspect of the system of land tenure. If it is collected, then rights to land use are matched by the duty to render up rent of the site; if it is not, then such rights are unconditional. The fact that taxes are assessed otherwise on incomes, sales, profits and whatever else does not mean that they have become an entirely separate issue. By implication such taxes mean that land tenure has become an unconditional system, allowing landholders to reap where they did not sow.

Modern economies are creatures of such a system. Absolute private property in land and taxation assessed upon output and wages stand together as two aspects of one phenomenon. How this acts upon the production of wealth, the level of employment and the allocation of resources of land, labour and capital has been explained in outline. In order to emphasise how the present structure of industry is so determined, a brief sketch of how it reached its present development is now given. Imposing a tax on rent in place of existing taxes would unwind the devious subdivisions of claims on output, and release the suppressed productive force of free labour working on free land. In many respects such a fundamental reform would reverse the process which has led over a long period of time to the current structure; but it would by no means return the economy to where it began. Much has changed since, in particular the productive power of modern technology, but nevertheless a brief theory of economic history, by tracing out the steps to where we stand now, may illuminate the path of a proposed reform.

Land Enclosure

Land enclosure in Britain in modern times began in the late Middle Ages and gathered pace in the sixteenth century. A second great wave of enclosures between about 1750 and 1850 completed the process. Virtually no common land has remained. Enclosure meant not only the destruction of common fields and common rights over pasture and waste land, but also the gradual elimination of landholders' duties towards the community – the payment of land taxes, in particular, but also duties towards tenants concerning security of tenure, rights over improvements and so on. In the seventeenth century Gerard Winstanley could exclaim with the passion of the expropriated, 'True freedom lies where a man receives his nourishment and preservation, that is in the use of the earth ...'[1]

Appearance of Scarcity Rent

Enclosure was not the main cause of greater agricultural productivity; that was rather the result of the improved efficiency of yeoman farmers and developments in agricultural technology. Where enclosure was by agreement between farmers, as opposed to imposition by landowners, it also tended to raise output. What enclosure did cause unequivocally was a reduction in wages and a corresponding rise in rents. After all, that was the main motive of the landlords. In short, scarcity rent appeared (Diagram 75).

DIAGRAM 75

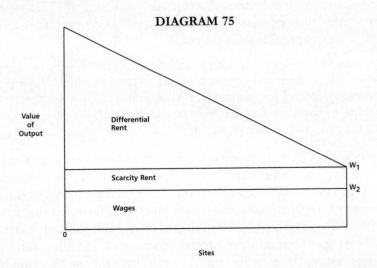

Wages fell from W1 to W2 as workers could no longer look to common land for additional sources of income, and were forced to compete more vigorously for employment as agrarian land was turned

1 Quoted in C. Hill, *The World Turned Upside Down*, p.134, Penguin, London, 1991.

to pasture or held out of use for future development. Greater labour productivity in agriculture, combined with inelastic demand for food, intensified the struggle for employment. Though population grew, extra mouths to feed also meant extra hands seeking employment, so that scarcity rent could only increase.

Industrial Revolution

Rural unemployment and the fall in wages led to migration to towns, where cheap labour coincided with technological progress through inventions and innovation in major industries like textiles. Cottage industry and merchant outsourcing gave way to the factory system. Farm labourers and self-employed artisans became factory employees at minimal wages. 'Capitalists' saw the opportunity to develop productive urban sites by borrowing money from landowners or obtaining credit from banks to finance buildings and machinery. Workers were employed without job security and at the lowest wages they would accept, often at piece rates which left them exhausted and indigent. The familiar horrors of the industrial revolution – the abuse of women and children, slum housing, high mortality rates – became endemic. 'Everyone but an idiot knows that the lower classes must be kept poor or they will never be industrious', wrote Arthur Young in 1771.[2] Worse, perhaps, even than physical degradation was the degeneration in the status and craftsmanship of workers.

> But increased competition overturned the sense of identity between workers and masters, and the development of specialization and minute subdivision eroded the property of skill, removing workers' general knowledge of the production process, and reducing the prospects of becoming an independent producer.
>
> M.J. Daunton *ibid.*, p.199

The new class of entrepreneurs was often not composed of wealthy men initially. They were especially adept at seeing the opportunities offered by the unique combination of low wages and technical development. By borrowing they could invest in a favoured site, where power, water and transport, for example, were available, and realise its full rent by contributing their special expertise of initiative, foresight and organisation. Interest, however, had to be paid and thus the levy extracted by loan creditors and bankers took its toll.

On the other hand, the industrial revolution greatly raised the output of manufactured goods and associated products like coal, iron

2 Quoted in M.J. Daunton, *Progress and Poverty*, p.177, OUP, 1995.

ore and transport services. Total production rose enormously in quantity, albeit falling in quality as handcrafts gave way to mechanisation. Hence both total rent and total wages increased, with perhaps *per capita* wages rising also but at the price of higher unemployment. Workers may generally have experienced a rise in material living standards, but relatively to unearned incomes derived from rent their share declined. As firms became heavily indebted, limited liability was introduced to protect entrepreneurs, enabling yet greater credit to be extended to successful firms through the extension of shareholding. Bankers, of course, looked to 'capitalists' rather than to relatively impoverished workers as worthy recipients of bank credit. The prospect of worker owned enterprises was more or less eliminated. Absentee owners and salaried directors became the masters of industry, though soon the former were to see themselves reduced to rentiers.

> The whole edifice of business rested upon the shifting sands of credit, and any disruption threatened large-scale collapse ... the 'credit matrix' of firms is complex and less visible than steam engines, spinning-jennies, and factory buildings, which embodied fixed capital.
>
> Daunton, *ibid.*, p.247

By 1834 poverty and unemployment were so widespread that a new and harsher way of treating workers beset by them was introduced in the Poor Law Amendment Act, under which workhouses replaced outdoor relief. The Act was

> ... based on a changed conception of society (which) rejected the notion that society was reciprocal and organic ... and substituted a view of society based on an interdependent market economy resting on self-interest, competition and contract ... part of a wider change which was expressed in the enclosure movement, the replacement of coincidental use-rights by unitary property rights ...
>
> Daunton, *ibid.*, p.493

Taxes on Output and Wages

Economic growth required more social infrastructure financed by government. War, and the steadily rising cost of supporting the poor, added to the need for higher taxation. Public debt also brought a burden of interest upon the taxpayer. The land tax had been removed by the ascendant interest of the gentry and of those who benefited from burgeoning urban rent. Thus tax was assessed almost entirely on output and wages, with harmful effects at the margin of production (Diagram 76).

DIAGRAM 76

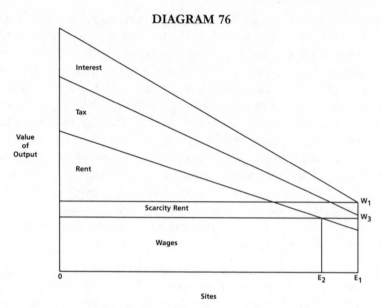

Wages could no longer be driven down, as workers were now receiving the least acceptable wage and fought to defend it by forming unions and supporting radical, and then socialist, MPs. Still, however, pressure upon them was tightened by the impact of output taxes in the form of excise and sales taxes, and later taxes on income. Taxation harmed them more by its effect on firms than by actual reductions in workers' net income. For marginal firms could not pay higher taxes, and non-marginal ones put off workers at the intensive margin. Employment fell to E2.[3] Cyclical movements of trade and production became more severe, so that employment rose and fell around this reduced level (see Chapter 26).

Need for Welfare State

Disparity between rich and poor became greater. Poverty was indicated now by inability to provide for the vital needs of a family – education, medical care, housing and provision for the old. If families were to be left to the harsh conditions of 'the market' for work, then eventually such poverty, and indeed starvation for the poorest unemployed, would lead inevitably to revolution (as happened, of course, elsewhere). Britain, however, chose the Welfare State. Genuine economic reform was ignored, despite valiant attempts by some Liberal and Labour

3 The diagram exaggerates unemployment, since more intensive employment on better sites would occur.

politicians to shift taxation off production and on to rent in 1909 and 1931. A vast system of outdoor relief was slowly introduced under the guise of a beneficent State: pensions, unemployment pay, free education, public housing, a national health service, social security benefits. Why an economic system that was evidently highly productive and growing at an average rate of about 2%p.a. should need massive public aid to relieve poverty was not explained, except by the misconceived theories of Marxists. The Welfare State has temporarily saved 'capitalism', but the signs of how ephemeral is the solution are already upon us. As concealed poverty, both absolute and relative, increases, the tax necessary to relieve it becomes harder to find. For every tax increase depresses the margin yet further.

Growth of Monopoly

Today the economic structure is further skewed by monopoly. Firms that have captured rent by developing valuable sites, like sources of raw materials, high street stores, or supermarkets on ring roads, reinvest their 'super-profits' in further sites. Oil, chemicals, grocery retailing are just a few examples of industries in which a few firms dominate the market. Such firms usually make sure that they own freehold sites. Inevitably they capture suppliers and ancillary industries also under the euphemism of rationalising production. They trade under a multitude of product names to obscure from the public the degree of monopolisation that exists. The provision of credit undergoes similar concentration, until a handful of financiers, more or less in league with the central bank in the name of 'stability' or 'prudence', control bank credit, making it available mainly to those who own the better freeholds, including monopolists. Standardisation of products becomes the norm; consumer choice is limited to brands. Work is not merely narrowed to employment as opposed to self-employment, but increasingly limited to employment by firms caught up in the nexus of monopoly groups. If you enter the oil or chemical industries, which oligopolist do you work for? If you get a job in a supermarket, which 'household name' is it? If you want a career in banking, which one of the 'big four' employs you? Thus monopoly profits become another ingredient in rent, not in this case bearing so much upon the margin, since such monopolies eschew sites where rent is very low. Rather they absorb a fair slice of rent on better sites, denying it alike to independent landlords and to any public purpose. This in very broad terms is how we live now (see Diagram 72, p.182).

Examples abound of the multifarious distortions of economic life arising from such monopoly power – from influence over television channels through advertising expenditure to the mass introduction of computers into education at all levels – but one example may exemplify how far the drive to monopolise rent has gone.

> In the early 1990s, as local authorities' budgets collapsed, developers began offering inducements in return for planning permission which had nothing whatever to do with the schemes they were proposing. They would offer, for example, to build a swimming pool on the other side of town in return for planning permission for a new housing estate, or they would simply give the council a cheque, with which it could do whatever it wanted. While most people regard these inducements as bribery, local authorities describe them as 'offsite planning gain'.
>
> G. Monbiot, *Captive State*, p.133, Pan, London, 2001

These are not natural monopolies, where genuine economies of scale make production at minimum efficient scale uneconomic for more than one firm. They are firms drawing upon the community's rent to swell their so-called profits and upon the restricted life-blood of credit, which could be freely available to firms large and small, central and marginal, if they operated on a level playing field. Nor are these overgrown conglomerates notably efficient, since living off rent is prone to produce indolence and complacency rather than industry and initiative. The threat of take-over, when their profits decline and their share price understates their real asset value (including freehold land perhaps available for development) may stimulate them to greater efficiency, but dog eats dog is a clumsy way to achieve it. Needless to say, employees' and customers' interests are not in the forefront amongst the motives for take-overs.

Globalisation

Finally, these bloated giants in the economies of 'advanced' nations become multi-nationals, with much the same forces operating on a world stage. Globalisation becomes the order of the day.

> Identical products are now manufactured for distribution all over the world. Brands have become universally recognisable, their attributes signalled in the international language of advertisements on far-flung satellite television screens. Coca Cola has been imbued with so much value that it has become the traditional drink at Indian weddings; the blue, red and white of a Pepsi can is now more identifiable than the Union Jack; the swoosh insignia on a pair of Nikes, as familiar in Milan and London as in Saigon, has spawned an entire new global industry of pirated swooshes. N. Hertz, *The Silent Takeover*, p.34, Heinemann, London, 2001

Probably the main incentive for multi-nationals when they relocate is the presence of cheap labour in the new host country. But what is this cheap labour? Why is it so cheap? Are Brazilians or Indonesians or sub-Saharan Africans culturally predetermined to subsist on a bare minimum wage, which even the unemployed in Brooklyn or Liverpool would refuse to accept? Perhaps so, but what underpins their poverty is landlessness. Their wages, if they have jobs, or their post-tax incomes from small plots of marginal land, if they are peasant farmers, are so low that the multi-nationals may pay them more. Yet 'more' is less than the wages of workers in 'advanced' economies. Land enclosure, unrestricted private property in land and the non-collection of rent by public authorities round the world opens up opportunities everywhere to predatory global companies. This is a vast area for economic study, but the fact remains that it all began with the system of land tenure and taxation in the home country. More importantly, it is these fundamental conditions of land tenure and taxation in all economies that determine how they operate now.[4]

4 For a summary of this historical process as it occurred in the USA, where land was especially held out of use in extensive quantities as settlement moved westwards, see Henry George's 'Savannah Story' in his *Progress and Poverty*, pp.235-42, Robert Schalkenbach Foundation, New York, 1962.

CHAPTER 17

Externalities

S INCE ALFRED MARSHALL developed the concept of external economies and diseconomies the subject has been greatly extended to become a major part of modern welfare economics. Social costs and benefits, previously overlooked, or thought inaccessible to analysis, are now the stock-in-trade of many economists, enabling such diverse problems as industrial pollution, traffic congestion and overhanging trees to be quantified and subjected to equitable remedies. Trading in pollution rights, electronic road pricing and the bribing of neighbours are some of the practical outcomes.[1] Yet the very diversity and complexity of cost/benefit analysis suggests that something is missing.

Rent from External Economies

Consider an inner city site devoid of all buildings, pathways or fittings of any kind, set amidst other sites fully equipped with everything needed for a modern city – offices, shops, houses and flats, petrol stations, banks etc. – and served by transport facilities, power supplies, water, sewerage, refuse collection and so on. Consider, also, a thriving population of workers and residents in the whole neighbourhood. What would be the annual value of the site? What would be its price were it to be sold? Unless there were very severe planning restrictions, the answer would be 'a great deal'. Why? It is bare earth almost identical in itself to any similar sized area of bare earth anywhere else in the country. Yet it is worth perhaps thousands of times the price of such an area in the remote countryside. The answer is primarily external economies.

Rent of land is far and away the greatest effect of external economies. Oddly enough – in view of economists' disregard of it – it is also far the easiest effect to measure. For, apart from natural causes

1 See, for example, Begg, *ibid.*, Ch. 15.

of rent, like micro-climate, soil fertility and mineral wealth, the remainder of the causes can be seen as external economies. In other words, rent is largely the product accruing on a site exogenously, from the presence and work of people on other sites. Consumers, workers, firms, local and national authorities and a host of other agents, like schools and hospitals, create benefits (and costs) outside their own endogenous activities. No man is an island.

Industry Supply Curves

The external economies and diseconomies of firms may be considered under two heads: those acting within an industry and those acting on society at large. The former effect a change in the industry long-run supply curve which does not enter into the individual firms' cost curves. As the industry expands along its supply curve, it experiences new conditions brought about by its expansion as a whole, not attributable to actions of any one firm, such as economies of scale amongst suppliers, the growth of a skilled labour force or the profitability of new services for the industry, like transport; or, conversely, rising costs of suppliers, shortages of skilled labour or transport congestion within the industry. Hence the industry supply curve falls or rises respectively, and is not just the summation of constituent firms' long-run marginal cost curves (Diagram 77).

DIAGRAM 77

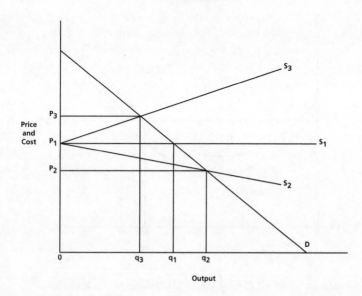

Long-run output and price may therefore be q2P2 or q3P3 rather than q1P1. This is after all, or possibly only some, firms' costs curves have been adjusted downwards or upwards, so that *ex post* the new industry supply curve becomes the sum of firms' adjusted costs and prices.[2] These shifts will probably affect the distribution of firms' revenue between rent and wages, depending upon the configuration of cost curves and the precise impact on each firm of external (dis)economies, since there is no reason why this need be equal or proportionate. However, the main point here is that any such impact remains within the industry and is not a social benefit or cost. Landlords may receive a gratuitous gain or loss, but only those within the industry. (Although there may, in fact, be an additional effect upon other landlords of the type outlined below.)

Social Economies and Diseconomies

On the other hand, firms create external economies or diseconomies for society at large. The latter – social costs – mean that a particular firm's marginal private cost curve (MPC) may be below its marginal social cost curve (MSC) owing to its polluting air, land or rivers, or otherwise damaging the environment or causing difficulties for the community, such as excessive local traffic (Diagram 78).

DIAGRAM 78

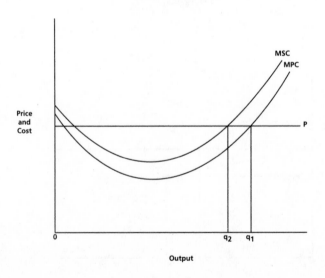

2 For a fuller analysis, see Lipsey and Chrystal, *ibid.*, pp.231-2; Blaug, *ibid.*, pp.363-7.

Such a firm's output at q1 is above the socially optimum output at q2, which suggests that a pollution tax might be beneficial.[3] General acceptance in society of the principle to keep land in good condition would probably pre-empt most problems of pollution, but in its absence more complicated measures are needed. In practice, much of what is called social costs is borne by nearby landlords rather than by society at large. Land and water pollution, if not air pollution, may despoil nearby sites; very loud noise may reduce the value of adjacent sites. Rents are correspondingly lower.

Social benefits arising from the activities of firms are also usually treated as though they were received by the population at large. Their incidence, in fact, is heavily directed towards landowners. Begg's example of a farmer's pest control system which benefits neighbouring farms is an obvious case, but so too are those of factories or shops which attract customers, ancillary services, competitors, skilled workers and so on to the immediate neighbourhood, where landlords can charge higher rents. Likewise, a supermarket may create greatly enhanced rents nearby, especially in a shopping centre, if it is a household name. Cumulatively this process generates whole areas of high rent. Firms interact via external economies, so that markets, labour forces, housing – in short, communities – develop largely by means of this process:

> Manufacturing has developed partly in areas or regions of largest markets and in turn the size of these markets has been augmented and other favourable conditions have been developed by the very growth of this industry'.[4]

Were the rent created by firms' external economies to be collected by society, then they would truly be social benefits. Under a system where rent is taken by private landlords, such benefits are largely private benefits, which are like windfalls over the neighbour's fence.

Locational Externalities
What is sometimes called 'the new economic geography' identifies locational externalites, which lead to clustering of firms, on a ring road, for example.[5] If minimum efficient scale occurs at a high level

---

3 See Begg for discussion of various methods of dealing with this, *ibid.*, pp.248-53.

4 Harris, C., 'The Market as a Factor in the Localisation of Industry in the United States' [Annals of the Association of American Geographers 64, p.315], quoted in P. Krugman, *Development, Geography and Economic Theory*, p.92, MIT Press, London, 1997.

5 See Begg, *ibid.*, pp.278-9.

of output, i.e. a firm's long-run cost curves fall over a large range of output, locational externalities may not be easily realised, because no one firm will make profits if it is the first to open. Locational externalities only begin when several firms are in operation. This raises issues about public subsidies and the function of property developers. However, locational externalities, by definition, create rent, not profits. Were land controlled by a public authority, it could charge a rent which did not deter first arrivals, and then increase rent later as locational externalities actually occurred with the arrival of later firms. Private landlords, on the other hand, may charge an initial rent (or price for freeholds) which anticipates future externalities and thus deters first arrivals. Furthermore, when an area is owned by several landlords, unless they co-operate, development is stifled by the difficulty of realising locational externalities in the early stages.

Public Goods

Beyond externalities derived from the production of firms, however, stands another category at least of equal weight, namely those arising from public expenditure. Public goods, or collective consumption goods, defined as those which are non-rivalrous and non-excludable,[6] clearly create externalities. For example, national defence, from which anyone benefits without depriving others and from which no-one can be excluded, provides security for the whole population, whether or not it operates at any one time to protect someone or no-one in particular. Similarly, law and order offers everyone the protection of the law, even when being enforced only in favour of certain people i.e. the potential victims of crime. Street lighting is another familiar example, where provision for some amounts to provision for all. In terms of individuals, the demand for such services can be represented as a group of demand curves, the vertical summation of which constitutes collective demand (Diagram 79).

Optimum output of the public good is at q1, where Dc (= D1 + D2 + D3) equals the marginal cost of providing it, a point beyond the optimum at q2 for D3 alone, which is the greatest individual demand, if each individual sought to buy it. Were 'D3' to buy q2, 'D1' and 'D2' would be free riders i.e. they could share in the benefit of the public good without paying for it. There is a consumer surplus to the left of q1, since public expenditure of PE per unit is spent and, to the left of q1, DC is above PE.

6 See Begg, *ibid.*, pp.262-3.

DIAGRAM 79

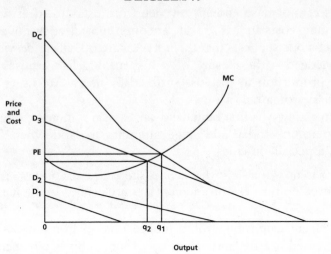

However, that is by no means the end of the matter. Not only individuals *qua* citizens benefit from defence, law and order and street lighting. If land is privately owned, so too do landowners. Land values respond very precisely to most changes in the provision of public goods. Street lighting raises rents and land values in the street concerned and perhaps nearby also. A higher degree of law and order does the same for the area concerned. Within a city, for example, house prices may vary greatly with the extent of local crime. And on a national level, both domestic and international security affect land values. Landlords are the greatest of all free riders under the present system of private receipt of rent. Public expenditure on public goods enhances rents, but landlords pay nothing for this, since taxes are not assessed on rent. As individual citizens, of course, they pay taxes on income etc. like everyone else.

Enhanced Rent from other Public Expenditure
Finally, there is another major kind of public expenditure which does not provide strictly public goods, since the provision may be rivalrous or excludable to various degrees. Such goods and services may indeed be publicly or privately produced, and in the UK have been the subject of nationalisation and privatisation. A tendency to experience increasing economies of scale is not here the issue, nor are arguments about natural monopoly, regulation and so on. Transport services best exemplify what is here relevant. A railway, for instance, may charge

users a series of prices which may or may not cover costs. Most railways cannot raise enough revenue from users to meet both fixed and running costs and, as a result, are often subsidised by governments. This fact alone suggests that the full measure of railway services is not acknowledged – the closure of a loss-making line arouses protests out of proportion to the loss suffered by users. Are users the only beneficiaries of a railway?

When a railway is first built, land values near it increase dramatically. Rail extensions today add huge amounts to landowners' nominal wealth, especially in cities:

> Access to mass transit is what defines site value today, just as proximity
> to a river, or to an exit of a motorway, once defined land values.
>
> N. Cohen in *The Financial Times*, 20 July 2001

The recent extension of the Jubilee Line in London cost £3.5bn and increased nearby land values by £13bn.[7] This is not recouped by railways, so that once again landowners are free riders, even if they do not personally use the railway. Were railway systems able to finance their capital expenditure out of rent created by them, whilst charging fares commensurate with running costs, i.e. marginal cost, they would certainly be viable. The urban transit extension in Hong Kong is partially financed in this way. Proposals to build a railway link with the existing Crossrail scheme at Liverpool Street in London, extending via Whitechapel, Docklands, London City Airport and the Thames Gateway corridor, have the support of property companies at Canary Wharf, which would benefit from the extension. Regenerating East London and creating employment throughout the area affected are substantial social benefits, but who in particular would receive the lion's share? Commuters and workers pay fares and earn wages. Landowners receive rent. All pay taxes as individuals which might subsidise the new rail extension. The direct connection between railway provision and enhanced rents is ignored, yet if recognised it could convert the idea of externalities into a cost/benefit analysis which was really social. Society's gain from a railway is measured by the rise in rent. The rise in rent is the natural source of funds to pay for the railway.

This is but one major example of how rent and public expenditure are related. The natural connection between the two is symbiotic. At present, however, it cannot function fully, for one side of the symbiosis is interrupted by private claims drawing off rent and obstructing its use in the provision of public goods and services. As a consequence,

---

7 S. Brittan in *The Financial Times*, 30 August 2001.

the necessary funding of public expenditure draws upon sources not suitable for taxation, notably wages, consumption and so on.

> Increases in land values give not only a good indication of the benefits of infrastructure investments, but also provide an efficient and just way of financing their costs. It is efficient to tax these values because the tax would reduce the size of a windfall, while other taxes used to pay for infrastructure reduce effort, penalize the division of labour or discourage capital accumulation. It is also just, because the chief beneficiaries bear the cost.
>
> Martin Wolf in *The Financial Times,* 9 June 2006

Effect of New Technology

Some might argue that modern technology is making location of less importance, that cell phones and laptop computers eliminate the need for centrally sited offices and proximity to colleagues, clients and markets. Yet city land values still accelerate in the major economies of the world. The need to site firms near raw materials, power, and large labour supplies may have gone, but it is replaced by the demand for 'wired-up' localities, skilled scientists and technicians, light-industrial buildings and good schools. In the USA, for example Boulder (Colorado), Austin (Texas), Santa Monica (California) and Cambridge (Massachusetts) grow, whilst older industrial cities, like Newark, Detroit and St Louis decline. In the former places, rapid expansion has its costs:

> ... population density soars, traffic-gridlock appears, parking becomes scarce, and rents go through the roof.
>
> J. O'C. Hamilton in *Business Week,* 4 December 2000

Who Benefits and Who should Pay?

Individuals certainly benefit, both from the externalities created by firms and from those created by public expenditure. Should they not therefore pay as individuals for those benefits, either by higher prices or by taxes, like income tax? Yet landlords clearly benefit also. Should they not pay likewise for their benefits? Such questions are confused. Were rent to be collected by the community, landlords would no longer benefit and would by that very fact be unable to pay. At the same time, individuals would all pay equally for their benefits were rent so collected. For rent is caused by the presence of the whole community in its multifarious life as producer, consumer, public authority and the rest. Marginal workers and marginal firms contribute to rent accruing on non-marginal sites by their living and working in the community.

All create rent equally, even though all do not create output equally. Hence by collecting rent, the community would collect equally from all. Hence everyone would be contributing to the benefits received as an individual from externalities.

This way of thinking cuts across present attitudes. It may appear that the owner of a high rent site would be making a greater contribution to public revenue were rent publicly collected, than would a worker in a marginal firm. But such an appearance is an illusion, arising from the idea that rent belongs initially to landowners. In fact, the community creates it, so that it belongs to the community in the first place. Landowners lay claim to it. Let their claims be examined. Likewise, if tax-free workers were to believe that public provision of defence, law and order and street lighting were a free gift from the community, they might reassure themselves that they have the same right to it as everyone else, though paying no taxes. For their work and very existence give rise to the natural fund that provides those benefits. There are no free meals, yet some would claim them.

CHAPTER 18

Natural Monopoly

I T IS A WELL-KNOWN problem in economic theory that, at least for some industries, long-run cost curves appear to slope downwards at output levels close to the saturation of industry demand. Where long-run average total costs (LATC) are falling, long-run marginal costs (LMC) remain below them. Hence a price equal to LMC generates a long-run loss, which is unsustainable. On the other hand, where LATC is rising, LMC must be above it and hence an industry equilibrium may be possible with marginal revenue equal to marginal cost and with average cost below or equal to price. In this case the resulting market structure may be perfectly competitive if there are many competing firms, imperfectly competitive if firms have differentiated products, or oligopolistic if industry demand only allows a few firms to operate at minimum efficient scale. Replication of plants means that U-shaped, or saucer-shaped, LATC for one plant does not prevent firm expansion, where there are economies of scope. These may take the form of multi-product, advertising, marketing, management and financial economies, some of which may be merely pecuniary i.e. the firms' gain may merely be equivalent to a loss by another firm, as in the case of forcing discounts on a weak supplier. Which 'economies', both of scale and scope, are genuine, and which are pecuniary or even illusory, is a vital question, to which the introduction of a true assessment of land and rent is highly pertinent (see Chapters 6-7).

However, even were it clearly answered, there would remain one further related question. Namely, after taking full account of such matters, if there are some industries still exhibiting cost curves which are falling near the saturation of industry demand, what is the correct or equitable solution to the inevitable monopoly position? Are there natural monopolies and what can be done about them?

DIAGRAM 80

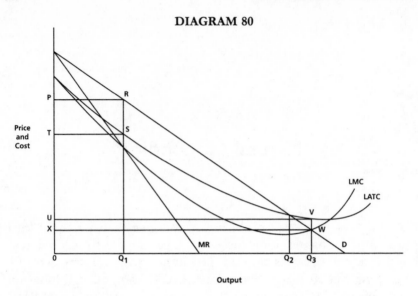

Output

How to Deal with Natural Monopolies

The standard answers to this problem can be briefly summarised
(Diagram 80). The industry may be allowed to operate as a private
monopoly, making LMC = MR with output Q1 and price P, and receiving supernormal profits of PRST. Regulation may force it to invest
most or all of these profits. Allocative efficiency is seriously disrupted,
since P is much higher than LMC, so that consumers would willingly
buy more at prices above social cost of production.[1] The industry
could be forced to break even by producing at Q2, but this has little
rationale beyond that of excluding both monopoly profits and the need
for a subsidy. Regulation could make it produce between Q1 and Q2
with pricing and investment policy determined by social and
political considerations. More acceptable to many economists, however, is production at Q3 where P = LMC. At this output the welfare
optimum is satisfied (subject to 'second best' considerations). There
is no dead-weight loss of consumer and producer surpluses[2] and
allocative efficiency is met in the long run by the provision of the exact
amount of industry capacity to make P = LMC. A subsidy of UVWX
is required.

There remains the possibility of discriminatory pricing, as used by
many existing public utilities, like the UK electricity industry, where

---

1 The theory of 'second best' complicates this point in an economy where price rarely equals LMC
elsewhere in the economy (see pp.177-8).
2 See Lipsey and Chrystal, *ibid.*, p.301.

consumer surplus is captured to some extent. This may be particularly useful where demand is insufficient to allow any uniform price to equal LATC (or even LMC). If price discrimination occurs from S to U with output Q1 then full costs PRQ1O are covered by revenue, provided STP > TRU (Diagram 81).

DIAGRAM 81

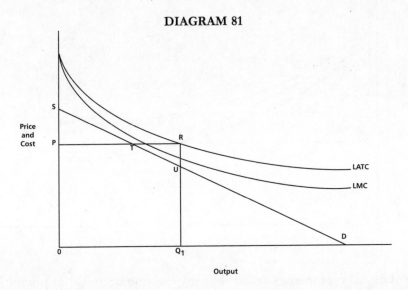

Land in Natural Monopoly

As always, most of the above analysis ignores the role of land. Since the types of industry experiencing such falling costs are invariably crucially dependent on locating correctly, this is a fundamental error. Transport industries, for example, almost by definition require land at particular places to operate at all as a public service. Roads, rail-track, stations, ports and airports, for example, need precise and permanent locations. Power industries similarly need large, accessible sites for generation, and extensive, continuous sites for cable and pipelines, as do telecommunication industries. Water supply needs extensive reservoirs, cleansing units and pipelines. Rent of such sites is high in relation to costs, as the price of acquiring them for new developments makes abundantly clear. As the principle of opportunity cost emphasises, the social cost of using such sites is the next best alternative use forgone, a value reflected in land acquisition prices. Hence land prices should be evaluated explicitly to determine optimum outputs and prices. In other words, all natural monopolies – like all other productive units – should show rent explicitly in their cost and revenue

analyses. This would make LATC, including rent, higher and even more
obstinately downward sloping. The outcome might be:

DIAGRAM 82

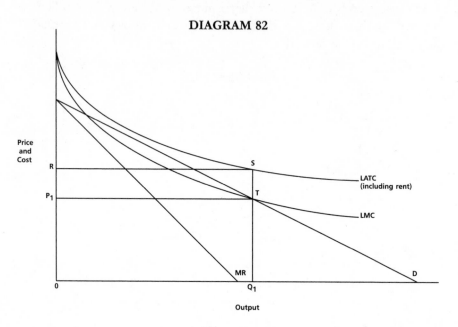

Marginal cost pricing would then give an output of Q1 at price P1,
with a subsidy required of RSTP1. To the extent that this subsidy is
augmented by the rent charge in LATC, such an outcome seems to
impose upon taxpayers a subvention to landowners. This, in fact, is
precisely what happens at present whenever a public utility buys or
rents private land for its activities, so it would be a progressive step to
make this more explicit. However, were the land held by a public
authority the rent charge could be purely nominal, if the utility were
publicly owned. If it were privately owned, as many utilities are at
present, the rent charge could be paid as taxation, or the subsidy could
be reduced by the rent charge.

What then of the remaining part, if any, of the subsidy? The
existence of the system itself benefits others besides users. Local
communities benefit from local services, the national community
benefits from a national system. Can these communal benefits be
measured? A minimum measure of them lies in the increased land
values that are attributable to the service. When a new railway or a new
natural gas pipeline is constructed to serve an area, all land values there,
both industrial and domestic, rise accordingly (see Chapter 17). Thus
if the remainder of the subsidy were financed by the public collection

of rent – for example by an annual tax on land values – the solution would be equitable.

Public utilities may charge two part tariffs, a standing charge to cover fixed costs and a variable charge to cover current usage. This reflects the distinction between the cost of maintaining the facility itself and the cost of providing a particular service at any one time. Yet users are by no means the sole beneficiaries of the facility, as the rise in land values on its creation clearly indicates. Why should only users pay the 'existence' costs? If they do so, landowners who benefit from the externalities of the utility are given a free ride. This is additional to any rent paid by the utility for the use of land. Both landlords' beneficial externalities and their claims for rent are dysfunctional elements in the natural operation of public utilities. The value they create is the natural source of funds to pay their standing charges.

The situation is different when many utilities have been privatized, as is the case in the UK at present. A privately owned utility that owns its land is benefiting from rent. If it also receives a subsidy, it is receiving a double benefit from the community in the form of rent and subsidy. Were the rent paid over as taxation, there would be good reason to finance the subsidy out of taxation on the grounds that the positive externalities created by the utility generate the public revenue required.

These complications arising from uncertainty about the proper ownership of utilities, however, would all be greatly simplified were rent to be made explicit in their financial analysis, and if their creation of positive external economies were recognized. The optimum balance between the public and private sectors of the economy can only be achieved if the phenomenon of rent is fully understood and accounted for.

Local Control

A vital feature of probably all public utilities is that they serve regional or local communities, who are well aware of the need for a reliable and good quality service. Failure of water or power supply is a local disaster; transport also is largely a matter of moving within a town or region. Although natural monopoly is often a consequence of economies of scale and scope on a national level, as in the case of the national grid or intercity trains, the actual delivery of the service is local. People take little interest in public utility supply in an area far-removed from where they live. Hence such utilities need a strong element of local or regional control in addition to a central management overseeing the system as a whole. They are therefore very well suited to democratic processes locally and regionally, a feature significantly lacking in the UK under the nationalisation regimes of 1945 to 1980s and equally so since privatisation.

Natural Monopolies in Europe

At the other end of the scale, natural monopolies derived from limitation by market size, are susceptible to expansion of markets by international developments. In particular, the European Union makes some national public utilities more prone to competition from similar foreign utilities. This perhaps raises the spectre of massive European wide oligopolies in such products as gas, electricity and water supply, but these could be subject to EU regulation or even ownership, subject again to the essential requirement of local or regional control. The principle of subsidiarity is relevant here, for such utilities may be examples of economic activities which naturally overstep national boundaries and lend themselves to maximum productive and allocative efficiency at supra-national level. The origin of the EU in the Coal and Steel Community and Euratom suggests this. Once again, however, the optimum scale of such organizations may not be as great as appears, if private land monopoly is taken into account. The accumulation of rent in private hands often gives rise to the illusion of large successful enterprises, whose real economic efficiency is low.

Rent from Locational Specificity

What in practice constitutes a natural monopoly with a constantly falling LATC may be to some extent a question of the current state of technology. The telecommunication industry especially has demonstrated that rapid technological change may make obsolescent the very conditions giving rise to natural monopoly in some, if not all, aspects of the industry. Telephone wires may remain a natural monopoly – though perhaps challenged by satellites – but their use seems to have become fairly competitive. Yet in principle the whole issue reverts once again to the fundamental distinction between natural resources and capital. Whatever is capital, which includes the embodiment of the latest technology, has a supply price and can be produced under more or less competitive conditions if genuine free entry is maintained (which includes the central condition of free access to land). Whatever is natural resources has no supply price and cannot be produced at all. Natural monopolies probably possess the defining feature of falling LATC over a more or less unlimited range of output because they occupy land in ways which are both indivisible and incapable of replication. For example, railways' infrastructure can be easily replicated as capital equipment *per se*, but not as usable capital equipment *in situ* (two sets of lines, stations etc. in the same place). Power stations can be manufactured *seriatim*, but in one place only one unit of the most economically efficient scale is required. Gas pipelines could criss-cross the country in any degree of latticework, but no two alongside each other are economically viable. In short, location is the ingredient which converts certain kinds of capital into unique and thus monopolistic assets. Much public utility capital is indeed highly specific: power stations and a national grid cannot be put to other uses, but specificity creates quasi-rents, not natural monopoly. It is what might be termed locational specificity that counts most.

This means that what appears to be a return to capital is really a return to location. Whilst the return to unimproved land is easily acknowledged to be rent, the increased return when the capital asset, like a pipeline, is in place is less obviously so. Yet it cannot be a return to capital, since the capital is identical with other capital elsewhere in the economy receiving no return above its supply price. Why land may claim this extra return as rent is because location is an intrinsic quality of a particular site and includes the potential return derived from the site's best use in the existing state of technology. Thus a site selected for capital investment by a natural monopoly acquires an additional rent as soon as its potential is known.

Natural Monopolists and Landowners

Provided the site concerned is uniquely suitable there is no further problem about this question of returns. The landowner captures the return available above the supply price of the capital. Thus owners of natural monopolies, like railway companies, are quick to buy land for railway development along new routes in advance of publishing their plans, if they are allowed to do so. However, a problem presents itself if several sites are more or less equally suitable for a capital project by a natural monopoly, and the monopolist can bargain with the several landowners. Obviously he could capture some of the land rent by forcing down the purchase price of the land which he finally buys. The problem is the practical one concerning who knows what the potential actually is. Just as the railway directors would lose out to existing landowners if they published their development plans in advance of bargaining for the land, so would any natural monopolist lose out to any particular landowner who knew in advance precisely which pieces of land were intended to be developed. If several sites are suitable, no one, including perhaps the natural monopolist, knows in advance which particular one will be used, but nevertheless the potential attaches to whichever one turns out in fact to be used. The question is one of how the rent is apportioned. But the problem evaporates if both rent and the profits of natural monopolies are regarded as public revenue, for then no apportionment is necessary. (See Chapter 6 for other aspects.)

Only certain types of capital are associated with natural monopolies, and these types change as technology advances. Yet monopoly returns arising from a particular technology cannot be seen as returns due to the capital embodying the technology (or its producers or owners), if it is itself produced under competitive conditions (subject to patent rights for the inventors). Monopoly returns of utilities are mainly attributable to the use of capital in locations naturally possessing monopoly characteristics. Whoever controls the sites of public utilities controls their monopoly profits, if they are allowed to make them. If a gas pipeline were auctioned off, the aspiring buyers would not be bidding for pieces of piping as such, but *in situ* piping linking supplies of gas precisely to the market. The question of ownership, regulation and control of natural monopolies cannot be discussed sensibly in isolation from the greater issue of land ownership and claims upon rent of land.

The above argument seems relevant to any industry where significant amounts of capital are used, since all capital needs a location.[3] The illusion that capital in a particular location itself generates an extra return is strong for such capital-intensive industries. Once again the principle bears reiteration that a surplus arising from capital located in one place over similar capital located elsewhere – in particular over capital on a marginal site – is by definition rent of land. Basically it is the same principle as that which identifies rent as the surplus that labour produces in favourable, non-marginal locations. The law of rent is ubiquitous.

Examples of Natural Monopoly
British experience of nationalisation and privatisation could be examined at length in the light of this analysis. Perhaps a few aspects may be mentioned. The coal industry has moved into and out of

---

3 Most capital can be replicated by different firms without exhaustion of the market. For the question of multi-plant firms becoming oligopolies, or even monopolies, see Chapter 7.

public ownership with no regard to the simple principle that the land containing the coal is properly a public resource, but that the work of digging out the coal may be an appropriate activity for private firms. Were firms to lease mines from a public authority, the rent would return to the community, but returns from mining sufficient to pay wages and capital costs would be available where coal seams were economically viable. The same distinction applied to tin mining in Cornwall, and even to gold mining in Wales, would revivify those industries, provided – a crucial proviso – they were relieved of taxes on production. State ownership of North Sea oil fields, the national grid, oil and gas pipelines, rail infrastructure, motorways, the Channel Tunnel, ports, airfields and other land-based assets associated with natural monopoly is compatible in most cases with private operation of the services concerned, though not all may be possible in competitive conditions. Alternatively, a system of regulated private owners paying rent for the land occupied, including a full contribution for the locational aspect of capital and technology employed on that land, might suitably demarcate public from private economic participation. Institutional forms might vary; what matters is the principle of demarcation, which for so long has been ignored.

CHAPTER 19

Housing

EVERYONE NEEDS somewhere to live. This undeniable fact implies that everyone needs to occupy some land, however small, as living space, for even an apartment near the top of a block of high-rise flats requires that some land is used for its construction and maintenance. Hence all living accommodation involves both a building and a piece of land. The distinction between these, however, is fundamental to any understanding of the 'housing problem', which has been an endemic feature of modern Britain and is acute in many other countries. Buildings are the products of industry; land is a basic natural resource. The former have a supply price; the latter does not. Land for particular uses, like housing, may have a price which indicates its relative scarcity for that use, but the supply of land for all uses is for practical purposes completely fixed. Buildings, on the other hand, have a long-run supply which is elastic, since workers and materials can respond to wage and price changes with a high level of mobility within all likely ranges of demand. Indeed, shortage of land suitable for housing is usually the most effective brake on housing output. Hence separate analysis of house building and land for housing markets is possible. (Obviously the demand is inter-related.)

Separate Supply and Demand for House Building and Housing Land

Diagram 83 shows supply and demand for house building, exclusive of land. The short-run supply is inelastic because workers, especially skilled ones like bricklayers, and materials may not be easily available. Hence a shift in demand to D1 may raise price to P2, but in the long run it falls to P3 with an elastic supply.

In the case of land for housing, since location and other factors make it vary greatly in price, supply and demand analysis can only

DIAGRAM 83

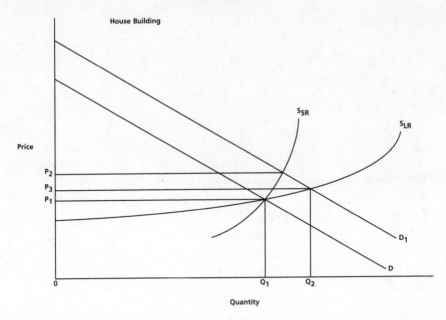

present a broad view by assuming either an average price or a price for land which is marginal between housing and other uses (see Chapter 8). UK average prices of land for housing have fluctuated within a steeply rising trend for decades, whilst house building costs rose much less (both in real terms).

Housing land may come onto the market from 'brownfield' or 'greenfield' sites, from the sale of existing houses, where the land is, of course, 'tied' to the building, and from land attracted from other uses. The complete inelasticity of the total supply of land makes elasticity in any one use move towards zero as that use increases.

In Diagrams 83/84 rises in demand for buildings and for land have very different long-run effects on each. Land prices rise greatly from P3 to P4 and quantity only from Q3 to Q4, whilst building prices rise only slightly and quantity expands easily in theory from Q1 to Q2. As house building requires land, the land constraint is obvious. Builders may respond by a greater density of building i.e. a substitution of building for land, in accordance with any other two factor production function. Planning conditions affect all this, of course, but the economic situation facing the planners is also dominated by an apparent shortage of suitable land.

DIAGRAM 84

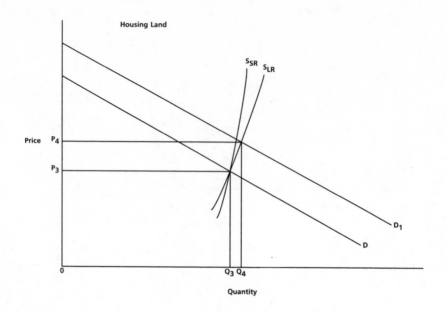

DIAGRAM 85

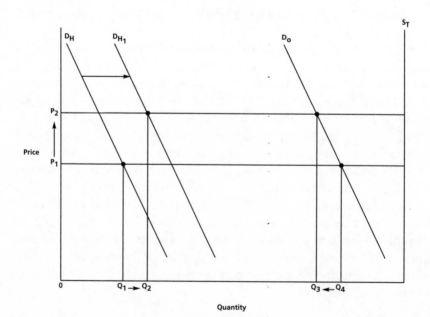

DIAGRAM 86

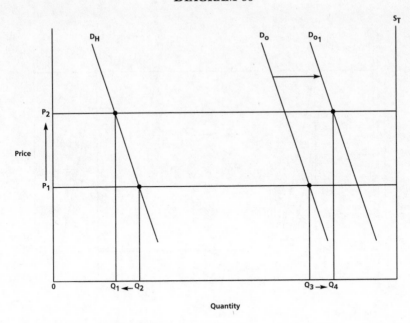

Effect of Fixed Supply of Land

The fixed total land supply can be examined further if demand curves for housing and all other land uses are compared. Many examples and outcomes are possible, but a recognisable set might be an increase in housing demand, when other land use demand remains constant.[1]

In Diagram 85 as demand for housing land shifts from DH to DH1, land is induced to switch to housing from other uses (Q2 – Q1 = Q4 – Q3) by a price rise for such marginal land of P2 – P1, with 'other' demand rising along D0. Similarly a rise in demand for land for uses other than housing raises all land prices, including housing land (Diagram 86). A rise in demand for both housing and other land may leave less land in housing use at a higher price (Diagram 87).

It is obvious that the constraint exerted by the total fixed supply of land is responsible for sharply rising land prices if demand increases. Planning restrictions, or any other reason for land not being available,

1 See below and pp.87-9 for limitations on the accuracy of this analysis, which uses average or marginal prices for each land use.

DIAGRAM 87

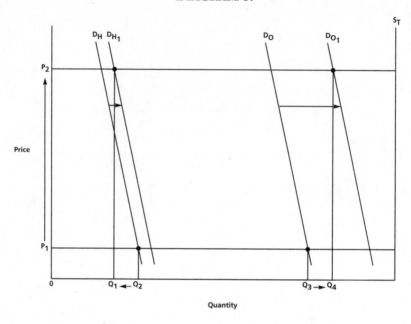

must raise prices further. Greater elasticity of supply between uses cannot significantly affect this underlying condition. Factors of production, such as building workers, may be mobile between uses, and legal or other constraints on switching uses may be minimised, but nevertheless any increase in demand for land must raise its price throughout all land uses. The needs for land for housing and production are both so basic that elasticities of demand are bound to be low, which means that price rises are substantial.

Land Held out of Use
What intensifies this situation is the holding of land out of use. This may be done through inertia on the part of landlords or owing to legal problems like loss of land titles, but mostly it arises from landlords speculating on future price rises. Negotiating a lease at a fixed rent may leave the landlord worse off than allowing a vacant site to appreciate in price. The absence of any tax or rates on vacant sites makes this inevitable. The more valuable the site, the more prevalent this tendency to prevent land being used; and urban building land is, of course, very valuable.

Price Differentials and Location

In practice land for housing is by no means uniform, so that any analysis based upon an average or marginal land price is only a crude measure of outcomes. Land prices vary from region to region and within regions between beneficial, or fashionable, sites and sites with poor amenities and low social estimation. A terraced house in an ex-mining village in South Wales sells at present for about 5 – 10% of a very similar property in Richmond, Surrey. Building costs would not vary greatly, hence the difference is largely land value. Rebuilding costs for insurance purposes are a fairly precise measure of the house, as opposed to land, value. At the higher end of the property scale, rebuilding costs comprise a diminishing proportion of the combined price. If costs are measured per acre for building and for land, the general relationship is shown in Diagram 88.

DIAGRAM 88

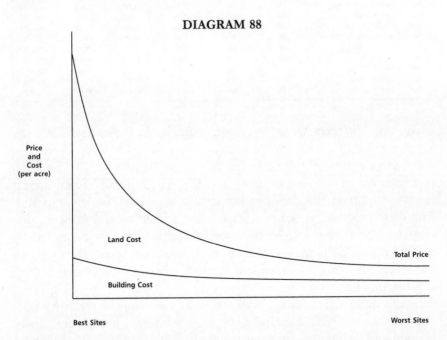

What are called house prices, but in fact are house plus land prices, show remarkable differentials from place to place which have steadily increased, especially in the last thirty years. Individual cases include houses in the west end of London which have risen in price by up to 3500% in 25 years, whilst general inflation showed a 570% increase. A prime-property index for central London showed an increase of

1,567%, almost exactly 1,000% above inflation.[2] If rents for the best central London property are compared with the salaries needed to pay them in the year 2000, the result shows that only a tiny minority of Londoners, and foreign workers in lucrative employment, can afford them.

DIAGRAM 89

(*The Times*, 11 January 2001)

London's Soaring Rents: Year 2000

		Weekly Rents per Property (£/Week)			Salaries Needed to Rent Properties (£/Year)		
Postcode	Area	1 bed	2 bed	3 bed	1 bed	2 bed	3 bed
SW3	Chelsea/Knightsbridge	410	698	975	107,677	183,313	256,061
SW1	Belgravia/Pimlico	375	650	850	98,485	170,707	223,232
SW7	South Kensington	413	600	1,100	108,465	157,576	288,889
W8	Kensington/South Kensington	400	500	650	105,051	131,313	170,707
W11	Notting Hill/Holland Park	375	485	738	98,485	127,374	193,818
W2	Bayswater/Paddington	325	463	650	85,354	121,596	170,707
W11	Mayfair	375	450	1,100	98,485	118,182	288,889
SW5	Earls Court/South Kensington	320	450	800	84,040	118,182	210,101
SW10	West Brompton	295	450	650	77,475	118,182	170,707
NW1	Regents Park/Primrose Hill	325	450	650	85,354	118,182	170,707
NW3	Hampstead/Swiss Cottage	343	425	595	90,081	111,616	156,263
NW8	St John's Wood	275	405	800	72,222	106,364	210,101
W9	Maida Vale	255	395	675	66,970	103,737	177,273
SW6	Fulham	215	390	600	56,465	102,424	157,576
W14	West Kensington	285	375	550	74,848	98,485	144,444
NW6	South Hampstead/Kilburn	240	330	475	63,030	86,667	124,747

Regional differentials are very considerable. At the end of 2001 the average price of a London property was about £180,000, whereas in the north of England the average price was about £62,000. The gap had widened in one decade from £32,000 to £118,000.[3] Since then it has widened further. Obviously land prices accounted for most of this. The economic and social problems arising from such a growing discrepancy are numerous. Mobility of labour is seriously restricted by difficulties of changing housing to high land cost areas like London; the reverse situation is a problem because workers believe that buying a house in a low land cost area is a once and for all move, if high cost areas continue to accelerate. National wage rates impose a relative burden on house purchase, including mortgage interest, in high cost areas, yet regional differentials in wage rates appear to be unfair. This is especially a problem for public service industries, like health, education and transport. Furthermore, local authorities' revenue, assessed as rates on house values, is seriously deficient in some areas and high in others, requiring massive central government redistribution. Since local

2 *The Economist*, 12 February 2000, p.36.
3 *The Financial Times*, 17 January 2002.

authorities are largely paying public sector workers national wage rates, their financial condition is precarious and local government suffers.

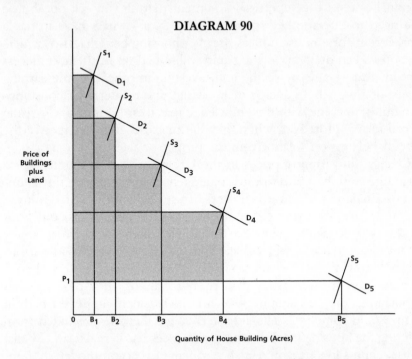

DIAGRAM 90

Quantity of House Building (Acres)

Regional differences in house land prices are broadly shown in Diagram 90. By grouping houses into bands according to total building plus land price, a kind of composite supply and demand diagram indicates how regional and local differences combine to produce an approximate profile. Each region (e.g. B2 – B3) has a local demand and supply of houses (with land) and an equilibrium price. Cross-elasticities of demand between one band and another and interactions between supply curves caused by the total fixed supply of land would complicate any shifts of demand or supply. Bands get larger as price falls, which is a realistic assumption. If P1 represents building-costs only, i.e. if B4 – B5 is marginal land of zero price, then the shaded area shows capitalised rent.

Effects on Distribution of Wealth and Income
Such facts exemplify the law of rent operating in conditions of unrestrained private ownership of land. What then are the effects of this? Firstly, owners of high-price houses gain vis-a-vis low-price owners, and the distribution of wealth is affected accordingly both on a

regional and local basis. Since property values represent potential claims on production, there is a real shift in wealth and not merely a nominal one, as the superficial argument that 'if you sell one house you need to buy another' would suggest. Non-owners have to pay a market rent for a house, unless they get housing benefit. Also owners of houses can draw upon the equity value tied up in them, if necessary by a mortgage, by selling and investing in other income earning assets, or simply by reducing their savings and raising their consumption out of income with the knowledge that their house price is rising in real terms. Moreover, when they die their beneficiaries receive the potential claims on wealth from the property value.

Changes in property prices in the UK must have accounted for a very large shift in wealth towards older generations, towards the southeast of England and towards owners of especially well-located houses, and away from the young, the north, Scotland and Wales, and poor inner city areas. Such a shift is clearly quite unrelated to effort, ability or any other rational way of allocating wealth. More broadly it has led to a growing gulf between owners of any kind of house and non-owners. The former group has risen to about 70% of the adult population; the remaining 30% are increasingly impoverished in relative (and sometimes absolute) terms, for they are precluded from entering the housing market as property prices rise in real terms. Whilst house owners live free of regular payments for accommodation, non-owners are burdened with them. The latter are more or less a genuine proletariat, reliant on public aid, not just for housing, but for much else as well.

> The big point is that higher house prices cannot make society as a whole better off. They merely redistribute income from the young to the old, which is socially destructive. If, in addition, there is an element of overshooting, that will prove particularly costly to those who turn out retrospectively, to have bought at the peak. For these hapless people, it would be far better if price overshooting had never happened.
>
> Martin Wolf in *The Financial Times*, 24 November 2006

When most land is in private ownership and economic rent is not paid as public revenue, workers are constricted in two fundamental ways. Their wages are set by the least that they are prepared to accept and, at the same time, they are forced to pay whatever they can afford to landlords for living space. Those who manage to buy housing land find their condition ameliorated, but the rest are permanently squeezed by rising rent for accommodation, either as landlord's rent or in the form of rising prices for houses including land. A housing market based upon land held privately, free of a public rental charge, traps workers without land in a vice of low wages and rising housing costs.

This detrimental effect shows itself strikingly at the present time in British cities. Workers in key industries, like transport, education and health services, can barely afford to live within the city boundaries because of the high price of housing. Acute shortages of bus drivers, teachers, nurses and other public service workers are becoming endemic. This is probably an early symptom of the breakdown of urban communities under the pressure of mounting urban rent, which accrues to private owners of land, whether corporate or individual.

'Doughnut' Effects

A further symptom of urban breakdown from the same cause is the 'doughnut' effect. This has a well-established American form and a more recent British one. The American consists of a sugary ring with an empty centre i.e. rich suburbs around a collapsed inner city. Land held out of use by speculators, or by landowners who individually cannot develop the city centre because it requires a collective effort, makes the centre into a wasteland, occupied by the poor and unemployed, whilst the suburbs prosper with good housing and commercial development. The British 'doughnut', typified by Birmingham, consists of a jam centre, surrounded by a stodgy ring of suburbs. Public and private investment, stimulated by local government, has revived the centre, where rent potential is high, while the suburbs have been left behind, with food retailers moving to out-of-town supermarkets and 'reverse' commuting from the centre to new greenfield site companies on the outer edge of the city.[4] Such effects may vary between regions, but all such distortions of a natural profile of development, in which housing location would be related to people's workplaces and leisure needs, arise from private 'rent-seeking'. Paying the full rent of a piece of land leads to a natural and efficient allocation of sites to uses, including housing, but private receipt of rent distorts this.

Mortgages

Yet another major problem has its origin also in the high land costs of modern housing. Most house buyers cannot afford to buy without obtaining a substantial loan by mortgaging the property. For many the loan represents about 90% of the house (plus land) price and the

4 See *The Economist*, 19 January 2002, p.26.

maximum that the lender will risk in relation to the owner's income. Prices are now rising to as much as six times annual wages of buyers. In exceptional conditions, as with rich foreign buyers in the west end of London, price rises are enormous. This is squeezing post-mortgage payments incomes. Many people spend much of their working life repaying mortgages and the interest on them.

Recently, as a higher proportion of women with families have become wage earners, house prices have become more closely related to a two-income family's ability to pay. This helps to explain the rapid rise in the price of housing land, but it also demonstrates clearly the constraint that the present housing system has upon households' real income net of housing expenditure. As household incomes have risen with women's earnings, house plus land prices have increased to cream off the surplus above other living expenses. In the process, women are often forced to work, even when busy bringing up children, in order to maintain living standards for the family. Hence the housing land system is a cause of both high land costs and greater female employment, with these two strongly interacting. The freedom of women to choose to become wage earners or not is greatly inhibited.

Windfall Gains and Losses

This question has many other aspects. In the period from 1970 to 2000 many people grew in wealth by holding houses the prices of which outstripped mortgage plus interest payments, because both inflation and real price increases were in their favour (mortgages being fixed in money terms). Measured in purchasing power over goods and services their extra wealth was absolute, but also it was relative to that of others not on the same 'bandwagon'. Yet other homeowners buying in the late 1980s just before real prices fell somewhat found themselves with 'negative equity'. All such windfall effects are contrary to the principle that wealth naturally accrues to those who create it by work. Indeed some workers found that their house prices rose by more in one year than they earned in that year. Such a system encourages the destructive idea of 'something for nothing', as does any system that allows the private collection of public revenue. However, the time of reckoning may be at hand!

> Household debt now stands at a record high in relation to disposable income. In a low-inflation economy this debt has to be repaid in honest currency. Borrowers can no longer rely upon inflation to do the heavy lifting for them ...
>
> *The Economist*, 25 August 2001, p.32

Government's Use of Interest Rates

Criticism has grown in recent years of the government and central bank policy of trying to control the economy by interest rate changes, when these have a dual effect upon the housing market and upon productive industry (quite apart from an exchange rate effect). When housing land prices rise very fast the government is tempted to restrain them by raising interest rates, yet higher rates may be completely inappropriate for industry, which requires new investment (and for exporters who do not want a higher exchange rate). Moreover, marginal interest rate changes can be ineffective when swamped by home buyers expectations that house (plus land) prices will continue to rise indefinitely. These rather obvious drawbacks of monetary policy are obscured by a failure to recognise that the cause of the problem lies in rising housing land prices, which can only be controlled by transferring the rent of land from private into public hands.

Mortgages in USA

The US economy exhibits even more severe forms of the mortgage problem. Mortgage debt there in 2001 was $5.1 trillion, of which 40-45% was held by two institutions: the Federal National Mortgage Association and the Federal Home Loan Mortgage Corporation. Their assets equalled two-thirds of the US government's publicly traded government debt, and the institutions were hoping that their debt, which they sell in bundles in the bond market, would become government guaranteed. They are obviously dependent upon a stable or rising price for the housing land that in effect secures their debt. Were land values to falter they could 'become the source of the next global financial crisis' (*The Economist*, 21 July 2001, p.78), a remarkably perceptive comment in the light of events in 2007, such as the collapse of Northern Rock. For such debt is not created by the granting of credit for future production. It is simply a future charge on incomes, whereby the mortgagor undertakes to pay, not just the price of bricks and mortar, but also the capitalised value of the annual rent of the land, and interest on both of these.

Zero Housing Land Values

How would the housing situation change were all rent of land to be collected as public revenue? Firstly the capital value of housing land would be nil. Differentials between house prices would represent only differences in building costs. Buyers would need to finance merely the

building cost minus any depreciation. Rent would be payable to a public authority at an annual value determined by the relative advantages
and disadvantages of the site, including proximity to a city centre,
shops, and other facilities, available transport and the public services
on the site, like refuse collection. These would be paid for once in the
rent, not twice over as they are usually in the present system where a
private landlord and a local authority each charge for them. Rents
would be payable periodically and not capitalised, so that no capital
sum would be due in advance. Hence the only capital sum involved
would be the initial cost of the building itself.

House Purchase with Free Land
In a society with free land where the community received the full rent,
wages would be high and the price of a house low in relation to them.
Nevertheless, the house price would still, no doubt, require several
years' payment out of wages. How might this be met? Some properties, as today, might be inherited, with the new owner simply assuming the public rent charge. Others might be rented from an owner at
a rent which amortised the initial building expenditure, less depreciation. Without interest payments on this initial sum, the rent would be
light. Credit from a bank would be required for the owner to obtain
the building in the first place from the builder, but this in turn could
be repaid out of the proceeds of the rent of the buildings. Since the
house yields a genuine benefit of occupation during its lifetime, such
a use of credit is not very different in principle from the financing by
credit of productive capital or infrastructure. Finally, if a house were
bought directly from a builder for occupation, the owner might expect
to receive credit from a bank upon his promise to repay during the
period of his beneficial occupancy. This is independent of any credit
the builder might receive initially during the construction period. Such
methods of payment for housing assume interest free credit in a
society where both free land and free credit were available. Since
interest on credit is primarily a result of unlimited private property in
land, or unfree land, this dual assumption is reasonable. Obviously if
a positive interest rate existed, any capital payments would necessitate
an additional burden on the house buyer.

Bank Credit for Housing Land
Under the present mortgage system, credit is given for land and building costs by banks or building societies largely against the security
of land values. How unreasonable and indeed precarious this is may

be shown by an analogy. Imagine a society where congestion in cities is so great that the local authority is forced to introduce draconian parking charges. These are not punitive; but simply a means to allocate parking space by a price system, so that only those most desirous of parking are prepared to pay. Suppose the charges amounted to thousands of pounds. Some people might need credit to pay these. Would a banker willingly offer credit for such parking charges? Obviously if the motorist were wealthy and believed to be honest he might, but the banker might regard such a transaction as of dubious security and perhaps even as a perversion of his function as a banker to finance productive enterprise. Yet paying for the price of land for a house is really only a kind of up-front payment for permanent 'parking' space. No tangible asset is bought. Whatever is bought – the right to exclusive use of a piece of land – may fluctuate in price in the future.

Allocation of Land to Best Uses

Capital values of land for housing are a form of compensation whereby the buyer acquires the right to use a site in return for others not using the site. He gains, others lose. If the payment goes to the community, these others are collectively compensated. If it goes to a private individual or corporation then the compensation has gone astray. Such payments are not fit objects for attracting credit, since no net product is created by them. Of course, rent of land also serves the very important function of allocating land to the best uses. It does this perfectly well when it is paid over to a public authority. When it is paid to private landlords, who do not themselves pay rent, the system is seriously incomplete, for the best allocation only occurs when everyone, without any exception, is subject to it. In principle a computer could make the allocation, if sufficient information about rent were available to it. The computer would not need a credit system to fulfil this function. Nor does a rent system, if rent is paid as public revenue and not capitalised. When individuals or corporations claim something for nothing in the guise of land values, they are creating a pyramid of credit built on shifting sand. Sound credit is built only upon foundations laid by labour and capital on land. The housing problem, like most economic problems, is ultimately a consequence of a lack of measure between what people contribute to the community and what they ask from it.

PART SIX

Macro-Economics

CHAPTER 20

Outline of
Macro-Economic Theory[1]

NOWHERE IS IT more true than in economics that the whole is not merely a sum of its parts. An economy is organic; parts of the economy interact with each other; each part has a function within the whole economy. Hence the fallacy of composition is only too common in thinking about economics, such as: if the price of a good or factor falls then more is demanded; therefore if all prices fall, total demand rises. Before Keynes published his *General Theory* in 1936, most people thought that a fall in the wage level would increase the demand for labour, and that if each individual saved more, all could save more.

Macro-economics concerns itself with the whole economy, rather than with questions about particular goods, services or factors of production. Since Keynes, who can be regarded more or less as its founder, the theoretical development has been considerable, and many schools of thought now do battle about such matters as the precise shape of the consumption function, the role of expectations and the time taken for the economy to reach equilibrium. However, all such arguments revolve around a roughly similar framework of concepts and models. A general summary of this framework is given below, with the proviso that exponents of macro-economics are sure to find points with which they disagree, but that these points may be inessential in relation to the critique that follows.

Real and Money Circular Flows
Macro-economics begins with the idea, derived from the eighteenth century French school of Physiocrats, that the economy consists of

1 The contents of this chapter will be very familiar to students of macro-economics, but it is included in order to establish a basis for the critique that follows.

circular flows of expenditure on one hand and of goods, services and factors on the other (see Diagram 91). Households offer factor services of land, labour and capital to firms, which pay factor incomes in return. Although much land and most capital is legally owned by firms, it is assumed that since the ultimate owners are individuals who own shares in firms, or are partners in them, and receive incomes in the form of interest and distributed profits, then all factor services are actually being hired from households by means of payments of rent, wages, interest and dividends. Firms produce final goods and services for sale to households, who spend their incomes accordingly, thus completing the circular flow. Intermediate goods and services, bought and sold between firms, like semi-manufactured goods, are left out of the model, just as they are, of course, from statistics for national income. This very simple model appears thus as two circular flows, one a real circulation of goods, services and factors – the real economy – one a money circulation of expenditure made for these – the money economy.

DIAGRAM 91

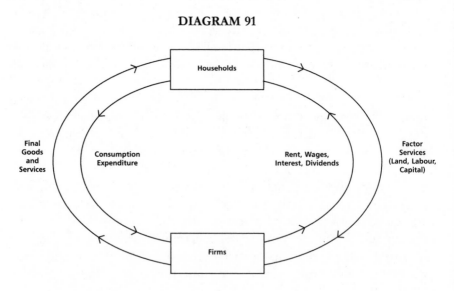

Injections and Withdrawals

To this model are added six additional flows, three inward and three outward, usually seen only under their aspect as money flows, so that henceforth the model becomes entirely a monetary one, though implications for the real economy are by no means disregarded.

Inward flows, called injections, consist of investment, government expenditure and exports; outward flows are savings, taxes and imports. Investment, defined as expenditure by firms on capital and land, enters the money flow in the time period in which expenditure is made and regardless of its source in savings or bank loans. Government expenditure includes all public spending on goods and services, whether purchased from firms, like military aircraft, or provided directly in the form of public sector services, like law and order.[2] Export expenditure is a purely exogenous item, since foreigners are buying goods and services in the economy from outside. (Balance of payment and exchange rate considerations are initially ignored.)

Outward flows, called withdrawals (or leakages) are corresponding aggregate movements out of the circular flow, consisting of savings by households of income not spent on consumption goods (firms' savings in the form of undistributed profits are treated as belonging to individuals as owners), direct and indirect taxes, whether paid by individuals or companies, and imports of foreign goods and services.

Ex Ante and *Ex Post*
Were investment to equal saving, government expenditure to equal taxation and exports to equal imports, macro-economists would join the ranks of the unemployed. Unfortunately, as Keynes long ago pointed out, there are no reasons at all why these three equations should hold, since decisions about each of the six items (with the partial exception of the second pair) are made by completely independent sets of people – businessmen, government, consumers and foreigners. Do injections in total then equal withdrawals in total? The answer is ambivalent. The values that are decided upon, sometimes called *ex ante* values, will not be equal, but the values that are finally achieved – *ex post* values – are equal by definition, since the actual measured flow of expenditure on consumption and injections must equal the actual measured incomes of factors, which are all spent on consumption goods or withdrawn. Any putative difference between *ex post* injections and withdrawals must be reflected in a difference between output produced and output sold, which amounts to a change in stocks of goods held by firms. As changes in stocks are a form of investment or disinvestment, the putative difference disappears. This identity of *ex post* injections and withdrawals is reflected in the fact that

2 The latter could be shown as expenditure directed at factor services, especially labour, rather than at final goods and services. Also, Government transfer payments, such as pensions, for which no value is received, are excluded, provided taxes are also shown net of the same amount.

national income can be measured in three ways, which all give the same
result in theory, i.e. as output, expenditure or income.

The Multiplier

A model of consumption expenditure only, without government or
foreign sectors, maintains a constant flow, since no injections or withdrawals disturb it. When *ex ante* injections (J), however, differ from
ex ante withdrawals (W), as they must in practice, the circular flow
moves to a new equilibrium level. If J > W, national income (NI) must
increase; if J < W, it must decrease. Yet it does not change by the
amount of the difference, for the model is not that of a single revolution to which is added a one-off J or W. In a given time period, say
one year, many revolutions take place. What happens in one revolution affects subsequent revolutions. If J > W, then the difference ΔJ
is a net increase in NI, but that increase is partly spent on consumption goods in the next revolution. Some of it will be withdrawn on
savings (S), taxes (T) and imports (M). The proportion spent enters
the next revolution and is itself partly spent and partly withdrawn.
Provided that the proportion spent remains constant, the succession
of extra expenditures accumulates as a geometric series of the form:

$$1 + r + r^2 + r^3 \dots + r^n \text{ to infinity}$$

where 1 is the initial ΔJ and r is the proportion spent. As the sum of
such a series is $1/ 1 - r$, the initial ΔJ is multiplied by that amount.
Thus, for example, if r = 2/3 then ΔJ is multiplied by

$$\frac{1}{1-\frac{2}{3}} = 3.$$

This ratio between an inflow of expenditure and the final increase in
NI (Δ NI) resulting from it, is the multiplier. Its value is

$$\Delta NI/\Delta J.$$

In practice what is happening is that the net injection of expenditure in the shape of, say, the government building a new school
costing £1m, falls into the hands of contracting firms, who spend it
all on rent, wages and profits (dividends). The recipients of these in
turn spend, say, 2/3 of what they receive, withdrawing 1/3 as savings,
taxes and imports. Again the recipients of this expenditure do the
same, and so on, creating the above series.

Consumption Function

It is evident that the size of the multiplier is a function of r, the proportion spent. This proportion is the marginal propensity to consume

(MPC), a measure of how much on average any additional pound of income is spent on consumption goods and services. Obviously $1 - \text{MPC} = \text{MPW}$, where the latter term measures the marginal amount not spent. Hence the multiplier also equals $1/\text{MPW}$. If MPW is say $1/5$ the multiplier (m) is 5, i.e. the reciprocal. In practice in the UK economy MPW is high because of the level of taxation and imports, and hence m may be as low as about 1.4.

If MPC is the same whatever the level of income, a curve correlating consumption and national income will be a straight line, with a slope equal to MPC.

DIAGRAM 92

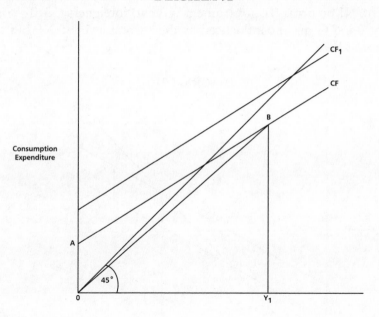

In Diagram 92 the consumption function (CF) starts at A because OA represents consumption expenditure made even when NI is zero, with people borrowing in order to buy essential goods. (In theory the goods would have to be bought from existing stocks or from abroad.) Thus the average propensity to consume (APC) at any particular level of NI is greater than MPC, and is shown by the slope of a line from that point through 0 e.g. 0B at NI of Y1. If consumption increases, but not as a result of a higher NI, i.e. not as a movement along CF, then CF shifts upwards to CF1. Such a shift represents an injection into the circular flow from new consumption expenditure and has a corresponding multiplier effect, depending, as before, upon the size of MPC or MPW. Much debate has focussed upon the shape and stability of the consumption function; in particular upon to what extent it is, indeed, a function of NI in any one year.[3]

Equilibrium National Income

When the consumption function and injections are brought together, a simple model of Keynesian macro-economics is created. Consumption (C) plus J, from the standpoint of monetary demand in the economy, represents the total demand made on all final goods and services produced, or aggregate monetary demand (AMD). C is a function of NI and J is a constant determined independently of the level of NI by firms (I), government (G) and foreigners (X). To some extent I and G may be influenced by the current level of NI, but this is ignored here.

DIAGRAM 93

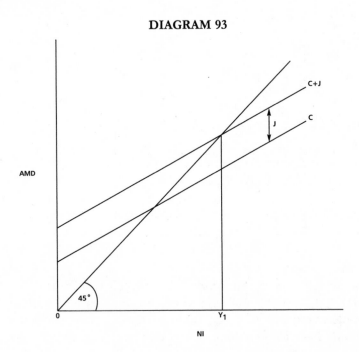

In theory, NI must be in equilibrium at Y1, where $C + J$ (AMD) = NI, for if it were lower total expenditure would exceed the total value of output and stocks of finished goods would diminish, forcing firms

3 Such theories as the permanent income and life-cycle hypotheses are discussed, for example, in Lipsey, *ibid.*, Appendix to Ch. 29.

to raise their output to meet the extra demand. (If they could not do so, lower stocks would mean a fall in I and equilibrium at a lower level of NI.) If NI was above Y1 then stocks would rise, since demand would be insufficient to purchase all that was produced and firms would cut their output, making NI less. At Y1 no forces make NI move either way. The same theoretical result is achieved by drawing W and J independently, without reference to C.

DIAGRAM 94

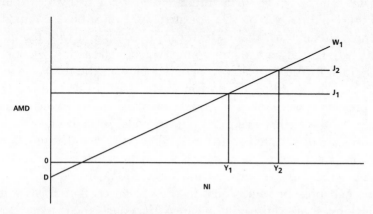

Equilibrium occurs where W1 = J1, for C + J = C + W (*ex post*). As W does not equal J (*ex ante*), NI must rise or fall until W, which is a function of NI, changes (along the line DW1) to become equal to J1. Prior to Keynes this *ex post* equality of J1 and W1 was thought to be brought about by changes in the interest rate, on the grounds that it equated the supply and demand for savings (i.e. S and I), but Keynes' theory claimed that when W does not equal J, NI must change value to bring W into equality with an autonomous J. The value of the multiplier is seen most easily on Diagram 94, since any rise in J1 to J2 raises Y1 to Y2 and makes *m* equal to Y2 − Y1 / J2 − J1

C + J may change through a greater or lesser desire to buy consumption goods (C), or by a rise or fall in I, G or X. Movements in investment expenditure are usually the most volatile element, and raise problems about borrowing and interest rates which lead on to monetary complications in the model. Firms are influenced by two main conditions when making decisions to invest. Firstly, they envisage the state of the market for their product, especially over the period for which the new capital goods will be in operation; and secondly they weigh up the returns on the investment against the rate at which they must borrow to finance it. If they already possess sufficient liquid resources, then they will charge the new capital with a notional rate of interest to represent the opportunity cost of the finance used.

Marginal Efficiency of Capital

These conditions were given a precise measure by Keynes in his concept of the marginal efficiency of capital (MEC).[4] A new unit of capital will only be bought if the future returns on it justify the expenditure. Future returns, net of all associated costs, must be discounted to give a present value for them which can be compared with the initial capital cost. If the rate of discount which makes the discounted returns equal to the capital cost were higher than the market rate of interest, then it would pay to borrow at the market rate and invest in that capital. If it were lower it would not pay. For any particular unit of capital, the rate that makes its returns equal to its cost, when the net returns are discounted at that rate, is the MEC for that unit. Since diminishing returns operate as capital in a firm is increased, the MEC must fall, because the returns fall and a lower MEC is required to give a discounted present value equal to the capital cost. It follows that firms will invest up to the point where MEC equals the market rate of interest i. Only at that level of I, will profits from new investment be maximised (Diagram 95).

DIAGRAM 95

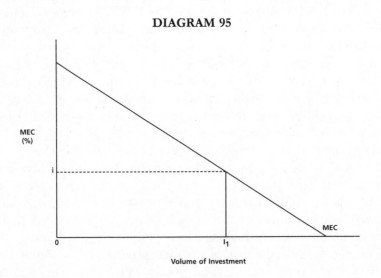

MEC (%)

i

0   I_1

Volume of Investment

MEC

4 See Keynes' definition in *The General Theory*, p.135.

An MEC for the whole economy is the horizontal summation of all firms' MECs, modified by the fact that the MEC for each industry will be steeper than each firm's MEC, as industry demand curves slope downwards, and by external diseconomies in capital goods industries.

Many questions arise about the slope, or elasticity, of MEC and about how much and how frequently it shifts. Movements along the curve will be induced by interest rate changes. Shifts occur when business expectations alter. Whether interest rates or expectations are the principal force acting on the overall level of I is a major issue. In any case such an analysis leads back inexorably to the question of what determines the rate of interest itself, meaning here the real rate of interest corrected for inflation. The answer draws upon Keynes' explanation of motives for holding money and his concept of liquidity preference, usually now called the demand for money (MD).

Motives for Holding Money

Everyone holds money as cash and bank deposits in order to be prepared for buying things when they are required. Since incomes and expenditure do not accrue exactly in time, a fair proportion of income for a given time period will be held for this transactions motive. Both individuals and firms will hold transactions balances of a size related to their level of income or revenue. In addition they will both hold extra balances as a precaution against contingencies, including the possibility that the disparity of receipts and payments will be greater than expected. If a worker loses his job, or a firm has unexpected bad debts, the disparity will increase; hence precautionary balances will be held, though these too will be more or less proportionate to income or revenue. Keynes' third motive is more subtle. Money is always held with the opportunity cost of 'investing' it in an interest bearing asset. If all interest bearing assets, including shares receiving dividends, are called bonds, then the opportunity cost of holding money is the rate of interest on bonds, or the market rate of interest. Other things being equal, the higher the rate of interest the less money will be held or demanded. Hence, although some money holdings will be a function of the size of NI (transaction and precautionary balances), some will be a function of the market rate of interest, giving an MD curve which slopes downwards. This is complicated by the fact that at low rates of interest people expect a future rise, which would cause a fall in the price of bonds to make their yield rise accordingly. This will deter further purchases of bonds, and make the interest rate intractable downwards. Thus the MD curve tends to flatten out at what Keynes termed the liquidity trap (see pp.145-8).

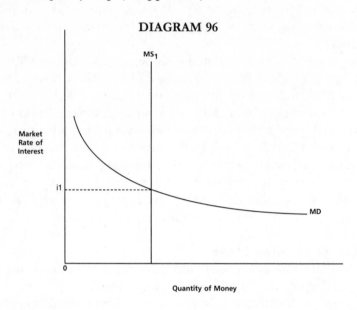

DIAGRAM 96

Money Supply
Money supply (MS) is controlled by the Government or central bank.[5] They may fix MS at a chosen level and accept whatever interest rate then prevails e.g. i1 at MS1, or they may choose to determine the interest rate, in which case they must make an appropriate MS available. The inability of Government or central bank to control MD prevents their determining both i and MS at the same time. Their choice is influenced by whether the exchange rate is fixed or floating, since a fixed rate requires that money is free to move across borders to maintain the rate and cannot therefore be limited in its domestic quantity. However, the UK government recently has allowed the exchange rate to fluctuate, whilst ceasing to control the money supply. It has also, of course, handed over interest rates to management by the Bank of England.

Monetary Transmission Mechanism
What is called the monetary transmission mechanism now puts together the MEC and MS/MD concepts to explain the role of

5 MS can, of course, be variously defined, but for these purposes it includes notes, coins and non-interest bearing bank deposits, though the recent introduction by banks of interest bearing current accounts on which cheques can be freely drawn complicates the issue.

DIAGRAM 97

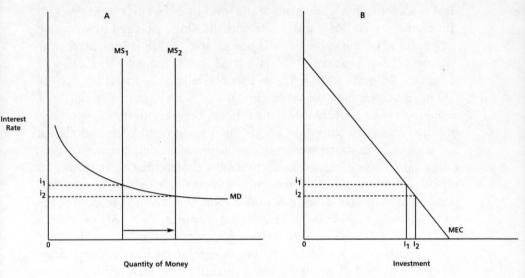

DIAGRAM 98

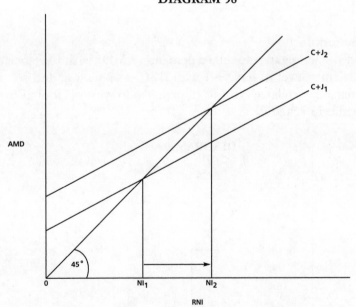

interest rates in the economy as a whole. A change in MS (or a shift in MD) affects the interest rate, which in turn causes I to rise or fall by a movement along MEC. As I changes, it has a multiplier effect upon national income (measured as real NI [RNI] to rule out

inflationary changes in nominal NI). Hence the initial shift in MS or
MD works through to determine the level of NI to an extent given by
the elasticities of MD and MEC and the slope of the consumption
function (or by the value of *m*) For example, if MS is increased from
MS1 to MS2 in Diagram 97 i1 falls to i2 and I1 expands to I2. C + J1
(Diagram 98) rises to C + J2, so that NI1 advances to NI2.

This assumes that the entire impact of a change in *i* is felt by I,
though in fact *i* influences also both consumption, exports and
imports. Some consumption goods, such as cars and kitchen durables,
are bought from borrowed money and hence a fall, for example, in
i raises C to some extent. Less directly, a change in *i* by attracting or
repelling foreign funds affects the exchange rate, which in turn will
produce a response in export and import demand for traded goods
and services. Hence both C and net exports (X – M) will be a
function of *i* to some degree.[6] However, since C, I and (X – M) are all
components of C + J, and moreover changes in each consequent upon
a movement of *i* all act in the same direction, the analysis in principle
is not upset by these complications. If *i* falls, C + J rises; if *i* rises,
C + J falls.[7]

The IS Schedule
Each level of aggregate monetary demand (AMD) is thus associated
with a particular level of *i* (C + J with i1, C + J2 with i2 and so on).
Hence *i* may be correlated with RNI, giving a downward sloping curve
known as the IS schedule.

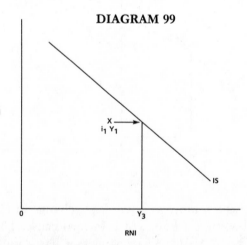

DIAGRAM 99

6 If the exchange rate is fixed, the effect on (X – M) is negated.
7 There may be some effect also on savings, which would alter the value of *m*.

The name IS can be misleading, as it really connects all points of i and RNI where $W = J$, rather than merely where $I = S$; but since G and T are not affected by i, and X and M are only affected indirectly under a floating exchange rate system, the name IS has become established. (The name also fails to recognise the effect of i on C.) However, the name does not invalidate the analysis: at all points on IS there is equilibrium in all markets for goods and services and factors of production. Any combination of i and RNI off the curve would result in a shift in RNI on to the curve. For example, at the point $X(i1Y1)$ on Diagram 99 demand for consumption or investment goods would exceed the available supply and firms would respond by raising output to Y3.

The LM Schedule

Corresponding to equilibrium in output and factor markets there is a similar equilibrium in monetary asset markets. At any given level of RNI there is a particular MD dependent upon transactions and precautionary motives. Therefore at different levels of RNI MD shifts up or down.

DIAGRAM 100

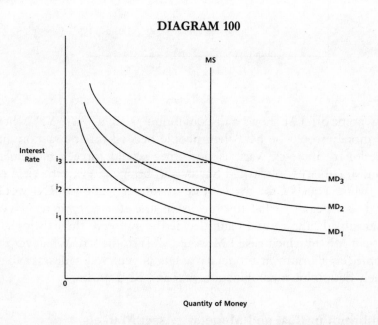

For a given level of MS, shifts in MD in response to changes in RNI will give a new level of i. It follows that i can also be correlated with RNI by means of a monetary asset schedule connecting all points of *i* and RNI where there is equilibrium in the asset market. In theory there are only two such assets: money and bonds. Hence this schedule shows for each level of RNI the *i* which will just induce people to hold the prevailing MS and the existing number of bonds. It also suffers from a misleading name, the LM schedule, which conveys a sense of liquidity and money, whereas the relevant dichotomy is between illiquidity (bonds) and money!

DIAGRAM 101

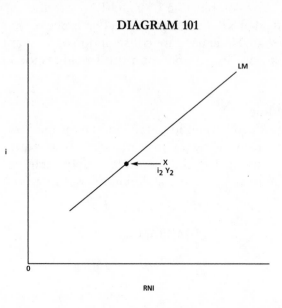

Any point off LM shows a disequilibrium, such as X (i2 Y2), where more money would be held than people needed for transaction and precautionary motives. Various outcomes would force a movement on to LM: either people would buy bonds, bringing down the yield on them (which equals *i*, the market rate of interest), and/or RNI would expand as *i* began to fall (by means of the monetary transmission mechanism). If the central bank decided to preserve the existing *i*, it might cut MS, in which case LM would shift to the left. Whatever the outcome, equilibrium in monetary assets is achieved at levels which uniquely determine a combination of *i* and RNI on LM.

Equilibrium in Real and Monetary Asset Markets
When IS and LM are put together, a single equilibrium combination of *i* and RNI is demonstrated. For any given IS and LM only one *i* and one RNI are possible. At any other combination of *i* and RNI

forces will operate, either in goods and factor markets or in monetary asset markets, or in both, to bring *i* and RNI to a point of equilibrium, like i1 Y1 in Diagram 102.

DIAGRAM 102

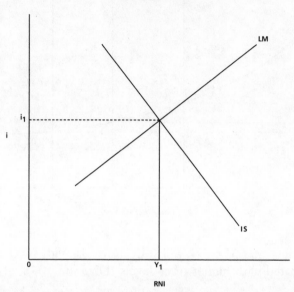

Construction of Aggregate Demand Curve

One final variable has been ignored in the analysis so far – the price level. It has been assumed that this is constant, or alternatively that variations in it are entirely neutral in their effect on all other variables and constants. Clearly this is not so. For example, a rise in the general price level makes the money supply fall in real terms i.e. measured against what it can buy. The assumption that IS is not affected by the price level is fairly realistic, since IS reflects real markets for output and factors, but monetary asset markets are sure to be affected by changes in the general price level, for this is equivalent to a change in the value of money. Hence we should expect shifts in LM to follow upon price level movements.

For any given nominal MS a rise in the price level is equivalent to a fall in real MS, and vice versa for a fall in prices. If prices rise in succession through, say, three levels, then this can be measured as a corresponding fall in MS in Diagram 103.

In Diagram 103 at any given level of MD associated with a particular RNI e.g. MDY1, there will be successively higher *i* for each rise

DIAGRAM 103

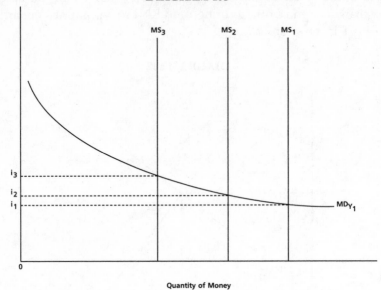

Quantity of Money

in prices. Thus the LM curve will shift upwards, with successive shifts being associated with higher price levels (Diagram 104).

DIAGRAM 104

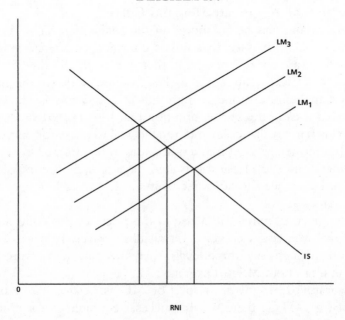

RNI

Shifts in LM generate new equilibria for *i* and RNI when related to IS. What is happening is that, as the price level rises, for example, the fixed MS has to do more work for transactions and precautionary motives and therefore bonds are sold to provide extra money holdings. As the bond price falls *i* rises. Higher *i* will move RNI back along the IS curve as C, I and perhaps (X – M) fall with multiplier effects. New equilibria in real and money markets are attained at a lower RNI.

This conclusion leads to the completion of the demand side of the analysis. For RNI is now correlated with the final variable of the price level (PL). LM1 etc. represent different price levels. As a result we can plot RNI against PL in Diagram 105.

DIAGRAM 105

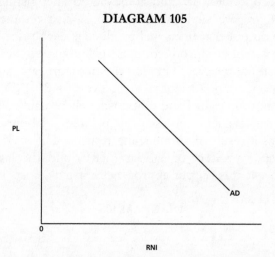

AD shows how much aggregate demand will be associated with each level of prices. It slopes downwards, not because it is a summation of the demand curves for all goods and factors – which would be an example of the fallacy of composition, since variations in the demand for one good have an influence on demand for other goods via income and substitution effects – but because a change in PL is equivalent to a reverse change in MS.

For two further reasons AD is flatter, i.e. more elastic, than it would be from the shift in LM alone. Firstly, there is the wealth effect. Higher prices mean a fall in the real value of all assets denominated in money. People who hold money balances and debts, including bonds, are worse off.[8] Therefore they will tend to spend less on goods and

8 Only assets that do not cancel out against corresponding domestic liabilities should be counted, e.g. debts of the Government or foreigners.

services. Secondly, as PL rises foreign goods become relatively cheaper and exports more expensive for foreigners (at any given exchange rate). Therefore both domestic demand and export demand fall. Thus there are several reasons why AD slopes downwards. AD has four constituents: $C + I + G + (X - M)$. C and I (and $[X - M]$ under floating rates) adjust to a new PL via changes in i as real MS changes; C and perhaps I (since firms hold money balances and debts – though they are also creditors) respond to the wealth effect, and $(X - M)$ to the foreign trade effect.

Short-run Aggregate Supply Curve

As in micro-economics, demand alone determines neither price nor output. An aggregate supply curve (AS) is also required, showing the aggregate output that firms will produce at each price level. In the short run the factors of production are given and so are the rates of income that they receive. The short-run aggregate supply curve (SRAS), however, is not horizontal at all levels of RNI (Diagram 106). At low levels both marginal and unit costs may remain constant, since firms have excess capacity and the principal item – labour costs – does not increase as a result of diminishing returns. The wage rate equals marginal revenue product of labour (MRP) and the latter remains constant. However, as output approaches capacity, costs begin to rise

DIAGRAM 106

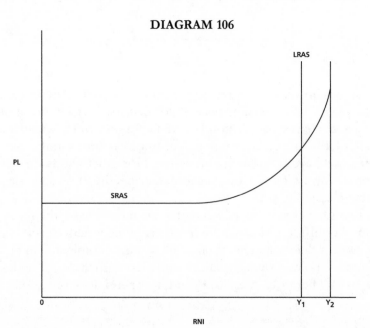

from diminishing returns and, in particular, labour productivity falls, even though the wage rate is unaltered. Why then do firms employ more labour at this point? The answer is that they raise their prices to cover the extra marginal and unit costs, which means that for the economy as a whole the real wage rate (money wages adjusted for the price level) has fallen, enabling firms to continue to employ labour up to the point where the diminished productivity of labour matches the diminished real wage. Thus the SRAS begins to slope upwards. When full capacity is reached SRAS is almost vertical, but the limit of output in fact occurs beyond full capacity, when, in the short run only, firms may employ labour at overtime rates and work capital and land round the clock. Full capacity is at Y1, when all firms' factors are fully employed, but not 'over-employed' as at Y2. Y1 is a sustainable level of RNI; Y2 is not.

Long-run Aggregate Supply Curve

What then of long-run aggregate supply (LRAS)? This is clearly the sustainable level of Y1, given existing factors of production and factor prices. Hence LRAS is a vertical line at Y1 (Diagram 106), where AS may remain indefinitely, regardless of the price level. This may sound unrealistic, but two points have to be considered: firstly, LRAS is a theoretical level of output where all adjustments of factors and output, both as regards prices and quantities, have fully worked themselves out, and, secondly, LRAS is sometimes called the classical supply curve in an economy – as envisaged by classical economists, like Ricardo – where there is perfect flexibility, or mobility, of land (between uses), labour and capital, and all markets for goods, services and factors adjust perfectly in response to prices and costs. At the least, LRAS can be understood as the macro-economic condition towards which the economy tends at any point in time, even if it never actually reaches that point. In practice there is much dispute amongst economists as to how far, if at all, the economy can approach to Y1 and even more dispute about the speed with which the adjustment can be made. Does the economy move smoothly and rapidly to a level of RNI where all factors are fully employed or, as Keynes suggested, in the long run are we all dead?

One final point remains concerning LRAS. Though PL may vary along the vertical LRAS without inducing any expansion or contraction of aggregate supply, the composition of supply may vary at different vertical points. For example, at higher price levels money denominated assets will be worth less in real terms and hence fewer consumption goods may be produced for a lower consumption demand. Also, at higher prices net exports (X – M) will constitute a smaller part of output than at lower prices.

Equilibrium

When AD and AS are brought together, an equilibrium is established where PL and RNI are both uniquely determined. This may be short-run or long-run, as in Diagram 107.

DIAGRAM 107

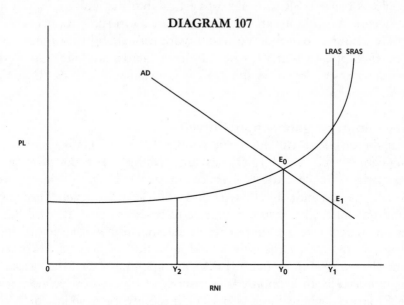

At short-run equilibrium E0 the economy has an output gap of Y1 – Y0, representing unemployed factors of land, labour and capital. At E1 there is long-run equilibrium at RNI of Y1. PL at E1 must be lower than at E0, because AD slopes downwards. Were AD to cut SRAS at or below Y2 RNI would be wholly demand determined in the short run, meaning that the level of output would be entirely a function of demand, and PL would be unchanged as AD shifted. Beyond Y2 costs and prices begin to rise as capacity becomes stretched and labour productivity, in particular, falls. Extra demand is then in part pulling output up and in part drawing up prices. In Diagram 108 the multiplier has a lower value as RNI rises, because a given increase in injections (ΔJ) is multiplied by Y2 – Y3/ΔJ at outputs below Y2 and by Y4 – Y2/ΔJ at outputs above Y2. Thus the closer the economy moves to full employment, the less effective are attempts to expand output by raising aggregate demand.

DIAGRAM 108

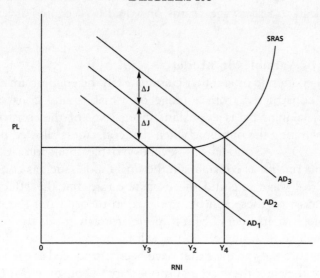

Demand and Supply Shocks

Any event which has an abrupt impact upon AD or AS so as to shift them appreciably in either direction, thereby instigating a movement along the other curve, i.e. AS or AD respectively, is known as a demand or supply shock. These may be within the economy (endogenous), such as a sudden large rise in wage rates negotiated by unions with employers' confederations; or from outside the economy (exogenous), such as the oil price rise of 1973 caused by the OPEC cartel. Both of these examples are supply shocks, which raise costs for most firms and shift SRAS to the left (upwards). Demand shocks might be a wave of business optimism, leading firms to raise their investment simultaneously (endogenous), or a surge in export demand caused by foreign inflation rates making domestic prices relatively low (exogenous). These would both shift AD upwards. Reverse phenomena would shift AD or AS downwards.

How government, or central bank, policy responds to such shocks is crucial to the outcome. They may be resisted or accommodated. For example, a negative supply shock, such as a sharp rise in import prices, may be met by a refusal to increase MS, thus allowing AD to fall and unemployment to rise, or by an accommodating increase in MS, with AD maintained and unemployment unchanged, but at a higher PL. The choice would be much influenced by the government's view of the longer term; in particular, whether greater unemployment would soon be relieved by a general fall in the real wage rate, and whether a higher PL would lead to large wage claims or would be accepted as a fall in real wages.[9]

Summary of Variables in Model

The macro-economic model that culminates in the equilibrium of AD and AS is constructed from a range of variables and constants. It proceeds by taking what is a constant at one stage of the construction and demonstrating the outcome when that constant is allowed to vary. Hence the AD / AS model has several variables built into it. Many determinants remain as constants in the final model, such as consumer tastes, the real wage rate and the exchange rate, but the effect of a change in most of these can be predicted in theory from the model. For example, if consumers begin to prefer foreign goods to domestic ones, AD will shift to the left and m will fall in value.

What then are the variables that have been introduced at each stage? In sequence they are: the marginal propensity to consume (MPC), the three injections (J) – investment (I), government expenditure (G), exports (X) –, the three withdrawals (W) – savings (S), taxes (T), imports (M) –, the multiplier (m), the marginal efficiency of capital (MEC), the demand for money (MD), the supply of money (MS), the market rate of interest (i), short-run aggregate supply (SRAS) and long-run aggregate supply (LRAS). There are important internal relationships between these, of course. For example, the three marginal propensities to withdraw are in total equal to 1 – MPC and m = 1/ 1 – MPC = 1/ MPW. Nevertheless, these are the constituents whose values determine the position and slope of AD and AS and therefore the equilibrium size and price level of RNI. Hence the operation of the whole model is known as the theory of national income determination, the centre piece of macro-economics.

Three Kinds of Government Polcy

a) Fiscal Policy

From the development of this model – an intellectual achievement by a series of economists over almost half a century – has emerged the use by governments of three kinds of economic policy based upon it. Fiscal policy aims to influence the economy, especially the level of real output, the price level and employment, by means of directly

---

9 This example suggests that there is a trade-off between inflation and unemployment on the lines of the famous Phillips curve. See Begg, *ibid.*, pp.464-8.

controlling government expenditure and taxation. Variations in these shift AD, since G is a component of J whilst T is a withdrawal. Equal changes in the same direction of G and T do not in fact have a neutral effect, because by definition the whole of G is spent (on the first round) whilst T withdraws only what taxpayers would have spent in the domestic economy (i.e. some of the tax take would have been withdrawn in any case as savings and imports). Hence a larger balanced budget has a multiplier effect compared with a smaller balanced budget. More importantly, deficits or surpluses on the budget will expand or contract AD, with an effect upon RNI dependent upon m and the slope of SRAS.

b) Monetary Policy

Monetary policy uses either the money supply or interest rates, but not both at the same time. It acts through the monetary transmission mechanism to determine the level of investment, since firms will tend to equate MEC with i. Again AD is the final aggregate affected, for changes in i directly influence its two components, investment and consumption. If the central bank, for example, increases MS, i falls, C and I rise and AD expands by the multiplied change. The slope of SRAS again determines the impact on RNI.

The monetarist school of economists, associated with Milton Friedman, believe in a more immediate relationship between MS and AD. They argue that changes in MS feed rapidly into price changes, on the grounds that the velocity of circulation of money is fairly constant, and that prices in all goods and factor markets adjust to clear markets, including the labour market. This rules out the horizontal part of SRAS and brings the economy on to a vertical AS where shifts in AD only serve to alter prices. For monetarists control of MS becomes all important, not because of the transmission mechanism, but because the correct policy is to keep MS in a fixed relationship to RNI in order to avoid inflation (or, in theory, deflation).

Monetary policy is further influenced by the prevailing exchange rate regime. Fixed exchange rates more or less rule it out, since money flows into and out of the economy must occur if the rate is to be maintained; in which case control over domestic MS is waived. For the same reason interest rates are then largely determined by international rates and international flows of money. Under a floating exchange rate MS can be controlled, since higher or lower MS will move i independently (partly) of foreign interest rates. International flows of money then affect the exchange rate instead of domestic MS; in effect, the foreign exchange market continuously clears, so that MS is insulated from it. Fiscal policy, on the contrary, is more effective under a fixed exchange rate, since a floating rate converts changes in government expenditure or taxation partly into neutralising changes in exports and imports. For example, if G increases whilst MS remains constant, a greater MD pushes up i, which draws in foreign flows of money, so that the exchange rate rises and $(X - M)$ falls.

c) Supply Side Policy

The third kind of policy – supply side – emerged more recently, perhaps from the apparent failure of the other two to deal with such modern problems as stagflation, the combination of recession and inflation which was caused initially, at least in the UK, by the 1973 oil price rise. It aims to act directly upon the real economy to improve productive efficiency, that is to reduce real costs per unit of output, thus moving AS downwards, or to the right. Supply side policies include encouraging research and development, innovation and invest-ment, improving infrastructure, and probably, most characteristically, by raising labour productivity by reforming trade unions, training workers, improving management, and, most controversially, elimin-ating over-manning. Since monetarists believe that shifting AD by fiscal or monetary policy is usually inflationary and that MS should be administered as a neutral check on inflation, they have tended to favour supply side policies. All three kinds of policy, however, may be used according to circumstance, though matters like the prevailing exchange rate regime may curtail their efficacy. Political considerations obviously play a large part in their choice.

Influence of the Model

What is not often examined is that all economic policy assumes a framework of macro-economics, of which the theory of income determination and the AD/AS model are the chief elements. This acts as a sort of parameter, so that causes and effects are assessed within it, and policies judged according to how the model predicts their out-come. A symptom of this state of affairs is that terms have entered commonplace economic vocabulary which take for granted the operation of the model. Overheating, crowding-out, and the natural rate of unemployment, for example, are terms which imply severe limits on production, investment and employment. The limits of the model, such as the sharp rise of SRAS and the vertical supply curve of money, are rarely questioned. Despite its intellectual vigour and systematic operation, the model has weaknesses which call in doubt whether it truly represents how a modern economy works. As it stands, it certainly offers little prospect of how a radically different type of economy might operate.

CHAPTER 21

Critique of the Theory: Land

IN EXPLAINING macro-economic models modern textbooks virtually ignore land altogether.[1] The economy that such models represent is almost landless; it seems to operate without spatial dimensions, or at least without a land surface on which labour and capital can produce. The very best that can be said as an apology is that land is subsumed under capital, which hides a multitude of errors. Were land totally neutral in its economic effects this might possibly be justified, rather like the omission of ether from modern physics since the Michelson-Morley experiment. Enough has already been said above to rule this out. However, the particular ways in which the omission of land from the macro-economic model distorts it need to be investigated. A really precise study – which this makes no claim to be – might even enable the model to be rescued from its present limitations by the introduction of new conditions.

Rent in Circular Flow

Let us begin again with the circular flow. Labour services do, of course, exchange very largely for wages, except mainly where labour is self-employed. Land services, however, do not exchange against rent to anything like the same extent owing to the variety and complexity of forms of land tenure. This might not matter too much were there not huge flows of money exchanging against land in what are termed capital transactions. Since purchase of land – freehold or leasehold – really amounts to a premium, or 'up-front', payment for future land services, these are in fact rent. The effect of this error is dealt with below, when discussing investment (pp.257-9). Where land is owned by the firms that use it, no rent payment occurs. A notional rent charge

---

1 For example, see 'Land' in indices of Lipsey, *ibid.*, and Begg, *ibid.*

would distort the circular flow, as no money changes hands. Hence rent is greatly understated, as National Income Accounts amply demonstrate.

Other aspects of the circular flow regarding land are also questionable. As an item in payments by firms for factor services offered by households, rent is paid for the use of land for industrial or commercial purposes, excluding payments for buildings, which are capital. If the rent is paid to property companies, this can be treated as part of the rent flow to households, on the grounds that households ultimately own the land via shares etc. in the companies. But what factor service is really being exchanged? The rent is an inducement to the landowner to relinquish his possession of the land for a certain period. The land exists, as does its potentiality as a service, regardless of a landowner, unlike labour, which only 'serves' in response to a wage payment. The rent payment is analogous to payment to a slave owner to allow his slave to work. Nevertheless, under the existing system of land ownership such rent enters the circular flow in exchange for the dubious 'service' of releasing the land for use.

Obviously the National Income Accounts are correct by their own accounting standards, but as a measure of a productive flow of factors on one hand and of final goods and services on the other, the circular flow concept upon which the macro-economic model is based is inaccurate. Either the full annual economic rent of land should be included or it should be excluded. As things stand, the fortuities of circumstance and land tenure make its inclusion partial and misleading.

Treatment of Land as Investment

When injections are introduced into the model, further confusion arises from failure to distinguish investment in capital goods from 'investment' in land. Both I and G may include purchase of land by firms and by government. If Begg's definition of investment as 'the purchase of new capital goods by firms' (Begg, *ibid.*, p.326) is used, land purchases may be omitted altogether, but in view of their volume and value in modern economies, this must distort any representative model. If I includes land 'investment', then once more payment is made for something not produced and *a fortiori* not emerging from productive firms. This has three important implications. Firstly, J is taken to indicate an addition to demand calling forth a productive response from firms. The whole theory of income determination rests upon a demand led economy, or at least one in which supply meets aggregate demand and achieves an equilibrium where the aggregate value of supply equals both the aggregate value of demand and, at the same time, the aggregate value of all productive costs. Yet land services are not production in the sense of being created by labour, land and capital. They are not produced at all. Hence there cannot be productive costs associated in their production (again land management services must be excepted).

A second point follows from the first: since 'investment' in land does not yield production of land or its services, as they already exist, it can only act on supply and demand in the land market. Other things being equal, any new purchase of land raises land prices. Land, of course, may be switched from alternative uses, but there is still a net addition to demand for a limited supply of land. Land as a whole has a vertical supply curve, and land even in a particular use must have a rising supply curve. Thus any land purchase from injected demand raises land prices. No more land is produced. Hence to the extent that I, and therefore J, includes land 'investment', there is a rise in costs largely unacknowledged by the model, which is primarily concerned with wage costs. In practice when land prices increase, there are major repercussions in a modern economy. The cost of living rises directly for all workers, except house-owners, and firms face higher rents and/or capital payments for land use.

Thirdly, the multiplier effect of an increase in J is less than the theory would predict. For the initial rise in I, and therefore J, is not fully multiplied as regards the purchase of land. Recipients of land sales revenues, whether firms or households, do not spend the proceeds at the prevailing rate of MPC. Firms do not have to spend on the productive costs of the land, because there are none, except those of bringing it to the market. Households do not spend the proceeds of a land sale on consumption goods at the rate of MPC. In short, the proceeds are largely withdrawn. Hence m for this item in J is very low.

Imagine a firm buying a new factory for £10 m. Let the land value be £4 m. Then only £6m is spent on paying a construction company, which in turn purchases materials, pays wages and distributes profits. Hence if m is 3, the real impact of I of £10 m is £18 m, with an effective m of 1.8; similarly, if the Government builds a new school on purchased land. If the new property is a commercial one in a city centre, the land price may be a very high proportion of I and effective m very small.

The futility of regarding the purchase of land as I is perhaps best demonstrated by looking at total national saving and total asset formation. From the equilibrium equation $S + T + M = I + G + X$ (i.e. $W = J$) we get $S + (T - G) = I + (X - M)$, meaning that saving in the private sector plus the government's budget surplus equals investment plus the export surplus.[2] In other words, saving in the whole economy by individuals, firms and the government equals the net formation of domestic assets and the growth of net external assets in the form of debts due from foreigners, such as assets held abroad or foreign currency held in domestic banks. If I includes land purchases, to that extent there are no extra domestic assets, since the same land was there before it was bought. No land was produced in the period in question. If it was in use prior to its purchase then, at best, only its use has changed (it may even have been taken out of use after purchase). If it was not in use, then the purchase may have brought it into use. In which case the situation more or less amounts to capitalising a bribe as some kind of asset. But even victims of protection money are well advised to write off the expenditure! Are we really to treat the transference of a claim on land from one party to another as asset formation nationally? This is surely a pure case of the fallacy of composition. What may be asset formation for an individual is not necessarily asset formation for all individuals taken together. Of course, land purchase tends to raise land prices, but a rise in land values is no more net asset formation in real terms than a rise in any other set of prices.

Investment in improving land is a different matter. If money is spent on draining land, preventing land slip, sinking mines and so on, that clearly is genuine investment, creating wealth, with multiplier effects. Any increase in the land value as a consequence of improvements represents investment and is quite distinct from a rise in land value from the price being bid upwards by extra demand.[3]

Land Values' Effect on Consumption

Let us now look more closely at consumption. A large feature in most household budgets is housing (plus land) costs. These are mainly a

---

2 Both $(T - G)$ and $(X - M)$ may be negative.

3 This appears to raise a problem about the value of rent in the future, since part may be attributable to the unimproved value and part to the improvements, but all that is needed is a decision as to the date when the improvements are treated as 'sunk' in the land value for purposes of assessing the rent. Most land has been improved for centuries. The improvements become the collective inheritance of the community in so far as they merge with the land over time. On the other hand, those individuals or firms making the improvements should reasonably expect a return for their labour and costs out of future production, or personal use, on the land concerned. There is no reason, however, why the descendants of such individuals should receive any benefit. See pp.329-30.

function of land values, as building costs change little in real terms. Thus rapid changes in land values, such as the recent rises in areas like south-east England, have a substantial effect upon the make-up of consumption expenditure. Since expenditure on basic items like food tends to be fairly constant, a change in housing (plus land) costs is likely to affect other constituents of MPC disproportionately. In short, if housing (plus land) costs rise, less is spent on cars, consumer durables, holidays etc.

In addition, however, land values are not produced goods and services. Expenditure on them yields no output whatsoever. Hence MPC as a measure of m (since $m = 1/1 - MPC$) is inaccurate. A multiplied rise in C, apparently acting like a rise in J, may do little to increase RNI if the initial increase is largely spent on higher housing (i.e. land) costs. Moreover, the influence of changes in interest rates directly on consumption is also mainly through mortgage rates for house (plus land) purchase. Thus increased or reduced expenditure in response to a fall/rise in i is affecting primarily the price of housing land and only to a lesser extent the productive flow through the purchase of houses i.e. expenditure paid to building contractors. To the extent that rent of all land rises as a secondary consequence, there is a further 'withdrawal' effect. In short, the full impact of the housing sector in an economy where land is privately owned needs much closer attention by macro-economists.

Land and Marginal Efficiency of Capital

The concept of MEC suffers also from a disregard of land. Investment by firms includes a large element of expenditure on land, as when an industrial firm buys a factory or a commercial firm office premises. If MEC is derived from the purchase of capital only, then the omission of very large payments for land distorts the macro-economic model. If MEC includes land, then the shape, position and volatility of the MEC curve probably need serious revision. The longer the life of a piece of capital, the greater the influence of i upon the full value of purchasing it, since the stream of returns is longer and therefore the discounting effect is greater. If the total returns on two capital projects of the same initial cost are equal, but one lasts longer, then MEC on the longer one will be less because its returns are discounted over a longer period. Hence the investor will choose the shorter one. If i rises, longer life projects will, therefore, be sacrificed first, other things being equal. But the longest lasting asset of all is land, which is for practical purposes eternal. Therefore 'investment' in land is more interest elastic than investment in capital. This means that MEC often measures the yield on two kinds of 'capital' expenditure: that on capital proper and that on land, with systematically different elasticities.

DIAGRAM 109

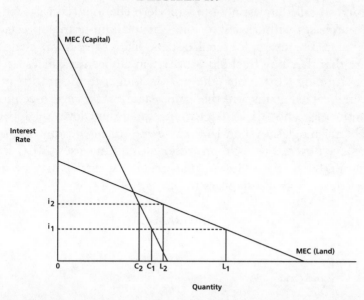

In Diagram 109 a rise in i from i1 to i2 moves land purchases from L1 to L2 and capital purchases only from C1 to C2. Thus the effectual impact of changes of i upon production, i.e. of capital goods, is much less than would appear when MEC is not analysed into its two components.

At the same time MEC for land shifts much more than MEC for capital. Firms base investment decisions upon their estimation of future prospects. Therefore capital investment takes account of future expected discounted net returns from the use of a new piece of capital, including buildings. Purchase of land, on the other hand, takes account of future expected discounted net returns of rent, plus expected changes – usually increases – in land values. The addition of the last item, which has no counterpart for capital expenditure since capital merely depreciates, makes MEC for land 'investment' more volatile. Future land values are unpredictable and generate speculative buying. The market for land, especially commercial urban land, experiences speculative disturbances caused by excessive optimism or pessimism and, moreover, these are related to – and are a cause of –

business cycles (see Chapter 26). In a recession, MEC for land 'investment' shifts to the left; in a boom it moves sharply to the right. Such movements may also be asymmetric in an economy which experiences long-term growth, since land is recognised as holding its value through the cycle in a way that depreciating capital cannot do.

Much so called investment in a modern economy consists largely of land purchases with a view to long- or medium-term appreciation in land value. For example, retail outlets, like coffee shop chains, may ensure that they buy freehold property in city centres. Sales of coffee cover running costs, but the major longer-term profits may be realising capital gains on the land values. The macro-economists' equation of i and MEC to give an equilibrium level of I becomes largely meaningless. When land values are rising steadily and expectations even exceed realistic projections of future rises, MEC for land may shift far to the right, so that genuine capital I may be a small proportion of what it appears to be.

DIAGRAM 110

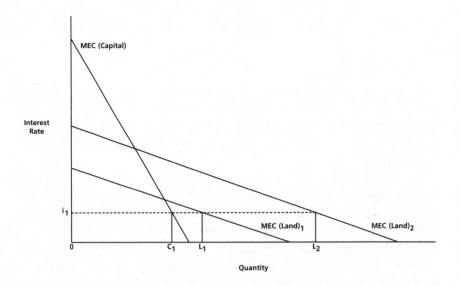

In Diagram 110 if MEC (Land) shifts to the right, capital expenditure may appear to rise from C1 + L1, at rate of interest i, to C1 + L2 at the same rate. In fact it has remained constant at C1. What of the multiplier effects? There are virtually none, since the whole apparent rise in investment consists of land purchases, which merely push up the price of (probably urban) land and generate 'capital' gains for landowners. The MPC out of these is very low, making m close to unity.

Effect on Monetary Transmission Mechanism

Where does this analysis leave the monetary transmission mechanism? Changes in i initiated by the central bank may be themselves asymmetric, in that rises may choke off I, but falls may not stimulate firms to invest if they are pessimistic. But the response is really much worse than that if the distinction is made between expenditure on capital and on land, for the measured change in I when these are aggregated grossly overstates I on real capital, because MEC (land) is both more elastic and more volatile. This is readily seen in practice in the UK, where the secular decline of manufacturing industry since about 1975 has been accompanied by a startling rise in land values considerably above the rate of inflation. Even the growth of the service sector is associated very much with investment in commercial property i.e. urban land. Monetary policy has completely failed to discriminate between investment in capital and purchase of land, just as economists have failed to analyse MEC into its quite disparate components. Hence the next stage in the transmission mechanism – the multiplier effect of changes in J – begins with a seriously inaccurate measurement of the change in I.

The next stage compounds the error by assuming that m has the same value for all kinds of I, whereas I spent on land has an effect close to zero. The total impact of a rise in I on the production of final goods and services can be reduced to the normal value of m multiplied by that proportion of I spent on capital goods. This means that the IS curve is much less elastic than appears. When i changes due to a shift in the LM curve, the effect on RNI when IS is inelastic is minimal (Diagram 111). So much for the monetary transmission mechanism, if land purchases and speculation in land values have a profound effect which is ignored.

A further question arises from failure to regard housing land prices i.e. all those involved in current expenditure on housing. These are a substantial component of the price level (PL). Thus a large rise in these will shift the LM curve upwards (see Diagram 104). People will be selling bonds in order to hold more money, so that interest rates rise. RNI falls in response to higher i. In effect, both consumption and investment in capital goods are cut back as i rises in order to accommodate the higher land prices. Of course, MS may be allowed to grow to

DIAGRAM 111

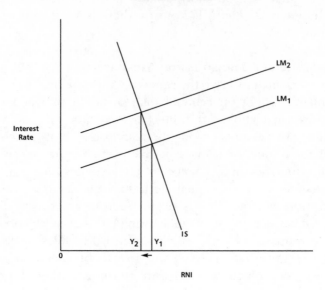

prevent this happening, but this allows the inflation driven by housing land prices to continue.

Wealth Effects
Housing land prices have a second effect on the model. The so-called wealth effect, whereby a rise/fall in prices makes money-denominated assets worth less/more, with a consequent change in consumption expenditure, is probably cancelled out, or even reversed, by rises/falls in land prices. Large increases in the latter in the UK have enabled house-owners to raise consumption expenditure in the confidence that they are wealthier; since mortgages are measured in depreciating money, owners with mortgages benefit in the same way. This reverse wealth effect means that, the AD curve is less elastic than the wealth effect implies, because as PL rises higher house (land) prices encourage houseowners to spend more, thus countering the other aspects which make MD contract.[4]

Treasury Predictions
How then does the Treasury achieve predictive and explanatory results from its model of the economy, if it ignores so many aspects of land transactions? No doubt the Treasury experts do take account of some

4 It could alternatively be shown as a shift in AD to the right as land prices rise.

of the 'land effects' which do not enter the economics text-books as aspects of modern theory. However, they also ensure empirical 'conformity' to predictions by only measuring what fits the model. For example, PL is measured either without mortgage repayments (RPIX) – thereby excluding housing land price changes – or with mortgage repayments (RPI) which include both interest payments and capital repayments at historical costs. Current house prices are not properly reflected in these repayments. Nor are current house prices included in the measure of inflation, so that published figures for inflation of a few per cent completely fail to indicate a house (plus land) price inflation perhaps in double figures. But the Byzantine complexities of Treasury accounting are, fortunately, not the main issue.

SRAS Curve

Inattention to land as a factor of production does not invalidate the SRAS curve, which only rises slowly, if at all, over low ranges of output, becomes steep as capacity is more fully utilised and finally vertical when factors are employed at overtime or round-the-clock rates. This profile of SRAS occurs because both land and capital are fixed in the short run.[5] Hence labour costs rise when diminishing returns to labour result in a rise in marginal costs, accompanied by a rise in average or unit costs. This is true whatever the market structure of industry, since perfectly competitive firms – price takers – will raise prices as they move along their MC curves to the right, and the others – price makers with falling MR curves – also experience rising marginal and unit costs at high levels of output.

LRAS Curve

As regards the LRAS curve, however, failure to appreciate the significance of land makes it exceedingly unrealistic. It is taken to be vertical at a long-run level of output at which all adjustments in goods and factor markets have been made and at which no further production can be extracted from any factors. Land, labour and capital are fully employed at equilibrium levels, implying that to force more factors, if they exist, into production could not be sustainable. The validity of the 'fully employed' labour market has already been questioned (see Chapter 10). In present day conditions can the labour market clear in the long run, so that there is no unemployment?

---

5 The macro-economic short run is not identical with that used in micro-economics. The former is the time period within which full adjustment of all factors to price and other market conditions has not been made.

On LRAS the real wage rate is such that all workers who wish to find employment have done so at that prevailing rate. Any who remain unemployed are 'voluntarily' so, i.e. the economy is at the so-called natural rate of unemployment. Whether this is a valid notion of labour market equilibrium is very much open to question. Those workers who are 'voluntarily unemployed', and hence disappear from the picture when the economy is on its LRAS, may in fact have legitimate grounds for withdrawing their labour at the prevailing real wage, notably because it does not offer them an acceptable standard of living, either in absolute terms or relative to other levels of income and wealth in the economy, especially those which are unearned. Would it be a natural rate of unemployment if the 'voluntarily unemployed' refused to accept a real wage which left them in dire poverty? Is it any more valid if the real wage leaves them very largely dependent upon the Welfare State to maintain an acceptable minimum standard of living?

Fully employed capital is also a dubious concept, since more capital can always be produced by turning resources over to it; but this is a question closely bound up with the provision of credit and with interest rates, which are discussed below (Chapter 22). Fully employed land is the immediate issue.

Not all the land in any economy can be used economically. Obviously some is more or less beyond productive use, except perhaps for leisure and tourism. Where then is the boundary of productive use to be drawn? If land were freely available, the margin of land use would occur naturally where the marginal revenue product (MRP) of labour, without any deduction for rent (since there would be no economic rent on marginal sites i.e. no scarcity rent), would equal the MRP on all non-marginal sites. MRP on the extensive and intensive margins would be equal. Free movement of factors, in particular labour, would ensure that this equality held.

In modern economies, however, land is not freely available. Setting aside the impact of taxation, which is discussed below (Chapter 23), we find that the current restrictions on free land give rise to scarcity rent imposed on marginal land. Because landless workers seek work almost at any price, landowners can force down the wage rate below the net product on marginal land in order to receive rent. It is on such marginal land that an unequal struggle between the countervailing power of workers and owners is fought out, not on the factory floor between workers and capitalists. The fundamental error that Karl Marx made was to assume that an initial conflict between landowners and workers had come to an end with the completion of land enclosure, to be followed by a more critical struggle between workers and the owners of capital. On the contrary, the hidden opposition between private landowners, who appropriate scarcity rent, and workers – of all types from professional experts to labourers – continues wherever and whenever scarcity rent is charged. In fact, scarcity rent is charged on all land in use, but it is on marginal land that its imposition is critical.

What has all this to do with the LRAS curve? Everything! The position of the vertical LRAS is set at a point largely determined by conditions of land tenure. Were land freely available, it would shift far to the right to reach a genuine position of full employment of land i.e. where workers choose to limit production at a margin of land use yielding an MRP equal to that available elsewhere on non-marginal land. Rent charged by land-owners on marginal land cuts the net return to productive factors, and pushes the margin in to where the product can bear both rent and labour/capital costs.

Another present-day aspect of land tenure further limits the use of land, and thus draws LRAS yet further inwards from a real full employment condition. Unlike labour, and to a lesser degree capital, land can be held out of use without any serious loss to its owner. On the contrary, if land values are rising, there may be a gain to the owner, especially if he avoids commitment to a long-term lease set at rents which are overtaken by rises in the land value. In short, speculation can be profitable in land, but not in labour or capital. As every trade union leader knows, labour can be withdrawn only for strictly limited periods. So too, capital deteriorates rapidly if not used. Land, on the other hand, can be withdrawn from use indefinitely. Hence, at any one time, much land is being held out of use by owners who are speculating on a future price rise, or even in some cases cannot be bothered to put the land to use, if they do not need a current income and feel assured of a maintained or enhanced capital value. This is especially true when real land values are rising with economic growth. In such cases, the land concerned may not be marginal at all, indeed it is often valuable urban land.

Example of Land Held out of Use
An individual observation of the author serves as an illustration. One mile from the centre of Oxford on a main road a row of shops was bordered by a plot of land held out of use for so long that not only weeds had overrun it, but even small trees! The plot was fenced off as

private land. Recently it was developed rapidly as the site of a large and apparently profitable furniture store. Why at that time? Presumably the owner was too idle, or was absent abroad, or was otherwise content to wait for the land value to rise as the local environment developed. That plot of land could have been used productively throughout many years before it was developed. Its use may not have been as a furniture store. It could have been used for whatever a free market chose – housing, workshops or whatever; but its site on a main road, surrounded by land fully in use, rules out the possibility that it was truly sub-marginal land. It was sub-marginal only in the prevailing conditions of private appropriation of rent and land values which induce the landowner to hold the land out of use until rent or rises in land values attract it into use. Economics is properly concerned with the most efficient allocation of resources for the whole of society; not with the seemingly efficient use of resources for the benefit of individuals at the expense of society.

Effect on Margin of Scarcity Rent

Examples of more scope are not hard to cite. Why do new firms find it difficult to enter an industry? Not just because of the need to raise finance and pay interest, nor just from barriers to entry like sunk costs in advertising and brand names; but also because they need, first and foremost, premises or land. Access to land is primary; without it nothing. But access on what terms? To prohibit access to land, as the Soviet State did for private firms in most industries, is not a great deal more restrictive than limiting access by imposing a rent, a lease premium or a freehold price which makes entry entirely unprofitable. Marginal land produces no excess over production costs, unless wages are forced down below the full product, i.e. no genuine economic rent. If scarcity rent is charged on it, then access is made more difficult. Such a rent is charged, not to create an available natural resource, but to bribe a landowner to release for use an otherwise available natural resource. That is why it is difficult for a group of workers, given the necessary capital, to set up in competition with, say, established manufacturing or retail firms (see Diagram 47, p.101). That is why, if they are determined enough, they set up under a railway arch or in a backstreet, where rents are relatively very low. Only established firms, usually operating as price makers and/or on freehold sites, can afford to produce on higher rent sites. Were land available on a margin free of scarcity rent, far more firms could enter production and compete on better terms.

Were land so free, primary industries like mining, forestry and agriculture could expand under the entry of self-employed producers. Marginal land, at present charged with scarcity rent, would yield a net product sufficient to pay wages. Land would come into use on a scale which would shift the LRAS curve significantly to the right. This, however, is only half, or less, of the story. For as scarcity rent disappeared from marginal land, so would it also disappear from all other land. Rent would become a true measure of differentials between any one site and the margin. Wages would rise to absorb the defunct scarcity rent and the entire structure of industry would undergo a profound change. Such a reformation of production is best considered later (Chapter 24), but meanwhile suffice it to say that the LRAS curve would shift further to the right, once forces of land, labour and capital were so released.

Allocation of Land between Uses

Finally, land would be more efficiently allocated between uses were scarcity rent and speculation eliminated. Differential rent, as the difference between what a piece of land can produce, after all input costs are deducted, and what could be produced on marginal land, is a true measure of how to allocate land to its best uses, since what land can produce refers to its potential in its best use. What it is producing, or failing to produce, at any point in time is irrelevant. Rent is a measure of land potential. Land values tend to reflect this potential, as any expectant buyer of a derelict site soon realises. Hence whatever interferes with the response of labour and capital to differential rent inhibits its function in proper resource allocation. This mechanism is the real invisible hand allocating resources to meet all needs and demands, if permitted. Scarcity rent and land speculation impede it by placing artificial values on pieces of land, which obscure the underlying differential rent and send false signals to factor markets.

For example, scarcity rent added to genuine rent makes an enterprise appear unprofitable, when free of scarcity rent it could make a profit after bearing all factor costs, including a genuine differential rent charge.[6] How often do firms close down when leases fall in and rent rises? Similarly, holding land out of use in expectation of future gains in land values raises rent charged on other sites. As cities grow this phenomenon is marked. Landowners on the outskirts wait for

6 This statement ignores tax effects dealt with in Chapter 24.

rents/land values to increase in the future and create a ring of withheld land which forces up rent of land within the city. Firms – and homeowners – also find that land further out becomes more expensive than it would be without the withdrawal of intermediate land. Diagrammatically the situation is shown in Diagram 112.

DIAGRAM 112

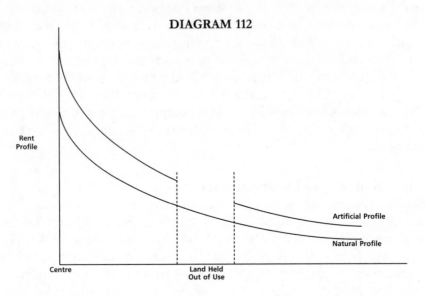

Rent
Profile

Artificial Profile

Natural Profile

Centre

Land Held
Out of Use

Any land so held out of use forces up rent on some other sites and therefore distorts the economic efficiency of resource allocation. When the Berlin Wall was demolished in 1990 a strip of land was released right across the centre of Berlin, which when offered for sale or leasehold fetched very high prices. While held out of use for political reasons, its potential value (economic rent) was totally inhibited, which is a measure of the extent to which labour and capital 'wanted' to make use of it. Meanwhile those particular factors were forced to deploy elsewhere, if at all. Land held out of use, because landowners in a so-called free market are permitted to leave it idle for their personal benefit, is just as much withdrawn from use at the expense of proper resource allocation. The right to land speculation creates a desert and calls it freedom!

Misallocation of labour and capital costs an economy perhaps as much as does the tight ring created by scarcity rent on marginal land. Both abuses of economic efficiency, in its usual sense of producing at the lowest opportunity cost, keep LRAS far short of where it might be in an economy with free land. All production of goods and services needs land. The conditions under which land is made available to producers is the most vital of all the influences bearing upon long-run aggregate supply. Why is LRAS a vertical curve in the first place? The reason is that all the factors of production are said to be utilised to the full; but what enables them to be so utilised? Most observers would agree about the need for free labour and free capital – who would agree about free land? Unless we are precise in our understanding of what free land actually means and just how it affects the position of LRAS, the existing barriers to the uninhibited expansion of output and prosperity will remain.

Summary of Criticisms

All this amounts to a considerable catalogue of criticisms arising from the omission of land from the income determination model. To begin with, rent of land is very inaccurately measured in the circular flow. More importantly, investment includes land purchases, which are not capital expenditure and not therefore a payment for production. Land purchases merely raise land prices, and have a multiplier effect which is far less than that for genuine investment in capital. Consumption expenditure also includes payments for housing land – effectively withdrawals – which affect other consumption items, especially when mortgage interest rates change. These items, unlike housing land payments, are produced goods and services. MEC has two components – land and capital – the former of which has a more interest elastic demand and is also more volatile. Moreover, land speculation may destroy any remaining precise relationship between interest rates and the volume of investment, with a consequent breakdown of any measurable multiplier effect. The monetary transmission mechanism is therefore obscured by land purchases, and monetary policy based upon it becomes nugatory. The IS curve is much less elastic than may appear. In addition, the wealth effect may be reversed when real house land prices are rising. SRAS remains, perhaps uniquely, a valid measure, but LRAS is extremely misleading. The concepts of both fully employed labour and capital are of dubious value as currently presented, whilst that of fully employed land is completely neglected. Marginal land is greatly reduced and bears a higher price owing to scarcity rent, and land is held out of use for speculative purposes, thus rendering the idea of full employment of factors of production illusory. Finally, the allocative function of differential rent is ignored, so that there is a false assumption that LRAS represents an optimum, and therefore full employment, use of factors. Land especially is not optimally used, but as a consequence nor are labour and capital. What should we make of the footnote in *Positive Economies* (given in the context of a discussion of growth)?

> ... nothing significant is lost by ignoring land in the analysis of an industrialised economy.
>
> Lipsey and Chrystal, ibid., p.634

These errors and omissions in the AD/AS model render it virtually useless in its present form. Yet major criticisms still remain in relation to money, credit and taxation.

CHAPTER 22

Critique of the Theory:
Money and Credit

OMISSION OF land from the income determination model is an error which seriously distorts how it represents the real economy. Criticism of the theory as regards credit and money takes a different form. MS and MD curves and the consequent IS/LM equilibrium provide an analysis of the monetary assets side of a modern industrial economy. They reflect, however, assumptions that drastically limit how the economy actually operates. Were these assumptions dropped, or at least modified, the economy would operate quite differently and indeed more efficiently and productively. Therefore the following critique is primarily concerned with exposing the severe limitations imposed on the real economy by these fixed, and generally unspoken, assumptions. In particular, it is in the function of the banking system and in the control of the money supply where rigid assumptions are found.

Obscurities in the Model

In the circular flow of income 'profits' appears as the return to households for providing the services of capital. This is usually justified as a useful simplification, on the grounds that households own the shares, bonds etc. which are equivalent to direct ownership of the real capital used by firms, for which the latter pay shareholders a return in dividends and interest. Whilst this may not invalidate the model, it leaves it open to damaging misunderstandings about the nature and source of real capital, which is in fact provided entirely by capital goods industries, financed ultimately by the banking system responsible for all money creation in the first instance.

Secondly, the whole concept of a circular flow of money may be questioned. Money is created by banks allowing customers to hold overdrafts by drawing cheques (or cash), which when deposited in a bank create money as deposits. When an original debtor of a bank repays his overdraft, usually out of the proceeds of work, or production so financed, he cancels the debt and deposits are equivalently reduced. The whole process amounts to an extension, followed by a withdrawal, of funds. Credit is given and then withdrawn. All money is involved in this outward/inward movement, which hardly amounts to a circulation. For example, funds are withdrawn from a bank account by a firm to pay wages. Workers spend the money, which very soon finds its way via shops etc. back into a bank. Nevertheless, the circular model is fruitful in explanation and may be a fairly accurate representation of particular money flows, which are continuously being recharged, as it were, by inward and outward movements between firms and households on one side and banks on the other.

Limiting Assumptions of the Model

a) Money Creation

What then are the limiting assumptions made about the banking system and money supply? They mainly affect how savings and investment play their part in the model. There are three assumptions, which may be described as unduly restrictive, or perhaps as just wrong! The first of these is a failure to distinguish between creating money and lending it. This error would never be made in the case of manufactured objects, like tables, but since money is a claim represented by a token, i.e. cash or bankers' promises in writing, the error is harder to discern. Banks create money.[1] Financial institutions which are not banks, such as building societies, may lend money.[2] To lend money is to hand over money which one possesses, usually for a fixed term, to a borrower, who normally would pay interest on the loan. To create money is to make a generally acceptable promise, usually in writing, to pay a determinate sum. Such promises can then be lent and borrowed, since they are money. A bank deposit is a holding of promises to pay, which in the UK means a commitment by the bank to supply legal tender. When a bank gives an advance it creates money, since 'every advance creates a deposit' (the old textbook dictum now frequently forgotten). Any person or institution whose promises to pay are not generally acceptable cannot create money i.e. operate as a bank. Any

---

1 A logician might regard this as an analytic statement.
2 Recent changes in UK financial institutions blur this distinction, and indicate the same failure to appreciate it.

explanation of money must imply this function of banks, whether or not the word 'bank' is used. Those whose promises are generally acceptable, and only those, are bankers. Money is not manna from heaven to be lent and borrowed by a population of Israelites. It has to be created by men, not by God. The significance of this distinction appears below.

Even Keynes failed to get this aspect of banking into focus when he wrongly described its proponents as ignoring the double entry nature of bank transactions.[3] In fact, when a bank gives an advance it debits the customer's advance account and credits his deposit (current) account. The customer then draws cheques against the deposit, retaining the debited advance account as a liability (an asset of the bank) to be repaid subsequently. Alternatively the bank might simply debit cheques drawn against an open and empty account and credit the amount to the recipient of the cheque, or to his bank if he banks elsewhere. Creating money does not break the rules of double entry bookkeeping.

b) Borrowing and Lending

The second assumption takes the form of a fallacy of composition. It appears succinctly in Lipsey and Chrystal:

> Remember that banks have to take in deposits in order to make loans. They borrow from one set of people or firms and lend to another.
>
> Lipsey and Chrystal, *ibid.*, p.683

An individual bank may sometimes do this, and oddly enough many bankers think that this is what they always do, but it is certainly untrue of all banks i.e. of the banking system. Banks as a whole 'lend' their own promises to pay, which creates money in the form of deposits. From whom could the whole system receive loans in order to make advances? From the non-bank sector? But whence does the non-bank sector get its deposits? All deposits have their origin in the banking system's ability to create them *ab initio*. Of course, the apparatus of reserve ratios, and government or central bank restrictions, inhibit the process, but they do not remove it. Different, and more productive, rules could be laid down. For example, banks could follow the principle of only giving advances to productive enterprises which were credit-worthy i.e. those who could be trusted to repay an advance out of the proceeds of future production. Such banks would still keep cash reserves, needless to say.

3 See pp.81ff *The General Theory.*

c) Finance for Investment

A third assumption, partially but not entirely exposed by Keynes, is the view that investment is financed out of savings. This misleading view is rendered especially harmful when coupled with the so-called 'classical' corollary that the interest rate is the price which brings them into equilibrium.[4] Investment is financed out of money available to the investor, i.e. the purchaser of capital goods, which may be money he already holds, money he borrows from the non-bank sector or money advanced by a bank. Each of these three cases needs examination.

Money held by the investor (i.e. purchaser of capital goods) probably represents past saving by a firm, but this can be misleading. New investment may well be in response to profits already earned, especially as profits indicate good future prospects. However, in most businesses profits are not literally saved as money. Profits in the profit and loss account have their counterpart in a growth in net assets in the balance sheet, and this growth may be largely in the form of greater stocks, work-in-progress and debtors and/or a reduction in creditors.

A growing firm, especially, may have an overdraft or even a cash flow problem. The decision to invest will not usually be based on having cash savings lying about waiting to be spent on more capital goods. Firms do not invest because they have accumulated bank deposits, though they may accumulate bank deposits because they have failed to invest! Hence, investment out of firms' money savings may be of little consequence in the economy; which is not to say that investment 'out of' profits may not be important.

What then of money borrowed from the non-bank sector? Clearly this is a very significant element in modern conditions. Firms borrow on a large scale from private 'investors' and from other firms, particularly pension funds, by issuing shares and bonds. The deposits they borrow come largely from savings. Nevertheless the distinction remains that lending and borrowing of funds is not at all the same thing as saving out of income and investing by the purchase of capital goods. Not all savings are lent; not all investment comes from borrowing deposits. Hence the interest rate is not the price which equates savings and investment.

Present confusion over savings, investment and interest rates stems to some extent from failure to observe the now well-accepted distinction between *ex ante* and *ex post* equalities. *Ex ante* saving (S) does not

---

4 A view still extant, for example in Begg pp.314-16.

equal *ex ante* investment (I), since the decisions to save and to invest are made by different people with different motives. Transformation into an *ex post* equality is brought about by the shift in national income required to remove unplanned items of I, such as over- or under-stocking.[5] Planned S also becomes an unplanned *ex post* S. The interest rate in no way brings about this equality. Nor does it bring about a long-term equality of I and S, especially as the longer the term the more I responds to future prospects in markets and other (non-interest) conditions.

Finally, investment may be financed by bank advances. In response to proposals by firms of new investment opportunities which will generate the income to repay an advance of money, banks will give credit i.e. make their promises available to pay for capital goods. The interest rate need play no part in this. Banks need as the supply price of their advances only their costs, such as wages and bad debts, and a normal rate of profit as entrepreneurs (which can be seen as wages of management and enterprise). If the money supply is limited by the government or central bank, banks are able to charge more, and may use the market rate of i on the lending and borrowing of deposits held by the non-bank sector as their benchmark. Without restrictions on credit and money, however, banks would be obliged in a competitive banking system to cover only their costs and normal profits. Nor would there be as much need for the non-bank sector to provide funds. Firms would not be dependent on non-bank deposits, nor forced to pay high interest rates for them.

Of course, this whole issue is not just in the hands of the banking system. Whilst a resolve to give advances only for productive enterprise, rather than for land purchase and current consumption, would help matters, the banks alone cannot change the structure of the economy. The non-bank sector has funds available for lending largely because the present distribution of income, wealth and land leaves huge deposits in the hands of those who receive or hold major shares of one or more of these. A more equitable distribution would leave more in the hands of the actual producers, i.e. workers of all types and abilities, who would need funds for the purchase of the equipment and tools that they use. In other words, industry could be more self-financed.

---

5 The equality is, of course, between total injections and total withdrawals, so S = I *ex post* is a simplification.

Non-bank Financial Institutions
In view of the present day role of investment funds, pension funds and building societies, it is necessary to look briefly at precisely what part they play. Superficially they appear as major sources of finance for investment in industry and house-building. They are often collecting money savings from large numbers of people and lending them on to industry by buying shares and bonds. Hence they are intermediaries in the lending and borrowing market. Their interest rates for both are prices in the loan market, the differential representing their costs and profits.

Pension funds appear to have a special function of their own. Are they transferring purchasing power into the future by saving premiums in order to pay future pensions? In so far as present premiums equal present payments on policies maturing, they are not doing this. Instead they are simply transferring deposits from premium payers to policy beneficiaries. In theory this does not affect the level of consumption in the economy, except when marginal propensities to spend differ. Saving on one hand is matched by dis-saving on the other.[6] Whilst such funds are growing, of course, purchasing power would seem to be transferred into the future. Even this is questionable. Whether the denial of present claims on current output can be matched by an equivalent addition to future claims on future output is most doubtful in view of all the variables of price and equilibrium national income involved. The fact is that whereas an individual may well transfer a claim from one time to another (subject to problems about changes in the value of money), it is most doubtful whether a whole society can do so (see below pp.279-81). If most people decide to save more, national income falls and firms are unlikely to expand their investment in response. Only perhaps government action can help to carry out the wishes of a whole society to save for the future. Infrastructure investment, education and research, for example, may raise future living standards. Firms are usually investing on a time-scale of a few years, and do not respond in any case to the wishes of savers. The present crisis in regard to both private and public sector pension funds tends to confirm this scepticism about the ability to transfer purchasing power into the future.

What of building societies? They transfer saved funds from one group of individuals to others who need to borrow for house

6 Whether maturing policies are paid as lump sums or pensions affects this.

purchase. They too are in the market for loanable deposits, using an interest rate that tends to equate supply and demand. To some extent they transfer deposits from old to young. The total volume of deposits is not affected, unless bank advances are introduced. Since banks now act as lenders for house purchase, advances are in fact given for this, thus creating fresh demand in the economy, largely for land, since land values are a major element in so-called 'house' prices. The inflationary consequences of this are obvious, as land is not produced. Were advances purely for house-building costs, banks would conform to the principle of creating money only for productive enterprise, though the need for such advances to be repaid by house buyers, rather than by productive firms, complicates the issue (see Chapter 19).

Present versus Future Production

If the interest rate is not the mediator between savings and investment, how does society express its decisions to provide for the future? In other words, what enables the value of investment to express the will of society to consume future goods in preference to present goods to a particular level of substitution of one for the other? There is no collective decision about this, except in special cases where public opinion might favour a really large project like a Channel tunnel, but nevertheless there may be a shift in individuals' time preferences. For example, people in general might decide that a prosperous old age is more significant than before. Putting aside money as savings does not

DIAGRAM 113

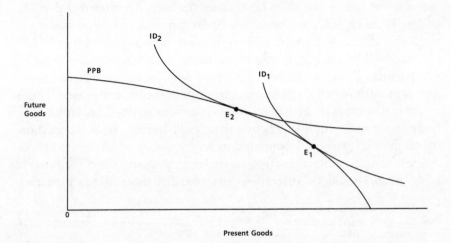

provide the means, though lending it to industry would help. The choice is shown in Diagram 113.

PPB is the production possibility boundary for producing combinations of present and future goods, both under diminishing returns. ID1, and ID2 are indifference curves representing different groups of choices by society, which express time preference.[7] If production is at E1 and society decides to value future goods more than before, how does the economy respond by moving to E2? Begg's analysis using i as the mediator has been criticised already (see footnote 4, p.276). There may indeed be a small shift as extra S are loaned and extra I stimulated by a fall in i, but this cannot achieve much. Nor can the price mechanism help. There is no rate of exchange between present goods and future goods (except in the highly specialized futures markets). Nor is there any way in which private investment in capital goods can respond to a general desire to consume more in the future and less in the present.

Some meaning, however, can be given to this social choice, since some goods and services marketed in the present have a long-term use and may thus qualify as future goods. Amongst these are infrastructure – roads, railways, buildings, drainage etc. – education and research and development. In so far as consumers can express their longer time preference by buying these, their prices may rise and stimulate greater output of them. Obviously this raises issues about public authority demand and its democratic expression. But for consumption goods and services that have a short life, it is difficult to see how a price mechanism can solve the problem. The fact is that every economy has to provide out of current, not future, production for those unable to support themselves by work, especially the old. Whether this is done within families, by State pensions or by privately financed pensions makes no difference whatsoever to this fact. The 'problem', for example, of the UK having more private pension funds available than its EU partners is, in this respect, a bogus one. The real goods and services for pensioners come out of current production in all cases. There is no special stock of actual goods and services to draw on. In the UK there is a greater fund of claims; that is all. Indeed the accumulation of claims may well be detrimental to an economy, which is then beset by past claims rather than free to make a spontaneous choice about how much should be offered to the old. Inflation or stock market

7 This analysis suffers from the serious defect of what meaning can be given to a collective indifference curve, but the main conclusion may still loosely hold. Such a concept assumes a given distribution of income, wealth and land.

collapse may ruin the accumulated fund. A spontaneous choice could be more generous, either by family or community or State benevolence.

What then of investment in capital goods? Can that move also towards E2 as a response to ID2? Why should it? Investment decisions usually relate to a medium term of say 5 to 10 years, hardly a long-term provision to meet society's future needs. Moreover a firm's rationale in investing is in response to its own estimation of markets. It takes a view about present and future demand over the life of the investment only, as do those who provide the finance. Neither can be cajoled to move collectively to E2, which is an illusory point, except in so far as some goods and services have a very long life and yet may be bought in the present, like a good education.

Money Supply, Interest Rates and Equilibrium

Such questions are peripheral to the theory of income determination. Let us return to the role of the rate of interest. This does not equate savings and investment. It does, however, act as the price of loans, when these are forthcoming out of deposits derived from saving and are borrowed by investors, who neither have their own funds available nor receive bank advances. A limited money supply and restrictive rules over banks, however, make bank advances also appear to be loans which are subject to market rates of interest, whereas they are really the original source of all deposits and could be offered at their supply

DIAGRAM 114

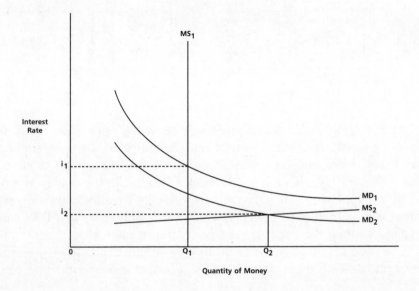

Quantity of Money

price i.e. at marginal cost. Joseph Schumpeter was right when he described bankers, even in modern conditions, as the ephors of the exchange economy.

So let us waive the assumption of a fixed money supply. If bankers gave advances to productive enterprises at rates of interest which only covered their costs, the theory of income determination would look very different.

In Diagram 114 the MS curve would become almost completely elastic (MS2), sloping upwards only slightly with more bad debts at high levels of advances. MD would shift leftwards, since the speculative motive for money would be greatly reduced in a much smaller bond market. Transactions and precautionary motives would remain. Hence i would fall from i1 to i2, and the quantity of money expand from Q1 to Q2. The LM curve would also become much more elastic (see Diagram 115) as monetary expansion would proceed *pro rata* with the size of RNI (compare Diagram 101, p.244).

DIAGRAM 115

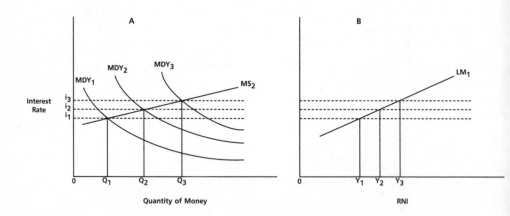

At the same time a lower interest rate would raise investment as firms equated MEC with the new rate. As this extra I was multiplied RNI would rise, shown as an expansion of RNI down the IS curve (see Diagram 116). RNI expands from Y1 to Y2. In the real economy what is happening is that finance from banks for productive investment and its multiplied effects is easily forthcoming, so that RNI can expand without the constraint of high interest rates.

The absence of restrictions on money supply depends for its efficacy on bank advances only being made available for production (see

DIAGRAM 116

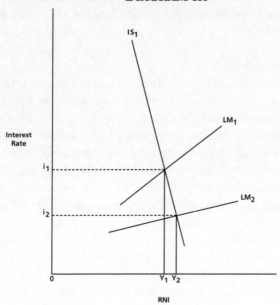

Chapter 13). If they continue to be made, as at present, for land purchase and consumption, then accommodating increases in MS merely
fuel inflation. This is precisely why the authorities now feel bound to
restrict MS. Unfortunately they do not see the underlying reason, which
is not that the total quantity of money is a problem, but its composition. Money to finance production should be unlimited; money for
non-productive activity should be nil. Milton Friedman and the
monetary school of economists have singularly failed to perceive this.

On the supply side the free availability of bank advances for
genuine investment would mean that LRAS would shift to the right as
more capital goods could be produced. Marginal projects would
become intra-marginal, though growth would depend upon conditions
of land availability (see Chapter 21). The elimination of non-productive
bank advances for consumption and for land purchase would be more
than compensated by the multiplier effects of higher productive investment, so that it would also be easier to keep RNI at full employment
levels in the short run.

As for monetary policy, freer banking would largely remove the need
for the central bank to control MS, except perhaps in crisis situations.
Instead, bankers would undertake their real responsibility of judging
the merits of investment projects. Interest rates in normal times would

be beyond the control of government, since money would be available at its supply price, and private lending and borrowing would take place at interest rates set without pressure upon the borrower.

Summary of Criticisms

We may summarise the critique of national income determination theory from the point of view of money and credit as follows. The 'profits' item in the circular flow may obscure the real sources of both capital and its means of financing. Moreover, the circular flow may be a misleading concept in some respects. Creating money is a function of banks and is quite distinct from lending it. To think that banks in general need to receive deposits in order to make advances is to commit a fallacy of composition. Investment is not primarily financed by savings; nor – *a fortiori* – is the interest rate the price which equates them. Investment is financed principally by banks, and partly by money held by investing firms and deposits held elsewhere in the non-bank sector and lent in return for shares or bonds. Non-bank financing constitutes a loan market, not a savings market. The interest rate equates loan supply and demand, rather than savings and investment. Bank advances, as the fundamental source of investment, are charged at the loan interest rate, if banks are limited by government. They could charge a money supply price, if free from restrictions. It is the existing unequal distribution of income, wealth and land which makes non-bank sector loans an important current source of investment finance.

Pension funds only match saving by some people with dis-saving by others. Building societies similarly transfer demand from lenders to borrowers using the interest rate as a price to equate deposits and loans. If banks were in fact free, MS and LM would be elastic and interest rates would be very low. Higher investment from more available bank advances would shift LRAS to the right, and AD would shift to the right to meet SRAS more easily at full employment. Monetary policy would become peripheral.

Questioning the assumptions of the theory of income determination in relation to credit and money opens up substantial possibilities, both for the model of the economy that it employs and, more importantly for the real economy that it seeks to explain. Yet these possibilities are not isolated from others, especially those previously discussed concerning land. Free land and free credit are like two arms of a pair of scissors; one alone may not cut the knot of poverty and injustice. Moreover, there is more to be said on how taxation has a strong bearing on the matter.

CHAPTER 23

Critique of the Theory:
Taxation

T HE EFFECT of the current system of taxation on the demand side of the income determination model is generally acknowledged. Taxes are a withdrawal, reducing the circular flow and playing their part in the equilibrium condition $W = J$. However, their real impact on the supply side is largely ignored. Since most taxes, like income tax, national insurance, VAT and excise taxes, appear to be paid by, and largely incident upon, individuals, their effects are taken to be essentially re-distributional between individuals and allocative between firms and markets i.e. they redistribute income and they induce or deter production of particular goods. Elasticities of demand, of course, have a strong bearing on the latter effect. But as regards their impact on the productive, i.e. supply side, of the economy as a whole they are regarded as being more or less neutral. It is as though taxes were drawn from the economy after the productive process, and thus do not make much impact upon it. Of course, there is a school of thought that views personal taxes, especially progressive ones, like income tax, as a serious deterrent to effort, but research suggests this may not be important (see Begg, *ibid.*, pp.448-9). Even this, however, misses the real point about supply side effects.

Effect of Taxes on Labour
There is no doubt that most present day taxes initially fall upon labour as a factor of production. Direct taxes are assessed on income (some income, of course, is unearned) and indirect taxes are assessed mainly on goods and services bought by workers. Corporation tax is perhaps the only major exception. What then is the full impact of taxes on labour?

In Diagram 117 the standard analysis shows a falling labour demand curve, derived from diminishing labour productivity, rising labour force

285

DIAGRAM 117

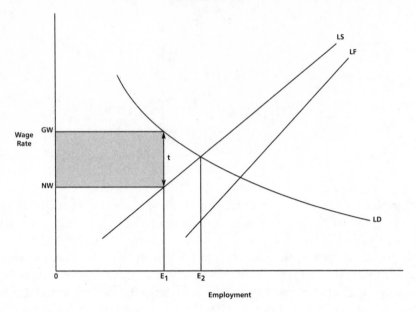

Employment

and labour supply curves (separated by the so-called voluntarily unemployed), a tax on labour of t, and equilibrium employment at E1, below the untaxed level of E2. GW and NW are the gross and net wage rates respectively.

There are disregarded lessons to be drawn from this analysis. The tax on labour is proportional to the wage rate, yet labour productivity varies greatly at different levels of employment within a firm. Tax is therefore proportionately higher, from the firm's point of view, the less productive is the labour. Hence such a tax deters greatly the employment of more labour. The least productive labour is that in marginal firms and in marginal employment in non-marginal firms, i.e. at the extensive and intensive margins.

A tax, however, that was proportional to that part of the marginal revenue product of labour which exceeds the wage rate would have a zero impact on employment, even at a rate of 100% (Diagram 118).[1]

Such a proportional labour tax can be related to the concept of value added by labour and land. If all other costs of production, including

1 It is of crucial importance that the *ceteris paribus* qualification of equal labour effort, skill and equipment is assumed here, since the concept of labour productivity can then be related to locational variation. See Chapter 8.

DIAGRAM 118

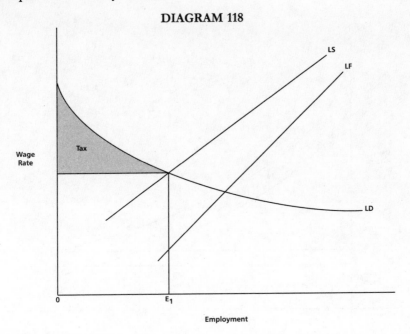

capital, are treated as 'below the line', then value added can be presented in terms of average returns to labour, where these vary systematically with location. In Diagram 119 the wage rate is more or less constant, but rent as a measure of variable labour productivity varies with location.[2]

With a tax proportional to the wage rate, however divided in incidence between firms and workers according to the elasticities of LD and LS above (Diagram 117), production contracts to M1 as firms M2 – M1 close down. Their value added is insufficient to pay gross wages plus firms' tax. Normal profits, derived from rent, are generally squeezed by the tax burden. In so far as workers react to tax increases, both direct and indirect, by wage demands which are granted, tax paid by labour may be minimal, increasing the marginal impact of taxation paid by firms and creating even more unemployment. In the long run higher unemployment may force down the wage rate, effectively driving workers to a lower, least acceptable real wage. In which case employment may recover somewhat. But the actual outcome is unquantifiable, especially when the effect of lower real wages on aggregate demand is also considered. What is certain is that any tax not

2 Rent can be understood as a measure of labour productivity as a function of location.

DIAGRAM 119

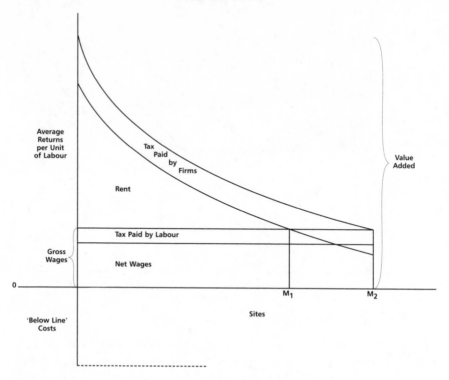

related to locational variations in labour productivity must have dele-
terious effects on output and employment.[3]

Effects on SRAS

This throws light on the effect upon aggregate supply of the present
tax system. SRAS rises to the right, mainly as a result of diminishing
returns yielding lower labour productivity and of firms on less productive sites entering production (Diagram 120). A tax proportional to
wage rates clearly hits output harder where labour productivity falls.
Hence such a tax raises SRAS above its untaxed level and does so
increasingly as full employment approaches.

In Diagram 120 AD1 is sufficient to maintain full employment at M2
with no tax burden, but when taxes are added to SRAS1, AD1 gives
unemployment equivalent to M1 – M2. Were demand only AD2,
employment would be greater by M3 – M4 if taxes were not paid by

3 This analysis ignores scarcity rent, which does not greatly affect the outcome.

DIAGRAM 120

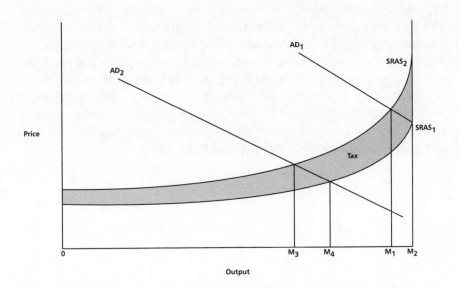

firms for labour. A tax proportional to the excess of labour productivity over wages i.e. to rent, however, would have no impact on employment or output, leaving SRAS1 unchanged, since SRAS measures only variable costs, especially labour charges.

Labour/Capital Ratios

The principal and most harmful effect of levying taxes on labour without paying heed to labour productivity is the severe limitation imposed on output. A secondary effect, however, is that labour intensive firms and industries are restricted more than capital intensive ones. The natural balance between the use of labour and capital, according to the technological conditions of production and the relative prices of labour and capital goods, is distorted by a tax proportional to labour units i.e. to the wage rate. By favouring capital intensity, the tax system promotes inefficiency, quite apart from other questions like the soul-destroying character of much large-scale production. Hence the total value of production is less than it might be if taxes were neutral as regards labour/capital ratios. AS could shift further to the right.

Summary of Criticisms

In conclusion it may be said that the present tax system inhibits the efficient employment of labour and land, by making the former too expensive at both the extensive and intensive margins of production, and by doing nothing to prevent the dereliction and misuse of land. Labour and land lie idle because firms do not find it profitable to employ them, and because workers find the rewards of present activity too low and landowners the penalties for present inactivity non-existent. Shifting taxes off labour and onto rent, which amounts to a tax proportional to labour locational productivity, would transform the economic model of income determination, and, more importantly, enhance the size and quality of RNI.

CHAPTER 24

The Model Reformed

THE PREVIOUS three chapters have suggested that many aspects of the theory of income determination are incorrect or misleading in view of the prevailing conditions regarding land, money and credit and taxation. How then would the economy itself, and the model of it, operate if these conditions were changed beneficially? Let us make some far-reaching assumptions: firstly that land values are zero, so that there is no market for land; secondly that money and credit are available at a very low supply price; and thirdly that there is no tax assessed on labour, either directly or indirectly.

The Demand Side

The most obvious consequence is that the circular flow of income and output would now entirely represent flows of production of goods and services and money payments for them. No payments would be made by households or firms for the purchase of land, nor for the rent of land held by private owners.[1] The consumption function would shift upwards, since households could spend more on consumption goods. The investment component of injections would represent capital goods purchases only and not land purchases. Government expenditure, also, would exclude payments for land. Exports would benefit from the tax relief on labour. Some investment might be financed by savings, but the banking system would provide advances for any rational investment project, without the need to finance land purchase.

Withdrawals from the circular flow now include only savings (used partly to finance investment but mainly to repay bank advances), imports and whatever taxes are not assessed on labour. The multiplier is also higher from the absence of the withdrawal effect of payments for land purchase.

1 Such private rent would create private land values, which *ex hypothesi* do not exist..

The marginal efficiency of capital becomes more inelastic, for the land element in investment was what made it elastic. With very low i (i.e. supply price of money), investment in capital goods is not restricted by a shortage of finance. Moreover MEC is less volatile, shifts in MEC indicating genuine changes in investment opportunities and not speculative or other movements in land purchases. Capital goods industries respond directly to such shifts, the multiplier effect of which is greater for reasons already given.

MS becomes very elastic, with banks responding at the supply price of money to changes in MD. Since with permanently low interest rates the bond price become largely irrelevant,[2] shifts in MD at different levels of RNI become the main determinant of actual MS. In other words, the transactions and precautionary motives dominate and the speculative motive is removed. The amount of money in the economy adjusts easily to real changes in demand for money, resulting principally from changes in RNI, and to a lesser extent from price movements or supply and demand fluctuations (see Diagram 115, p.282). Hence the AD curve becomes more inelastic.[3] Real aggregate demand, therefore, is not much influenced by the PL, except through the latter's impact on imports and exports. The land market and credit and money systems do not interfere with the real demand for goods and services. Prices may be flexible upwards and downwards without diverting consumers' demand for output into other channels, particularly into land purchases and bond speculation. Thus the demand side of the economy is freed from these trammels.

Impact on SRAS

Yet price flexibility might be expected to have serious disruptive effects on the supply side of the economy, as the damaging impact of both inflation and deflation in the past has proved. What then happens to aggregate supply curves under the assumed conditions of zero land values, cheap money and credit and a nil tax on labour? Zero land values have no direct impact on SRAS, because in the short run land does not vary as a factor of production and no land changes use or ownership. Interest charges, however, fall to the supply price of money, shifting SRAS downwards slightly. More importantly, the elimination

2 A speculative market in bonds depends upon an interest rate that can fluctuate significantly, thereby changing their capital value.

3 This result is modified by elimination of the 'reverse wealth effect', since house land values are zero and inflation no longer encourages house owners to spend more. However, this is probably cancelled out by the demise also of the wealth effect itself. Money denominated assets, like bonds, are no longer significant, though money balances remain so.

of tax on labour shifts SRAS yet further to SRAS2 (Diagram 121), and has most impact on the right hand end of SRAS, nearer full employment, owing to the disproportional effect on unit costs of a tax that strikes hardest on marginal labour (both on extensive and intensive margins). In the short run such interest and tax reductions may induce a small rise in the wage rate, which would shift SRAS back upwards to SRAS3. Thus in the short run total costs would fall, raising employment and output, for example, from Y1 to Y2.

DIAGRAM 121

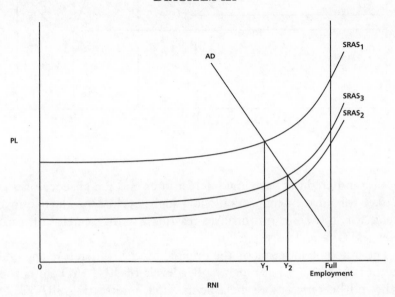

Shift of LRAS

The principal impact of the new conditions regarding land, money and credit and taxation, however, falls on LRAS. This shifts very substantially to the right for a variety of reasons (Diagram 122). Scarcity rent disappears (see pp.268-9), opening previously marginal land and marginal employment on intra-marginal sites to productive enterprise. Resource allocation is much more efficient, as rent becomes entirely a differential measuring out of the potential productivity of sites, and as land held for speculation is released for use. Previously unemployed labour may find work on land made available without either scarcity rent or a tax burden, taking advantage of capital provided by bank advances offered at their supply price. The general availability of

DIAGRAM 122

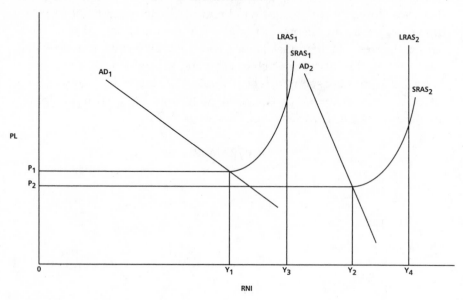

money and credit at very low interest rates and the absence of a land
market for 'investment' encourage a high level of productive investment, for 'there are no intrinsic reasons for the scarcity of capital'
(Keynes, *General Theory*, p.376).

The outcome in terms of the original model is therefore an equilibrium of AD and AS at much higher levels of RNI. AD shifts to the
right and becomes more inelastic at AD2, intersecting SRAS2 at Y2
with PL at P2 rather than at P1. Demand for goods and services for
consumption and investment is greater, and supply is at lower cost and
much higher levels.

Equilibrium in the Reformed Model
A central issue remains to be settled. Both models show unemployment, of Y3 – Y1 and Y4 – Y2 respectively (Diagram 122). Does the
reformed model also suffer from an endemic problem of unemployment, albeit at a greater level of RNI? More land and capital are
employed at Y2 than Y1 and some more labour, but can AD still be
insufficient to give full employment at Y4? This question is closely
related to the long-running dispute between Keynesian and 'classicist'
macro-economists about the ability of markets, especially that for
labour, to clear in response to price changes. The latter school of

DIAGRAM 123

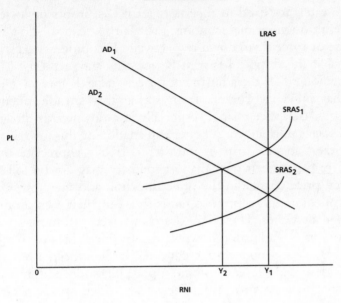

thought envisages a rapid clearing of the labour market as price changes stimulate a responsive adjustment of wage rates. If, for example, prices fall as AD shifts to the left at full employment (Diagram 123) SRAS falls as workers accept lower wage rates, so that full employment is maintained.

Keynesians, on the other hand, argue that the inflexibility of wage rates downwards prevents this, leaving unemployment of Y1 – Y2 and the need for government action to revive demand. The use of the dubious concept of 'voluntary unemployment' is a spurious attempt by the 'classicists' to defend their case by suggesting that workers who do not work at the new lower rates are not really unemployed. However, changes in trade union law and the weakening of inflationary expectations in recent years make it more plausible that 'money illusion' is now weaker and that workers may accept cuts in money wages in the hope that real wages are maintained.

The relevance of this issue here is that the reformed model reacts to price changes in a more 'classical' way than the unreformed one. The present-day economy is inflexible in response to price changes caused by shifts of AD or by supply shocks, like an oil price rise, because workers are employees earning wage rates not directly related to the prices of goods and services that they themselves make. If the price of a good changes the firm takes any resultant profit or loss, since wage rates are fixed in the short term. As profits or losses in general, i.e. throughout the economy, grow, firms tend to allow wage rates to rise or force them down respectively. This process takes time, which is what the dispute between Keynesians and 'classicists' is all about. How long does the adjustment process take? Is there a 'money illusion' that prevents workers from seeing that an adjustment of money wages to a price change, especially in a downwards direction, leaves real wages unchanged. A better explanation of this myopic view is that workers in one firm or industry correctly appreciate that a change of prices in their own firm or industry may not be followed by a general price change in the same direction and therefore would not be compensated, except in so far as they buy their own products, by a change in wages. Hence the 'ratchet' effect of money wages moving up, but not adjusting downwards, on price changes. Workers justifiably fear that a money wage cut does, in fact, mean a real wage cut. The widespread presence of monopoly, oligopoly and imperfect competition also serves to justify their fears, since only a pervasive climate of genuine competition is likely to induce rapid and general price reductions.

How then would the reformed economy react to changes in PL? This question elicits the degree to which the new conditions of land, credit and taxation really affect the whole structure of the economy. An economy like todays, in which the vast majority of workers are employees, paid a wage rate by their employers, is the product of land tenure, banking and tax systems that have developed over a lengthy period. Access to land demands a high price, credit is mainly available only to landowners and shareholders, and taxation is assessed on labour. Typically the limited joint stock company with land and capital owned by shareholders and directors is the outcome. Under the reformed conditions such economic servitude of workers to the minority who lend money to firms disappears. Workers themselves now have easy access to land and credit and pay no tax on wages. Marginal land is available for production free of rent, since scarcity rent is absent, and banks offer advances at very low rates of interest. Free associations of workers may take up production in all industries, except perhaps those where natural monopoly requires public control. Firms may become partnerships or workers' co-operatives.

A chief feature of such 'reformed' firms is that the prices of their products and the wages of their workers are no longer separated. The firm does not make profits after deducting wages as a cost, for wages are no longer a cost of production; they are a share in production, the natural reward for the value added by labour. As the price of the product rises and falls, other things being equal, wages rise and fall. This is not even an adjustment process; it is simultaneous, just as it is for a self-employed individual today. Wages become the firm's revenue, minus all its non-wage costs. Hence there is no problem of how the economy deals with changes in PL as regards wages. The 'classical' model comes into its own, in this respect at least.

> Flexible wages that fell rapidly during periods of unemployment would provide an automatic adjustment mechanism that would push the economy back towards full employment whenever output fell below potential.
>
> Lipsey and Chrystal, ibid., p.612

Say's Law

This whole problem of inflexibility in modern economies is related to more than the structure of industry. At root the issue concerns the famous Say's law, which Keynes was so ready to attack. 'Supply creates its own demand' has been replaced, since Keynes, by the dictum that demand creates supply. The real question is 'what interferes to prevent the smooth operation of supply and demand?' Clearly the structure of present day industry does so, in separating wages overmuch from prices. Yet behind this lies the interference caused by the chimera of land values. If land – given freely by God or nature – acquires a price, owing to private claims on the rent of land, money and credit flow towards it and away from the circulation of production. Money is absorbed from the circular flow by land sales and only returns to it with delays and difficulties. It is as though the river of production is diverted into ox-bow lakes of land prices. Worse still, these land prices feed a secondary effect back into the economy, for their prices have to be paid by productive enterprises for sites and by individuals for housing land. This fact alone accounts for much of the inflation of the past fifty years. For money that flows into land values and out of production is either withdrawn from the circular flow or replaced by fresh money. If withdrawn there is a fall in demand and consequent unemployment. If replaced, there is inflation, since money has been advanced, not against production, but against nothing i.e. against the artificial 'value' of a free good. Were the circular flow restored to itself by the elimination of land values the endemic problem of inflation would be solved.

The Keystone of the Reformed Economy

This account of how the economy and its model may adapt to the three basic conditions of zero land values (i.e. no land market), money and credit at their supply price and no tax on labour leaves several fundamental questions unanswered. The second condition has been explained at some length (see Chapters 13 and 22), but the practicality of the first and third remains to be explored. How can a land market be dispensed with? How can land values be zero? How can differential rents remain without private individuals receiving them? And how can taxes on labour be removed without denying government its main source of revenue? The answer to all such questions is so simple that it may be regarded as the keystone in reconstructing the economy. Rent of land becomes public revenue. Land itself remains, as now, largely in private hands, held by firms for production and by individuals for housing. Security of tenure remains a necessity for the economy, and indeed for civilised life, but the receipt of land rent by firms or individuals does not take place. (Unless they act as intermediaries and themselves pay the full rent over as public revenue.) Land then has no capital value, since it yields no income; hence there is no 'investment' in land, nor a land market. Differential rents, however, remain essential. Firms and households are prepared to pay whatever particular sites are worth to them as producers or house-owners, and compete for such sites, thereby creating a rent profile similar to the present one, but without the surcharge of scarcity rent. In fact, the profile would change considerably over time as firms and households relocated in new conditions.

Such a source of public revenue amply replaces a tax on labour. Present statistics of land rent greatly understate it for a variety of reasons,[4] some of which are technical, some obfuscations by landowners. The following chapter deals at greater length with the case for public receipt of land rent. From the point of view of macroeconomics, however, the case rests upon the far greater efficiency of an economy which operates under the three conditions outlined above. If rent becomes public revenue, these conditions fall into place. No more is the economy inhibited by the severe limitations imposed by privately owned land values, a government controlled money supply (and the high interest rates that accompany it) and a punitive tax on labour, which damages firms and workers in almost equal measure.

4 See Chapter 8 and, for example, K. Cahill, *Who Owns Britain?*, Canongate, 2001.

A New Model of the Economy

Lest the 'reformed model' argument strips the picture of the real economy too far down to bare essentials, let us consider more expansively how the system would operate were all three conditions in place, under the keystone of public rent revenues. The fundamental division of value added output between land and labour would no longer be obscured by taxes assessed on wages. Nor would scarcity rent depress wages below their full value at both the extensive and intensive margins of production (see Diagram 124).[5]

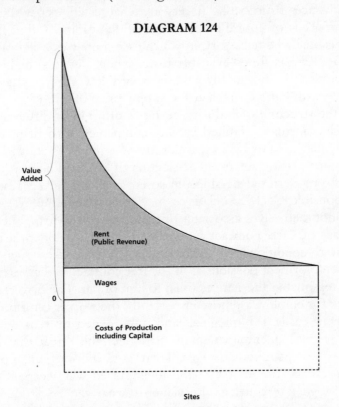

DIAGRAM 124

Value Added

Rent (Public Revenue)

Wages

0

Costs of Production including Capital

Sites

The very considerable increase in wages as a larger share of a greatly enhanced output is obviously a chief feature of the reformed economy. The implications of this extend far beyond a better material standard of living for the majority of people. Throughout the economy workers are no longer faced with the necessity to pay rent or the

5 Since Diagram 124 represents a three-dimensional circular model rotating on 0, wages are probably a larger share than rent.

price of a freehold or leasehold site to landlords. Land becomes freely available, subject to some reasonable method of administering it (see p.332), under the condition that users pay rent as public revenue in lieu of any other taxes. Firms or householders occupying marginal sites pay neither rent nor taxes. Hence entry to an industry is not burdened with insupportable charges that firms cannot bear. They do not need to turn to money-lenders or banks for loans to buy sites. *A fortiori* they do not bear interest (mortgage) charges for land. Nor do firms necessarily turn to outside finance for the purchase of capital. High wages enable them to buy their own capital. For large capital projects they obtain advances from banks at very low charges and repay them out of the proceeds of future employment of the capital. Other finance may occasionally be necessary, in which case money can be borrowed from whoever has funds available from saving, but this might be of small significance and, in any case, is at very low interest rates commensurate with bank charges at the supply price of money.

Thus the structure of industry becomes profoundly different from present day norms of limited liability companies, with firms owned legally by absentees or by a tiny minority of employees entitled directors. In short, firms are free associations of workers akin in several respects to modern partnerships, in so far as all are equally respected and responsible. Such associations may themselves employ workers who are not themselves associates or members of the firm, but this is on the basis of a free contract where the worker is not under the duress of modern conditions of employment. What makes such non-onerous employment possible, as in any free contract, is that each party to it has reasonable alternatives open to him or her. The firm can turn elsewhere for employees; more importantly, the worker can find other employment easily, for marginal land unburdened by rent or tax is available. Hence unemployment is no longer the threat that forces workers to accept minimal wages. There is no pool of unemployed; no wage level at the least that the unemployed will accept. On the contrary wages are equal to the value of what can be produced by applying one's labour on a free site. This does not mean that the worker's alternative is 'three acres and a cow'! Work is available at the extensive and intensive margins, both of which are unencumbered by taxation or other charges. On the former, new firms are easy to set up.[6] Marginal land would receive its full entitlement of public services financed by rent, such as drainage, roads and power lines. In these

6 In most industries small, marginal units are viable in free conditions. They may be, for example, ancillary to those requiring central sites.

conditions most workers may prefer to be associated in firms or self-employed, so that employment for wages becomes a sellers' and not a buyers' market. Firms seek to find workers with good potential who will become associates.

In these benign circumstances everyone has the opportunity for a genuine choice of work which suits his or her talents and aspirations. No longer faced with the dire necessity for a job of any sort at low wages and with little responsibility and respect, workers reveal their real abilities. The rare present day worker who loves what he does and enjoys the chance to serve the community is no longer the exception. Output rises greatly in quantity, but above all in quality. Creativity becomes a mark of the workplace, rather than of spare-time activity. Society is raised up by the daily endeavours of all. Fulfillment through work becomes a natural feature of the economy. So, too, people may learn to co-operate naturally, rather than compete ruthlessly for jobs and markets. Rivalry to excel may flourish, but the life and death struggle to undercut or outsell, both in the labour market and in markets for final goods and services ceases.

Modern industrial economies concentrate upon the quantity rather than the quality of output, although there are, of course, important exceptions, usually in markets where purchasers are wealthy. Most products are standardized and produced under severe cost restraints. Service to customers also suffers from the need for firms to minimize labour time and training. Firms in the reformed economy are free to emphasise the quality of their products, and to enjoy the exercise of skill and care in producing them. Service to customers is free of unnecessary cost restraints, and benefits especially from workers' awareness that they themselves constitute the firm which offers the service. Training of workers is an essential part of a firm's self-respect and development, for the trained worker does not become merely an addition to the labour market but a new recruit to a body of skilled professionals. Apprenticeships are once more the life-blood of firms.

Monopoly no longer occurs, except where natural monopolies in public utilities, like the electricity grid or road system, continue under public control. For private collection of rent is the root of private monopoly (see Chapter 6), and free associations of workers can challenge a would-be monopolist. Oligopoly also faces the same solvents of its power, though economies of scale in capital, where the minimum efficient scale occurs at a significant share of market demand, may remain. Capital/labour ratios, however, may change in favour of labour when tax is removed from the latter, reducing the use of capital per worker and therefore shifting the long-term average cost curve of the oligopolist to the left. At the same time, non-technical economies i.e. economies of scope, such as cheaper finance, tend to disappear. Technical economies alone are unlikely to create problems of oligopoly, at least not to the extent that firms can indulge in predatory pricing, excessive advertising and so on (see Chapter 7).

In such an economy credit also flows freely. Belief or trust in others is not soured by fear of losing a crucial extra payment that turns survival into bankruptcy. Firms no longer run on narrow profit margins, the residue left after paying the heavy charges of employees' wages, landlords' rent, taxation and interest. Their 'margin' is the value added by work i.e. their wages, which are ample enough for firms to give and receive credit fearlessly. Credit for the purchase of capital becomes largely the prerogative of bankers in the form of advances. It is available at very low cost to anyone whose capital project is sound and whose word that he will repay the advance is trusted. Only foolish projects and dishonest people are unworthy of a banker's trust, for the banker himself earns his living by the skill and extent to which he makes productive advances. No more do bankers look to speculative 'investment' in shares, still less in land, for the land market is rendered defunct by the withering away of private land values.

What now of land for housing? Householders pay a rent to a public authority for the land they occupy. If they choose to live in a city centre it may be high; in a rural village it may be negligible. Finance is required in advance, therefore, only to pay building costs or the second-hand price of the house itself. Banks may advance this, if they trust the house purchaser to repay. The rate of interest is determined primarily by the rate charged for advances to industry, which is the supply price of money. High wages make such advances and charges acceptable to borrowers, or even sometimes unnecessary. However, in addition, there are opportunities for firms or individuals to hold houses, whilst paying the land rent, for letting. Such a service, rewarded only by the going rate for the work of management, offers an alternative to buying a house, as at present but without the burden of an extra charge for landlords' scarcity rent. In effect, renting a house becomes payment for a proportional share of building costs, plus management expenses, with land rent payable directly or indirectly to a public authority.

Land itself, of course, remains – as it always has been – a prime necessity for work and for living, a natural element, like air, water and sunshine. All that has changed are the conditions under which it becomes available. The land in itself is free at all times and places, but at present access to it is more or less restricted. Absolute private land ownership, scarcity rent and taxation on wages severely restrict access. Public collection of land rent, with security of tenure remaining, frees land from all three restrictions. Access to land is available under conditions of freedom: that payment is made to the community for what the community itself creates, that quiet enjoyment of tenure is allowed, and that the land is maintained in good condition. Free land, like free men, is the reward for recognising the duties due to others.

Aspects of Natural Law

Of the seven aspects of natural law referred to earlier (see Chapter 2), mention has now been made of how five of these – work, land, co-operation, capital and credit – might reveal themselves in a reformed economy. What then of the economic surplus and of human freedom? Enough has already been said to establish that the natural surplus of an economy is the rent of land. Every society throughout history creates and always will create rent, for it is in the nature of mankind that land is occupied in such a way that natural differences of fertility, mineral resources, drainage, climate and so on, on one hand, and man-made differences of concentration of population, public services, markets, transport facilities and so on, on the other, make one site more productive or more highly valued than another. Once more the question becomes, 'How does human law and custom deal with this surplus?' It can be left in the hands of private landowners. It can be made to bear a range of charges, as it does today – interest, profits, taxes,[7] with a substantial residue to landlords – or it may be returned to the community which collectively creates it. Under free conditions of land tenure, the rent is so returned.

From rent as public revenue public expenditure may be generously financed, for that is the fund naturally available for such use. Those services which are unequivocally a public responsibility – defence, law and order, provision for those unable to support themselves by work, and maintenance and administration of publicly held land – may be all that society chooses to finance. Most societies may choose also to

7 Taxes assessed on labour still fall considerably on rent, even when not assessed upon it.

finance social infrastructure, like roads, railways, ports, airports, pipelines, the electric grid and the rest. Some may choose to include public health and education services. None would need to finance 'welfare state' payments for unemployment and excessively low wages. Bank advances to the State for infrastructure expenditure might be needed where especially large and long-lived capital projects could not be financed out of current rent. Some States might emulate Periclean Athens in the public provision of great works of art and architecture. Few would emulate the great dictators of modern times in vast expenditure on armed forces, for why would a free community sanction such a disturbance to their prosperity and happiness as an aggressive war?

The final aspect of natural law, the freedom of the individual, depends upon free conditions in both civil and economic life. In Britain, and all countries that derive their law systems from the Common Law of England, civil freedom has been strong, protected by impartial judges and a freely elected Parliament. Yet economic freedom has been gravely attenuated since its lustier days in Anglo-Saxon England and some periods in the Middle Ages. For law and custom regarding land have slowly allowed private landowners to gain more and more 'rights', while evading more and more duties. Especially has the duty to pay the full rent of land to the community fallen into neglect with the removal of land taxes and the introduction of taxes upon labour and goods. Land markets, 'investment' in land, so called capital gains from land, land speculation, land dereliction, land spoliation have all become commonplaces of our society. Only perhaps the last two have been seriously criticised in recent times, but all of them deny economic freedom. Access to land is an utter necessity for everyone at all times. If it is denied, or granted on unjust terms, people are at the mercy of those who so abuse their power. Freedom is a creature of justice, both in the civil and economic spheres. It is high time that we ask ourselves the question, 'What is the justice from which flows economic freedom?' That is the great question of our day for economists, not questions of how to produce more and more, how to get rich, or how to predict the next few months' share prices.

Green Issues

The recent prominence given to green issues by politicians and the media raises the question of how 'green' the reformed economy would be. This has been touched upon in relation to external economies and diseconomies (see Chapter 17). Transport, as probably the most polluting industry, however, requires a rather different analysis. Green remedies for transport pollution, such as higher fuel taxes or road pricing, tend to take the existing need for transport services for granted. But the distribution of industry and population, both now and in the future, is the result of the economic conditions that this book examines. In particular, land enclosure remains as the principal determinant. People and industries are concentrated in areas where rent of land is high. Firms are rent-seeking. Workers must be housed within reach of firms. Thus transport systems have developed especially to serve densely populated urban areas. Motorways, railways and aircraft transport people, raw materials and finished goods mainly to and from and within these industrial and commercial areas. More and more people commute, with some now 'reverse commuting', for example from west London to firms on the M4 corridor. More and more supermarket lorries traverse the country from national depots to out-of-city stores.

All this is the outcome of a 'free' internal market for labour, capital and products. But also of a 'free' land market. How would the distribution of firms and population change if land itself were really free? Were the extensive and intensive margins of production free of any charges, especially of scarcity rent and taxation, the location of firms, and with them of population, would be profoundly different. Firstly, the rent profile would be much less polarized between very high urban rents and low rural ones. Secondly, land would not be held out of use for speculative reasons, if private rent were not available. Thirdly, monopolies and oligopolies would no longer dominate markets like retailing, oil and chemicals. Firms would locate according to the economic advantages of geography, access to labour, markets, commercial services and transport facilities, just as they do now. The difference would be that their choice would not be distorted by the very severe restriction of land supply and by taxation charged on production. Labour and capital would no longer be driven into employment as appendages of very large companies with many sites, but would be free to establish themselves independently wherever a site was available at a suitable, even nil, rent. Rent-seeking would no longer be a motive. There is every likelihood that in such conditions the volume of polluting transport, both of people and goods, would be greatly reduced. Would farm produce be transported long distances to food processing plants and then to supermarkets? Would commercial centers require armies of commuting office workers to unravel the complexities of 'capitalist' organization? Would huge manufacturing firms still make mass, standardized products, maintained by heavy advertising and predatory 'competition'?

What of other green issues besides transport? A free land economy would turn naturally to the use of raw materials made available without scarcity rent and taxation. Agriculture, forestry and mining would fulfill once more their prime function as sources of materials. The enormous areas of land in the UK held out of production and settlement, except as estates for private use, such as hunting and shooting, would be redeemed for the whole community, since the present landlords would be unable to pay a full rent for such land. The Scottish Highlands, for example, could be restored to their rightful place as the home of a thriving population, undoing the gross injustice of 250 years. Cornish tin mines and Welsh gold mines, unburdened by taxes, might return to production. Free companies of coal miners might work the currently monopolised coalfields. Consider also a modern industry like chemicals. Would the giant chemical oligopolies continue to produce an immense output of technologically-based packaging, household goods, medicines and so on, if natural materials were readily and cheaply available? It would not require ingenious adjustments of the tax system and complicated regulations to eliminate wasteful and harmful materials, if natural resources i.e.land were free.

Yet could it not be argued that only private ownership of land encourages people to care for it, to avoid its pollution and neglect? Obviously some landlords take good care of their land, but how many do not, especially in cities? Payment of a full rent leaves a tenant in full control of his land. Security of tenure is the key to private care of the land, not claiming rent from it for doing nothing. Indeed landlordism encourages pollution and neglect by tenants, as any observer of landlord rented property may observe. Similarly workers, who in free association occupy productive sites, have a very much stronger interest in caring for it than do present-day employees, whose interest may not extend greatly beyond the weekly pay packet.

Finally, if land were to be recognized as the property of the whole community to be distributed and used as justice and need determine, a general duty of care might in time replace that of regarding only one bit, if any, as worth the trouble. Respect for land discourages spoliation of it more than does the idea of exploitation or holding it for 'capital' gains. The British may never aspire to the North American Indians' belief in the land as sacred, but free land might inspire in them a finer view of it than has the landlordism of past centuries.

A Practical Ideal

Is the vision of a free economy here presented merely a hopelessly idealistic and simplistic model, unsuited to modern conditions and contemporary attitudes and beliefs? Can people really refrain from the desire to own land unconditionally, to call it mine and demand a rent for its use? Can credit really be available only for production and not for land 'investment' and for consumption goods and services? Do we even want an economy where fulfillment and wealth are available from work and not from speculation, inheritance or mere chance? How are we to cast off the apparent limitations of such superfluous ideas as 'my land' or 'my security'?

It is wildly optimistic to think that such ideas can be easily over-turned in societies that have become accustomed to them. Yet to reject an ideal because its complete attainment is not foreseeable is naive. Bernard Shaw criticised Christianity on the grounds that he had never come across a Christian. He missed the point. He met people striving to be Christians, people living by the standards of Christ, though falling short of them. An economic ideal may not be fully achievable; but any move in its direction may improve matters. Any step towards freedom makes one freer. Any slackening of the bonds reduces the tension and the pain. The principle of free trade, for example, has not been fully realised, as the World Trade Organisation bears witness, but since Adam Smith and David Ricardo first wrote, there have been immensely beneficial advances towards it. To pay even some of the rent of land as public revenue, with a corresponding fall in tax on labour, would improve economic performance. To shift even some bank credit from land 'investment' to productive capital would raise economic growth. A true ideal is immensely practical. Indeed little else is.

CHAPTER 25

The Reformed Economy and World Trade

W HAT PLACE would such a profoundly reformed economy have in the world economy? Could it survive? Would it excel? How much would it trade with other countries? What would happen to its currency, 'capital' market and interest rate?

Comparative Advantage in the Reformed Economy

Let us assume that this economy has its own currency and that there is a floating exchange rate regime and a fair degree of free trade in world markets. We are not dealing with any transitional problems from the present bound economy to the free one envisaged, but with whether such an economy, once in existence, is viable internationally.[1] There can be little doubt that, at least unilaterally, the Ricardian ideal of free trade would operate. In the reformed economy the principle of comparative advantage is based upon underlying real factor opportunity costs and not upon opportunity costs distorted by the perversions of the present system. Prices of goods and services within the new economy are proportional to labour inputs at the intensive and extensive margins of production (see Chapter 14). Scarcity rent and taxes assessed on labour no longer distort them. Moreover, quantity and, especially, quality of production are greater. At the same time monopolistic and oligopolistic aspects of firms and markets have largely disappeared (except for natural monopolies). Price mark-ups caused by these, as well as the accompanying limitations of output, are eliminated. The combined effect of these features is to reduce costs, measured at purchasing power parity exchange rates, when compared with those of 'unreformed' foreign economies. Hence exports of the reformed economy increase and imports diminish. It acquires an export surplus, which tends to strengthen its currency.

1 Transitional problems are discussed in Chapter 27.

The trade pattern, of course, changes also. Money costs based on opportunity costs of labour lead to a switch from some goods and services previously cheaper in money prices towards those now cheaper because free from monopoly mark-ups, oligopoly, high interest charges and taxes on labour. Hence the pattern of trade now shows greater specialization in the latter and perhaps greater imports of the former. Underlying natural advantages of land and labour come to the fore, no longer suppressed by barriers to land use, lack of credit and inhibition of the creativity of labour.

Adjustment by the reformed economy to changes in prices and in other conditions, and to such changes in world economies, is much easier than previously. Firms of associated workers adapt to such changes by flexible wages (see Chapter 24, pp.294-7), and can readily re-site and re-equip, if necessary, when land and capital are freely accessible on easy terms. Most adaption, in any circumstances, takes place at intensive and extensive margins of production, and the radical freeing of conditions there is the hallmark of the reformed economy. Changes in the general price level lead to a corresponding rise or fall in the economy's exchange rate, with effects on export/import prices and volumes dependent upon elasticities of demand, as at present. However, inflation is no longer endemic (see pp.292-7). Where inflation prevails abroad, the reformed economy finds a ready market for exports and fewer imports, further strengthening its currency.

International 'Capital' Movements

What then of the crucial area of the international capital market? To observe that this is a gross misnomer largely answers the question. A real capital market is a market in capital goods. The so-called capital market is mainly a market in international loans and purchases of foreign currencies. Most of it has little to do with international trade and *a fortiori* trade in capital goods. The reformed economy has a permanently very low interest rate. Therefore it attracts no foreign loans, nor movements of currency concerned with a future rise in interest rates. Whether there is a 'capital exodus' is a transitional problem only. Foreign loans are not required. The needs for investment in capital goods are met fully by bank advances and domestic saving. There is no need for loans or currency movements motivated by speculation. Let the speculators depart, bag and baggage! The reformed economy's exchange rate is related solely to its productiveness and its ability to trade goods and services in world markets. May not ambitious bankers seek to make advances abroad and savers to 'invest' abroad at high interest rates? Such bankers deny their proper role of advancing money for productive enterprise, but if they so choose then they take the risk commensurate with the interest rate they receive. Recent experience suggests that foreign lending is not the road to fortune. However, the government might even decide to deny a licence for domestic banking to banks who look to make profits from lending abroad at interest, rather than to earning a living from creating credit for domestic investment. As for savers, they similarly face risks in 'investing' abroad, but if they take them then the reformed economy receives extra income from abroad, which in the long term 'compensates' the exchange rate for its initial loss of 'capital' A pension purchased abroad simply means that the foreign economy pays an income which, discounted at its own interest rate, is just equal to the value of the capital sum received. In other words, the 'capital' outflow has no real impact on either economy.

Foreign 'Investment'

Nevertheless there are at present more substantial movements of 'capital' into and out of the economy in the form of direct 'investment' in firms, e.g. by buying shares, perhaps a controlling interest, in foreign companies. This inward and outward 'investment' is more or less universally encouraged by economists and politicians. Yet what does it really mean? It represents merely the purchase of claims of dividends and interest against domestic firms. Such claims, especially at rates of interest set by a restricted money supply, are a burden on industry. Where new shares or bonds are purchased for a new enterprise to buy actual capital goods, of course, there is rather more sense in the transaction, though it then burdens future production with similar charges. All such foreign 'investment' is, however, no more than a poor substitute for bank advances at the supply price of money to be repaid out of future production. Firms would have no need for expensive foreign loans. Inward investment would have no point, not least for the foreign investor whose return would only match that of the domestic banker. Thus the economy would be free both from excessive charges and from the long-term strategic and political implications of foreign control. No committee of directors in Paris, Frankfurt or New York could close down a British factory and relocate in South Korea. Nor could an elderly widow in Bavaria be in the position to threaten the employment of British car workers in Longbridge or Cowley. As for the management and technical skills of foreign entrepreneurs, associations of free workers are seedbeds of productive abilities at all levels from manual work to high technology and intelligent and sympathetic management. Foreigners may be welcomed for their training and ability, but not on the back of so-called inward 'investment'. As for outward 'investment', why should an economy of autonomous groups of workers financed by banks and saving wish to send money abroad to finance foreign enterprise? Spare funds find a ready home in a dynamic, enterprising economy, where capital goods are owned by the labour that uses them. If some funds find their way overseas, they become a mere source of rentier income, like the 'investment' in a foreign pension. The return on investment in one's own firm is likely to be far more productive and satisfying.

If the exchange rate were fixed, which normally means that interest rates must conform to international rates in order to prevent massive movements of money to take advantage of interest differentials, the very low interest rate of the reformed economy would seem to imply a huge outflow of money. But, as argued above, genuine investment opportunities within the economy financed by bankers' advances make such 'hot money' dispensable. The economy functions perfectly well without it. If such movements force the currency to devalue, so much the better for trading prospects. Once again transitional problems, such as a large outflow of funds, must not be foisted upon the reformed economy once established. Since inflation is no longer a feature of the economy, the higher nominal return on money held abroad wherever inflation persists may amount to a negligible real return in any case. There is no reason, however, to conform to a fixed rate of exchange. A floating rate can become a true measure of relative goods prices, i.e. at more or less purchasing power parity, for an economy in which the opportunity for gain without work has been largely eliminated.

In the UK at present some privatised utilities, like gas, electricity and water companies, are foreign owned or controlled, particularly by French and German counterparts. This spurious 'free market' situation is nothing more than the purchase by foreigners of claims in the form of dividends and interest against vital domestic industries, most of which are natural monopolies. Strategic and political arguments for domestic control are yet stronger than in the case of competitive industries, as the utilities concerned deal in such essentials as water, power, transport, ports and so on. Public ownership is the simplest solution, but even public control in the form of watchdogs etc. is surely best exercised over domestic capital assets owned by domestic producers. Needless to say, the sites of such utilities, most of whose activities are intimately related to land, are no longer available for private ownership in the reformed economy, whether domestic or foreign. Indeed a major incentive to foreign 'investors' is thereby removed. Who would buy a foreign gas pipeline or airport or railway without receiving the rent of the land on which they operate and with no prospect of realising any land values? Only people interested in making an income from working in the industry, not from 'investing' in it.

The Reformed Economy as Exemplar

The condition of the reformed economy vis-a-vis its international partners is salutary. It competes under favourable conditions in world markets. It is not beset by international flows of 'investment' and speculative funds. Its currency is strong and can fluctuate in response to domestic or exogenous shocks without seriously disturbing the economy, for prices and wages are flexible in both directions. Indeed its success in promoting the welfare and prosperity of its citizens may make it a leader in world affairs and an object of economic emulation. Were other countries to make the same reforms, so much the better for all concerned. Just as Britain led the world in the nineteenth century into an era of free trade, so it may lead it into a greater era of broader and deeper economic freedom. So, too, might any national economy which underwent sufficiently profound reforms to its systems of land tenure, banking and taxation.

CHAPTER 26

Business Cycles

THE PHENOMENON of business cycles in modern economies has generated a huge volume of factual and explanatory literature without much consensus on the causes of cycles. Nevertheless there is some agreement on what features of the economy play a part in generating them. Perhaps the most obvious of these are time lags. Consumption expenditure may respond to the income of a previous time period; output may respond to sales of a previous period; stocks may rise or fall according to expectations of future market conditions. In particular, the full effects on output of investment expenditure are only experienced in future periods as the multiplier process works itself out, and moreover the response of investment itself to income changes is lagged. The latter relationship of I to RNI – the accelerator effect, whereby I adjusts to changes in RNI in previous time periods – combines with the multiplier to generate cycles. A simple model, where the government and foreign sectors are treated as constants, creates cycles when consumption and investment are given certain values:[1]

and
$$C_t = a0 + a1\ Y_t \quad \text{[with } 0 < a1 < 1\text{]}$$
$$I_t = b0 + b1\ (Y_t - Y_{t-1}) \quad \text{[with } b1 > 0\text{]}$$

Successive time periods are represented by $t - 1$, t etc. Consumption consists of a constant figure (a0), plus a linear function (a1) of RNI $(= Y)$, which equals MPC. Investment has a constant (b0), plus a linear function (b1) of the change in RNI, which is an accelerator coefficient. A difference equation is generated, which yields perpetual cycles when $a1 + 2b1 = 1$. Under other values for a1 and b1 damped or explosive oscillations occur. Generally, the greater the responsiveness of C and I to RNI the more the oscillations tend towards being explosive.

1 See M. Burda and C. Wyplosz, *Macroeconomics*, OUP, 1997, p.364.

Oscillations in a real economy have upper and lower limits. The former occurs as real resources are stretched to capacity: labour and capital are fully employed and available land is all in use, at which point any rise in output must come to a stop, with negative accelerator effects on I. The latter occurs when new or additional I has become zero and replacement I falls to a level where existing capital is insufficient to maintain the desired capital/output ratio. Firms then increase replacement I, which turns the cycle into an upward phase.

Such cyclical tendencies may be much enhanced by random shocks. Demand shocks include changes in the money supply, newly optimistic or pessimistic expectations, fiscal policy changes and shifts in export or import demand. Supply shocks include changes in prices, including import prices, new wage rates or factor taxes, new technology improving productivity or other productivity changes from, for example, better industrial organisation or management. Random shocks may trigger cycles by moving the economy away from an equilibrium trend or may exaggerate or dampen existing oscillations.[2] There are, no doubt, a thousand natural shocks that the economy is heir to.

If time lags, the multiplier-accelerator relationship and random shocks are applied to the AD/AS model of the economy, cycles are generated whereby the equilibrium price level and RNI at the intersection of AS and AD oscillate. The mathematics of this involves a system of linear difference equations.[3] However, a diagrammatic example may put flesh on the algebraic bones.[4]

In Diagram 125 a random demand shock (AD1 to AD2) shifts RNI from A to B. A time-lagged response of wages moving upwards to match higher prices shifts AS1 to AS2, towards a new equilibrium at C. Such inflation depends upon an accommodating growth in MS, allowing AD to reach AD3. A further lagged rise in wage costs shifts AS to AS3 with equilibrium at D. Falling output leads to revision downwards of investment and a multiplied fall in AD. Once more AS gives a lagged response, this time downwards, so that an anticlockwise loop is completed. This amounts to oscillations of RNI and prices, firstly upwards, then downwards, with prices lagging behind RNI. Empirical evidence tends to conform to such a model in several cases.[5]

2 See Burda & Wyplosz, *ibid.*, pp.365-7.
3 One such model is demonstrated in Burda and Wyplosz, *ibid.*, pp.383-4.
4 Burda and Wyplosz *ibid.*, p.368.
5 Burda and Wyplosz, *ibid.*, pp.369-70.

DIAGRAM 125

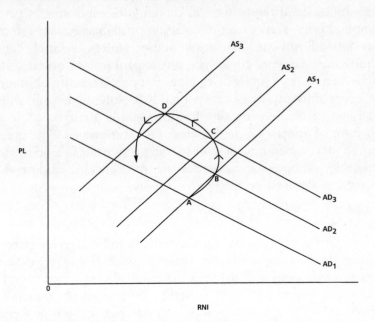

Such business cycles may occur in any economy. The serious question is why are their effects usually so harmful. Once again it is by identifying the role of land in the economy that this can be answered. On the one hand, the existing system of unrestrained land ownership is primarily responsible for the price rigidity that distorts the natural responses of the economy to cyclical movements (see pp.294-7); on the other hand, a so-called free market in land superimposes upon cycles a malignant series of consequences.

Price Flexibility
Complete price flexibility in both final goods and factor markets would render cycles more or less harmless.[6] Even without flexible price changes, if swings in output could be immediately matched by swings in income, there would be no major problem beyond the actual change in living standards. In no real economy, however, is this a possibility, since swings in total output are sure to be accompanied by changes in the composition of output. Shocks are discriminatory, because demand or supply shocks occur in relation to particular consumers or

---

6 Such an idea underlies the real business cycle theories, though their unrealistic assumptions, especially about the labour market, nullify their value.

producers. The multiplier/accelerator effect alone obviously has a relatively more significant effect on capital goods industries than on consumption ones. Hence accommodating price changes are essential for a smooth adjustment to swings in output. Unless all supply curves were horizontal, i.e. perfectly elastic, any expansion or contraction of output is certain to require a change in price, and any shift of a supply curve must move price up or down along a demand curve. If, however, prices are generally flexible, there is a correction in the composition of output as the business cycle progresses. The greater the degree of competition, of course, the greater the flexibility, since monopolistic/oligopolistic industries are price-making and tend to react slowly to demand or supply side variations.

Factor Markets

Price flexibility in final goods markets reduces the malignant effect of cycles, but there remains the key issue of price flexibility in factor markets. Capital goods industries, as suggested above, may respond by adjustments in capital goods prices and by expansions or contractions of supply, even though this process is itself part of the generating mechanism in a cycle.[7] Hence it is upon labour and land markets that attention must be focussed. Needless to say, modern economists deal extensively with the former and neglect the latter, but in this case at least their preoccupation with labour and wages is not entirely ill-judged. As Keynes emphasised, the wage rate is sticky, especially down-wards. What tends to happen to labour in the course of a cycle is that during the upturn the real wage rate rises somewhat (wage rates are mildly pro-cyclical), but more work is obtained from the existing employed workers by means of longer hours and overtime rates. Some extra employment is created. In a downturn the real wage rate falls slightly and workers are put off, though some labour 'hoarding' takes place in anticipation of a future upturn in the cycle. Hence the level of employment moves pro-cyclically with a time-lag, whilst the real wage rate is oscillating slightly around a general level of wage rates. This general level cannot fall significantly without throwing workers into poverty.[8] Of course, a large fall in the wage rate, were it possible, would not resolve the problem of unemployment in any case, since

---

7 The role of capital goods industries may be both exogenous and endogenous in the cycle.

8 This fact is nowadays obscured by the huge 'poor relief' of the Welfare State, whose payments are called, somewhat euphemistically, a 'social wage'. The Welfare State probably tends to lower the general level of real wages actually demanded, so that any large fall in a recession does indeed impoverish workers.

MPC would fall as income was transferred from wages to profits, thus reducing equilibrium RNI.

Since wage rates then are only slightly pro-cyclical, profits are considerably so. The wage share (as distinct from wage rate) in RNI is slightly counter-cyclical.[9] This means that in an upturn most firms are thriving, but that a downturn has a powerfully adverse effect on their fortunes. Profits are the residue after wages, interest, taxes and landlords' rent have been paid out of value added. Since all four of these claims, except taxes to some degree, are sticky downwards, then the residual profits bear a far more than proportional burden when trade is poor. Interest is a fixed charge. Taxes fall a little in so far as corporations tax and sales taxes are reduced, but the burden of labour taxes on firms increases when employment and the wage rate fall less than proportionately to turnover. Landlords' rent is only usually adjusted when leases fall due. Hence a recession cuts a swathe through firms rendered marginal by falling business. At the intensive and extensive margins firms can no longer pay the prevailing wage rates. Unemployment rises, even while workers retained in employment may not be a great deal worse off. Thus the business cycle does not merely involve all alike in minor adjustments of output and income, but causes major adjustments of entrepreneurship and employment. The well-intentioned aims of trade unions to protect their members may only exaggerate this tendency by maintaining the living standards of the employed, whilst enlarging the pool of unemployed.

Structure of Industry

Behind this dismal scenario lies the structure of modern industry. With the great majority of the work force employed by firms which themselves are dependent for their survival upon residual profits, the outcome during business cycles is inevitable. Whether wages are very sticky downwards or not, unemployment rises in a downturn. A natural adjustment to cyclical movements by a smooth adjustment of wages as the price of labour is ruled out. Output and final goods' prices are separated artificially from wages as the reward of the factor which actively produces them. In a free economy the reward of labour is the yield of labour; wages and both the quantity and price of its output are directly related. Once that nexus is broken there is trouble.

What is responsible for an industrial structure separating labour from its natural reward? Why are workers not proprietors of the firms

9 See Lipsey and Chrystal, Figure 43.4, p.845.

in which they work, so that as output and prices vary their incomes are synchronised with the variations? Enough perhaps has been said on this subject, but it is necessary to add that this is in no way just a matter of explaining the historical evolution of the economy towards this unfortunate state of affairs. The real issue is why, at the present time, workers are in the situation of being paid rigid real wages by firms dependent on risky residual profits. The answer is that private landlords are even now collecting rent of land and thereby both squeezing profits and forcing wages down to a minimum general level. The imposition of taxes on labour completes the process whereby the vital intensive and extensive margins of production are severely restricted. In short, the structure of industry is determined right now by the present acceptance of both landlords' claims on the natural source of public revenue and the misguided transference of the burden of that revenue onto labour. Provision of credit for industry inevitably follows a path set by these conditions. Business cycles in themselves need not lead to the collapse of firms and to heavy unemployment. A solution rendering cycles more or less harmless is obvious.

Disruptive Effect of Land Market

The land issue then lies at the root of the difficulties that cycles create when factor prices are inflexible. However, it has a second malignant role to play in the cyclical process. This time it is the land market which upsets the normal progression of a business cycle. If land is bought and sold at constant prices, allowing of course for huge differentials between sites, there is no impact on the cycle, since land is simply changing hands from one owner or leaseholder to another. As a recovery gets under way, however, the price of land tends to rise. If the extra demand for land were financed entirely out of the circular flow, i.e. by savings, this would have a depressing effect, for it would amount to extra withdrawals (assuming that sellers of land have a much lower MPC than the average). Since this is extremely unlikely, the extra demand must flow from bank advances, which generally serve to push up prices, but in particular land prices. Land as a factor of production becomes more expensive. Firms must either pay higher rents to landlords – there will be lags caused by the terms of leases – or pay higher 'capital' costs for land, usually by borrowing at annual charges of interest and repayment of principal. Either way firms are burdened with higher land costs and perhaps higher interest costs as well. Some firms may become highly geared i.e. their ratio of fixed debt to total value of the enterprise is high. All this squeezes profits.

Nevertheless, the combination of a rising land market, especially as some firms' own freeholds, and the rising prices usually attendant upon the recovery phase and enhanced by extra bank advances, help to promote optimism. Recovery continues and even accelerates. Nemesis, however, cannot be evaded. The greater the real recovery of output and the greater the optimism of firms, the more buoyant the demand for land. Rising land prices draw in speculative funds, which finance purchases of land to be held out of use, or in underused employment, such as car parks in city centres, in order to make future gains in land value. Land withheld from its best, or from any, use reduces land supply. Land prices rise faster than demand for use would warrant. Productive firms are forced to pay even more for their land. Investors may even sense that profits are being squeezed unduly and sell shares and bonds in order to buy land as a safeguard. Land prices rise further. Such a process cannot continue very long. Firms may draw upon credit to cover their increasing cash flow and profit margin problems, but interest charges rise and business optimism falters. They cannot cut wages, especially as production has expanded and unemployment is relatively low. Taxes remain the same, or even rise if the government follows an anti-cyclical fiscal policy, perhaps with built-in stabilisers like higher marginal tax rates. Sooner or later profits collapse for some firms. Then credit contraction sets in. Banks call in advances; firms offer less trade credit. Closures of firms rapidly lead to a fall in demand for intermediate goods and for labour. The process of the downturn is familiar enough. The largely hidden movement of land prices that intensifies it is not so familiar.

In a recession land prices fall, but not usually by enough to promote a quick recovery, because business pessimism may lead to continued 'investment' in land as a long-term asset. However, sooner or later rents are reduced to a point where firms are relieved of an excessive burden and may revive. This whole explanation, of recovery and recession, downturn, or crisis, and upturn, related to the land market in no way replaces or undermines those explanations which rest upon time-lags, multiplier/accelerator models, upper and lower limits and the rest. What it does is to explain further both the intensity and the virulence of business cycles in modern economies. Land speculation, especially, makes the downturn abrupt and damaging and may retard the upturn.

Expectations

There is indeed a further way of understanding the peculiar character of the land market here. Expectations about the future state of the economy are inherent in any developed society, and indeed are in the nature of entrepreneurship and of banking. How forecasting the future affects the buying and selling of assets, however, depends on what the law permits and on the precise characteristics of the asset. Labour cannot be bought for future use, except in a slave economy, and to a minor extent through contracts such as those used by football clubs and media companies. Moreover, extra demand for labour meets a slightly elastic work force supply. Firms may hoard labour, but not for long. In short, there is no real speculative demand, or price, for labour. Extra demand for capital meets a fairly elastic capital goods supply. Only in the short run can capital goods prices rise unduly.

What of financial assets, i.e. bonds in the Keynesian sense of all interest or dividend bearing claims? Here, of course, there is much speculative buying and selling, and bond prices may rise a long way above their 'real' value based on the productive potential of firms. Yet a speculative rise in such prices does not directly burden industry with a current charge. As bond prices rise, yields fall; the current charge is not a function of the 'capital' price. The central bank may intervene, however, by raising interest rates in order to choke off the speculative rise in the bond market. In this case, of course, firms are burdened with higher interest rates. Thus excessive buying of financial assets may indirectly damage productive enterprises through central bank action to inhibit the excess. It is the structure of firms, whereby they are dependent upon share and bondholders for their finance, that allows this constriction. Obviously the present credit system plays a part also.

Speculation in land, by contrast, has a more direct power to damage industry. To buy land for its future value limits present production. The land itself is needed now, in the present. Without it production is impossible. If a claim upon its future production or value is allowed, then its price rises and the current period must bear the charge. Either rent charges go up or firms must pay more in advance by buying freehold land or leases. Capital goods can be produced; the elements are given by God or by nature. Claims upon the former influence their supply; claims upon the latter only raise their price and restrict their use. Yet if there is a land market, people cannot be prevented from buying land with an eye to the future. Indeed, all land purchases are in some sense looking forward beyond present consumption. Banks could be restricted, with difficulty, in giving advances for land purchase, but the simple solution is to eliminate the land market by eliminating land values themselves. If land is not bought, it is not an object of speculation.[10]

Effect of Housing Land Market

A secondary effect of the land market upon business cycles operates via the housing market, and has become a significant feature of cycles in recent times. Real prices for house land tend to be pro-cyclical, though generally on a continuous upward trend. In so far as they are constant, then claims are simply being exchanged without effect on the cycle, but as before if land prices are rising, and bank advances finance the rise, there is an inflationary impulse in the economy. Workers buying or renting houses must pay more, and therefore pressure is put upon wage claims to maintain real wage rates. Whether firms can pass on such wage increases in higher final prices depends on the central bank's readiness to accommodate inflation with a greater money supply. As a recovery gets into its stride, house land prices may contain a speculative element, partly through direct speculation in housing land by developers, building firms who hold land banks, landlords and owner-occupiers who plan to 'trade-up', and partly by transference from speculative demand for productive land, since the land market is a single market, even if all sites are unique and rents have differentials. The phenomenon of rapidly rising house land prices is likely either to push up interest rates via the mortgage market or induce the central bank to put them up. Either way the recovery is slowed down or halted. Speculation in housing land, of course, also feeds back into the industrial land market, accelerating the damaging effect on production of a rise in rents and land prices there.

A further baneful consequence, becoming evident especially in urban areas, is the inability of workers to afford city housing and thus the emergence of a shortage of labour, especially in lower paid jobs in public services, transport and so on. This is yet another form of the harm caused by a land market, particularly when speculation in land prices transforms expected future gains into current charges on production. Shortage of labour results from the inability of firms or public authorities to pay the higher wages needed for higher house land

10 See F. Harrison, *The Power in the Land*, esp. Chapter 5, Shepheard-Walwyn, London, 1983, for evidence of the influence of land speculation.

prices. In effect, land prices above those commensurate with current production are once again hindering or stopping recovery. The 'housing boom' has become a leading feature – in both senses of the term – of business cycles, and a major target for central bank action in the form of high interest rates, even though these harm production as much or more than they do house-owners.[11]

11 The example of the Japanese economy's collapse in the 1970s following land speculation is examined in F. Harrison, *ibid.*, Chapter 12.

PART SEVEN

Conclusions

CHAPTER 27

Practical Problems of Rent as Public Revenue

THE ABOVE exposition has attempted to keep to issues that can be dealt with by economic analysis and has sought to avoid normative aspects, though the author's stance on some of these is no doubt evident. There remain to be considered various practical concerns about the collection of rent of land as public revenue, several of which involve explicit moral judgments.

Property in Land

Most obviously there is the view that land is legitimately owned by individuals, and that public collection of rent infringes valid property rights; in short that 'my land' is a fundamental principle of social life and individual liberty depends upon it. In what then does property in land consist? Essentially four rights might be claimed: to use the land, to exchange, give or bequeath it, to spoil or destroy it, and to receive rent from it. To use land must always be a basic right of individuals or groups. Security of tenure to enable use for production or for homes cannot be denied as a right in any reasonable society. Indeed, we may well ask why many people in present day societies, including the UK, do not have it. How many can be evicted by a landlord or building society at short notice? How many more can be evicted from their workplace at even shorter notice?

The right to exchange, give or bequeath land is less certain. What exactly is being transferred? Is it the right of use – in which case should an existing holder necessarily determine who should succeed him in the use, especially after he has died? Family businesses and houses raise searching questions here, to which society may give varied rational responses. As to any supposed right to spoil or even destroy land, there can be no justification for this, though it is permitted today in so far as land is allowed to fall into neglect and is sometimes polluted.

The central issue in modern conditions, however, remains the right to receive the rent of land. It is worthy of emphasis that this right is definitely separable from others. 'My land' does not imply an inalienable right to receive rent, even if – as Wittgenstein pointed out – it must involve rights to something![1] Indisputable security of tenure is perfectly compatible with no private receipt of rent. What grounds can there be for rent to be owned by individuals? Ownership of anything can only really rest upon rights acquired by work, exchange, gift or inheritance. Rent is certainly not attributable to the work of an individual or group of individuals; it arises from natural features of land and the presence and work of the community. How then can it be given in exchange, or as a gift or by inheritance, by one individual, family or group to another? Such a transference amounts to someone with a bad title passing to someone else the apparent right to future values created by the community. Work is the only original foundation for property in things, as John Locke explained,[2] and yet today the State confiscates property acquired from work by a whole range of taxes, whilst leaving untouched property claims that could never have been so derived. Far from landowners having a right to rent, they have indeed a duty to pay rent to the community. Were 'my land' to comprehend such a duty it would become no longer a title of greed, but a title of responsible tenure.

Land Acquired by Exchange

Yet many voices are raised against such arguments. In particular, there is the cry 'what about titles to land acquired for value?' If someone has given money or other property in exchange for land, surely he or she should not be deprived of what gives the land its principal value, namely its power to receive rent? Why should land purchasers be disappropriated when purchasers of other assets are not? Part of the answer to this lies in the fact that existing taxes affect property rights in all kinds of ways. No owner of an asset can claim any special immunity from government action on behalf of the community, for example, in changing a tax rate, unless he proves some absolute or inalienable right over it. Landowners have a much weaker case to such a right than do owners of most other assets, especially where these are acquired by work. More importantly, the claim to anything received in

1 N Malcolm, *Ludwig Wittgenstein, A Memoir*, OUP, 1962, p.31-2
2 John Locke, *Two Treatises of Civil Government*, J.M. Dent, 1962, Chapter V

exchange for value given depends upon the validity of the title of the seller. A bad title cannot usually be passed on in law, and even less so in morality. Does any seller of the right to rent of land have a good title, since he is selling the community's future right to the rent it creates? The claim of purchasers of land to land values is analogous to the claim of a purchaser of slaves to the slave's value. Neither the labour of one's fellow men, nor the land on which they need to live and work, are the proper subject of private claims to value. A man or woman may be employed in return for wages, and land may be used in return for rent.

The wages and rent should go to those who contribute the labour and the land value respectively i.e. the worker on one hand and the community on the other. It has been well said that the problem is not that some people have to pay rent, but that some people, i.e. land-owners, do not pay it.

Mortgagee's Responsibility

A peculiar problem of modern economies, though one familiar even to Solon in the sixth century BC, is the vast extent of land purchases on mortgage.[3] House buyers, especially, find themselves acquiring high land values and mortgages of up to 100% of the value. Were rent to be collected by the community, house owners would have to bear the double cost of paying rent on the annual land value and mortgage repayments with interest. More critically, land values would fall *pari passu* with the rent charge. Owners would find their land worth less than the share of the mortage attributable to the land, so that they might well experience negative equity. If all rent were so collected, land values would fall to zero, thus perhaps ruining an owner with an out-standing mortgage.

Would this be fair? On the strictest understanding of the question of who legally owns the land it would be just, but justice demands moderation in such cases. A gradual introduction of the new system is essential, as it is on other grounds. Moreover, surely the mortgagee, i.e. the lender, should bear part of the loss, on the grounds that he lent knowingly for the purpose of 'investing' in land. If payments to the mortgagee were reduced proportionately with the fall in land values, then the mortage debts would fall correspondingly in value as assets. This means that building societies and other lenders, including depositers and shareholders, would bear 'capital' losses, thus easing the

---

3 Solon 'uprooted the mortgage stones that everywhere were planted, and freed the fields that were enslaved before' Plutarch, *The Rise and Fall of Athens*, trans. I. Scott-Kilvert, Penguin, 1976, p.57.

burden on the mortgagor. A gradual innovation would enable them to accommodate this. However, such an equitable arrangement is a matter for reasonable debate.

Who is Better Off?

Apart from moral questions concerning the rights and duties of property in land, others are raised by the prospect of the public collection of rent. In today's circumstances of a 'property owning democracy' would not a lot of people, even a majority be worse off? Every home-owner would face a new 'tax' bill – for the annual value of the land on which his or her house is built. There are several answers to this. Firstly, an essential concomitant of rent becoming public revenue is that it replaces existing taxes. If it does not, but becomes merely an additional tax, then the total burden of taxes becomes unbearable. However, not only could it replace other taxes; at the same time the total yield of public revenue could be less, since at present much tax revenue is required for purposes that the present economic system necessitates. The 'reformed economy' needs no Welfare State beyond public provision for those genuinely unable to support themselves, such as the sick and the aged, and even these might be supported to some extent by the greater prosperity of families. Unemployment benefit, for example, becomes unnecessary when the causes of unemployment are removed. Moreover, how many house owners today would be worse off if they paid over the annual value of their land, but were relieved of all income tax, NHI, VAT, petrol tax and the rest?

Secondly, the removal of taxes on marginal enterprise and work, the elimination of scarcity rent paid by firms and the provision of very cheap credit for productive capital would release production from artificial constraint and empower a great rise in prosperity. The increase in output would not be maldistributed amongst the present multifarious claimants – landlords, land speculators, money lenders, shareholders, monopolists, tax collectors and, last of all, workers – but would be received only by those who contributed by work to produce it, on one hand, and those – the community itself – whose presence and public enterprise had created the rent, on the other. Justice yields a greater harvest and also apportions the fruits more equitably.

Yet more important than the material rewards of greater output of goods and services would be the profound improvement in the condition of people freed from the treadmill of modern employment. Most men and women would have the opportunity to be self-employed or to work in partnerships or in larger organisations where they would be principals and not employees. For land and credit would be available only on the conditions of paying rent to the public authority, which would be nil on marginal land, maintaining land properly and paying for bank advances at their supply price. Only those who freely chose to be employed would be so, and they could become self-employed as an alternative, subject to their terms of employment. The long established division of society between employers and employees would no longer be significant. Precisely how such a society would be organised cannot be foreseen, but faith in human nature offers the prospect of a society in which creativity and personal fulfillment would replace drudgery and frustration. Who then would be worse off?

Improvements to Land

Opponents of measures to collect rent as public revenue have usually made much of the question of improvements to land. They argue that if the rental value of improvements is not allowed to stay in private hands, then the work of improvement is not justly rewarded and little improvement will be undertaken. It is indeed important that improvements are rewarded and not deterred, but there are simple remedies for this apparent problem. The argument rests upon the assumption that improvements cannot be separated from the unimproved land. Physically, of course, this is often the case. Drainage, levelling, sinking of shafts, fertilising and so on merge with the earth and very soon can hardly be physically distinguished from its morphology and composition. Reason, however, is perfectly capable of separating in principle what may be inseparable in fact. The value of improvements can be separated from the value of unimproved land. Land values can be separated from improvement values. If work is undertaken on land, then the cost of the work in wages, materials and capital can be recorded, and is usually the subject of precise invoices of contracting firms. Such costs can be deducted from improved land values. Alternatively estate agents and other land valuation experts can compare improved land with similar unimproved land or use other professional devices in which they are well trained. If land changes hands, the record of improvements can change hands with it, although such records would no doubt be maintained by a public authority which collected land rents.

Expiry of time may seem to intensify the problem. Virtually all land has been improved in a modern economy. Are its land values therefore largely made up of improvement values? What one generation hands on to another is mainly a collective inheritance. Literacy, culture, a system of law and government are not individual bequests; they are society's gift to a new generation. So too are land improvements. If personal ancestors improved a particular piece of land – which is usually difficult enough to ascertain – why should their descendants gain a personal advantage? Perhaps the work of one generation may be credited to the next within a family, so that society may allow a son or daughter to deduct from 'his' or 'her' land values the value of improvements made by their parents, but even this is limited to the case where the same land is passed on, and that is an issue, raised above, which societies may answer in different ways. It may indeed be perfectly equitable that a son pays a rent for land improved by his father on the full improved value, since he did not himself do the work of improvement. Would fathers fail to improve land which they knew their sons would inherit merely because the annual value of the improvement would be paid as public revenue? Such questions merge into pedantry and cannot be allowed to influence the central and decisive one of whether society should be released from the bonds of economic slavery.

Effects on Agriculture

Since agriculture is the most land intensive industry, at least in terms of land area, there might appear to be reasons for fearing that public collection of rent would impose on it an unfair and insupportable charge. Nowhere is it clearer that such a measure in fact redresses a balance now destroyed by private rent and taxation. Agriculture very obviously varies in productivity with fertility and location. Agricultural rents and land values only prove the point. Yet the industry bears taxes and receives subsidies in a way completely unrelated to this. Marginal farms bear the cost of taxes on labour at the same rate as highly prosperous farms close to urban markets, even though the former are relatively more labour intensive and the latter capital intensive. Subsidies are paid more or less *pro rata* with output, rather than in relation to land fertility and location. Of course, where farmers have freeholds there is a shock-absorbing income safeguarding them from the system, unless they are on really marginal land where the freehold is almost valueless. Tenant farmers, on the other hand, are everywhere liable to be rendered precarious, for private rent leaves them only with sufficient, at the best, for costs, taxes and their earned income. The effects of the present land system in the UK are described by a Northumbrian farmer:

The UK is unique in maintaining a medieval system of land tenure in which so much power is held by the landlord. A three-yearly rent review procedure is invoked by landlords when farming profits might justify a rent increase, but ignored when farm profits fall. At these reviews, the tenant must pay the rent demanded or risk a potentially ruinous arbitration process which is often viewed by landlords as a hostile act which might result in unwelcome future repercussions for the tenant. Failure to agree leaves the tenant with the 'option' of losing everything: his business, his family home and his own as well as his childrens' place in the community ...

Aidan Harrison in The Times, p.20, 18 September 2002

Were all taxes and subsidies to be removed and rent received as public revenue, all farmers would be free to earn a fair income from their work, remitting only the differential benefits of soil, climate and location to the State. Those on marginal land would remit nothing, those on prime farming land a relatively high rent, though such rents would be small compared with inner city commercial rents. At the same time good farming land at present held out of use with a view to future gains in land values – on the edge of expanding cities, for example – would come into proper use. The nonsense of landowners, whether farmers themselves or not, receiving large windfall gains when development rights are granted would come to an end, since the annual value of land after planning permission would not be retained by the owner.

House Ownership

House ownership also raises some apparently perplexing issues. For many people houses seem to be their main form of wealth. For others, especially young people, houses are becoming increasingly beyond their means. Yet, once more, the real issue is land values. If rent is public revenue, land values are zero. House prices remain house prices. To buy a house is a matter of paying the supply price, which must always be close to the cost of construction, provided the building market is free from monopoly or other constraints. With no tax on labour or goods, construction costs fall. With higher general output and income from work, houses could be bought in a moderately short time period, if necessary with the help of bank advances. So long as advances are paid off at a similar rate to new advances, this would not be inflationary. Alternatively houses could be rented, without any heavy loading for land values. Security of tenure of houses would be greater in a society where tenure became the most important aspect in land use, and where excessive mortgages and interest payments were avoided.

Administration of Land

In the minds of people, like the British, familiar with conditions of civil freedom, for whom State interference is regarded with suspicion and individual responsibility highly valued, there may be resentment at the idea of public rent collection. It is crucial that the difference between outright public ownership of land and public rent is understood. Nationalisation of land, or State ownership, gives almost unlimited power to the State, as Lenin well knew when he made it Article 1 of the Soviet Constitution. Public rent gives the State only the right to the rent. It takes away from private landlords their *raison d'etre* as recipients of rent, and therefore leaves open questions of who determines tenure and maintenance of land. No longer would private landlords grant and deny access to land on payment of the bribe of private rent. There are more rational and more just ways of assigning usage. Since public rent would be paid for all land, except on marginal sites, those who offer the most would be granted tenure, subject to the community's right to use land for public or charitable purposes. But all such issues, the granting of individual tenure, the use of land for other purposes and so on, would be settled in accordance with the nation's own traditions, laws and customs.[4] Local government, democracy and, above all, the rule of law, would play at least as great a part as the State in its capacity as central government. There is a fine and ancient tradition of power administered by local communities in Britain, the revival of which would be hugely stimulated by the work of administering local land fairly. Nor would rent all need to be paid to central government, any more than taxes now are in the USA, for example. There are many possibilities here, all of which offer more grounds for individual freedom than does the present system of landlordism.

Transitional Problems

Finally there are a range of difficulties that any economy in transition from the present state of economic bondage to a reformed condition of economic freedom must face. So narrowly have the limits upon production, enterprise and fulfillment in the workplace been drawn that their removal is sure to render uncomfortable for a while the

---

4 An interesting contemporary example of how to discriminate between public and individual rights over land is found in the Constitution of Bahrain, which says that all natural resources belong to the State, but also protects citizens' property rights. If oil is discovered under someone's house, the State takes the oil and rehouses the citizen. Bahrain, in fact, has virtually no taxes. (I am indebted to the son of the Ambassador of the Gulf Corporation Council to the European Union for this example.)

prisoners released from the cave. Most present-day employees would not necessarily welcome the chance to become their own masters, exposed to responsibility, choice and fortune. The apparent security and regularity of employment might seem to be hazarded for the unpredictable autonomy of running one's own firm and dealing with one's own customers, suppliers and so on. A constant, if minimal, money wage may seem preferable to direct exposure to a market. Without a Welfare State some may feel too reliant upon their own and their colleagues' efforts, and unfamiliar with the decisions required by workers fully able to support themselves and their families out of their own earned income. Some too would regret the passing of unearned income and 'capital' gains from bonds and house values. The sense of well-being induced by the belief that one is growing richer by the mere passing of time, as the community in which one lives contributes steadily to a rise in house land values, is indeed soporific. The real cost of such apparent benefits has been overlooked for so long. For people to awaken from the dream of such a society, a dream that must end with a gentle awakening or a brutal shock, care is required.

The introduction of rent as public revenue needs to be a gradual process, taking many years before the full rent is paid. Thus the profound shifts in attitude and institutions that would follow would be slow and acceptable. As a portion of landlords' claims on output are paid to the State, other taxes would be reduced, so that marginal production would be relieved. As output rises, more rent would be collected and more tax relieved. Gradually workers would find the wage rate rising too, until their ability to finance their own firms were recognised, slightly at first but helped by a reduction in interest rates as bankers acknowledged their primary duty to assist industry and refrained from advancing money for land purchase.

Avoiding precipitate reform would also ease any problems in relation to foreign economies. Fears of a sudden shift to collecting rent publicly might engender a 'flight from the pound', as 'investors' take their claims abroad to safeguard their rights to unearned income. A slow transformation might lead to a less precipitous loss, as the consequent fall in the exchange rate stimulated production and cut imports. In the course of time prosperity might prove a greater magnet for foreign lenders than interest rates, though foreign 'capital' would not be needed in an economy with a proper banking sector. Foreign skill, enterprise and effort, however, would find a welcome.

Rapid changes would damage too the precarious conditions in the present economy of investment and pension funds, whose contributors' shares and premiums are 'invested' in modern industry and represent a very large proportion of its 'capital'. The market value of these 'investments' is heavily dependent upon the firms concerned receiving rent in the form of profits and landlords' claims. Removal of scarcity rent, of high interest rates, of private monopoly and the reduction of privately claimed differential rent as it became public revenue would greatly reduce the returns on such 'investments'. How then would the millions of pensioners and others receive what is due to them? The answer to this needs to refer once more to equity. What is due to them? To the extent that people have bought shares in land values the answer is, in strict justice, nothing. To the extent that they have lent money to productive industry, the answer is the return of what they have lent, plus a minimal amount for money lenders' interest. To the extent that as old or sick people they need help, the answer is whatever they need, not as a return but as a right. A gradual enforcement of public rent collection would make these distinctions. The land value element in such funds would disappear slowly and with it their return from land values. The productive industry element would get stronger and enable full repayment of this portion to be made. The State's duty to support the needy would be more clearly recognised with the development of proper public revenue and the reduction in unnecessary burdens upon it. Nevertheless, this transition could be fraught with danger if people remained ignorant of the real beneficent consequences of reform. An ignorant 'what do I lose or gain?' attitude destroys public faith. As Plato wrote, to reform a State already deeply embroiled in economic inequity requires freedom from avarice and a sense of justice.[5]

There are doubtless many more transitional and other problems associated with such far-reaching reforms of the economy. No one can predict the exact outcome. Trust is required in the operation of natural law and in the innate goodness of mankind. If reforms are founded upon justice, whose expression is natural law, no harm can come of them. Unreformed, the modern economies in which we live will offer growing injustice and suffering. For that in reality is how justice itself works. The face of injustice conceals the heart of the justice which it denies. Natural law operates, come what may. If it is followed, there is happiness for individuals and society; if it is ignored, all are forced by the consequences to seek painfully for the remedy. Justice will be done; how it is done is for us to choose.

5 Plato, *Laws*, V, 737, trans., B. Jowett, Random House, New York, 1937.

CHAPTER 28

Justice

T HE AGE of the great dictators – the twentieth century – is past. The works of Hitler and Stalin, of Mao and Mussolini linger on in historical consequence, but their distorted ideals have not survived the test of experience and the natural desire of mankind for freedom. Yet after their demise we do not see prosperous and happy peoples, nor have their policies been replaced by counsels of wisdom. At best we find a pathetic and misleading word – 'capitalism' – heralded as the principle of an economic order whose chief features are gross inequalities of wealth, an unjust distribution of income and the often mindless employment of great numbers, who become habituated to drab and passive modes of life. On one side, the new rich of media moguls, pop stars and property developers join the old rich of inherited land; on the other, the new poor of one parent families, 'drop-outs' and tenant farmers join the old poor of under-paid workers. Ignorance of the natural laws of economics affects the whole of society. As Keynes remarked, economists cannot offer civilisation, but only the possibility of it. For economic conditions influence all that goes on in every society, except perhaps the spiritual tranquillity of a true philosopher, and even he must avoid starvation and revolution if he seeks peace amongst the living.

Which Services are Genuine?

Despite all the appearances of economic growth, so meticulously and deceptively measured by the economists of advanced countries, we are not so far removed from calamity. An economy, like Britain's, whose national income consists of 70% services is unhealthy; not because we should revert to the production of 200 million tons of coal annually and cotton textiles for the millions of India, but because only some of those services represent genuine benefits to the population. Health services, education, law and order and much else are genuine enough, but a significant proportion are 'services' that amount to nothing, for they are largely jobs necessitated by the distorted relations of 'capitalism'. Mainly they are the adjustment of claims between individuals, firms and public bodies. Much of the work of the legal profession is directly or indirectly an outcome of our property laws regarding land and the crime engendered by economic injustice; much of the work of managers and accountants arises from the complexities of industrial organisation and absentee ownership; the size of the civil service, especially the Inland Revenue, is a direct result of the State's handling of issues that could be left to individual or group decision and enterprise in a free economy, or would simply disappear. Banking, management consultancy, stockbroking, building societies, and other financial services do little at present beyond adjusting claims on goods and services without producing any themselves, though some such work would be necessary, indeed vital, in a better economy. As for much information technology, one can only enquire to what extent it actually benefits the final customer.

The End of Capitalism

Nemesis approaches in other ways. Though recorded unemployment in the UK has fallen considerably from the three million of the early 1980s, it stands at about 8% in France and Germany, the basic structure of whose economies is similar to ours. Moreover, there is much hidden unemployment in the UK. Many school and university leavers do not seek permanent employment for some while. Many people take early retirement when they are perfectly fit for another ten years or more of highly productive work. Many of those on sickness benefit would perhaps be at work, if working conditions were less harsh.

Regional disparities in output, income, wealth and especially in land values are increasing. The implications of this for housing, transport, social services, mobility of labour and land use are profound, but largely ignored. Debt grows, accompanied only with platitudes from economists about ratios with national income. Ratios between debt and productive assets, excluding land values, would be much more significant. The burden of State welfare responsibilities is already being felt as the concealed poverty of workers is gradually revealed. Concentration and monopoly in industry advances steadily beneath the mask of advertising and company law that enable the real ownership of firms to be obscured. Modern 'capitalist' economies are shams. The thin crust of apparent prosperity may be on the verge of cracking.

Economic Freedom

Lest all this sounds merely like the complaints of an aging teacher outpaced by contemporary advances in economic organisation and technology, let us recall the essence of the argument. Human freedom is not the ability to do whatever one wants. Such is the freedom of beasts. In a society of rational creatures that freedom is limited, as J.S. Mill emphasised, to whatever does not harm others. To get what one wants without harming others is, however, a minimal degree of human freedom. That minimum is guaranteed by laws that punish assault, theft, false imprisonment and defamation. As English law has fully demonstrated, these laws establish civil liberty. Yet men and women are born, not just to be free from harm by others, but to live creative lives, for which they are given the natural gifts that ascend from hand and eye to mind and spirit. Shakespeare was protected by the laws of England from the malevolence of his fellows, but was that enough for his genius to flourish? What else is needed to yield a 'Hamlet' can scarcely be understood. What is needed in the economic sphere, however, to enable the mute, inglorious Miltons and the village Hampdens – if not the Cromwells! – to prosper, and for the economy 'to scatter plenty o'er a smiling land' is not hard to find, if prejudice and vested interest are set aside. Free men require free land. God and nature have enriched both sufficiently to allow their full co-operation to be eminently fruitful. All that is needed is to remove the barriers that separate or hinder access to land. These barriers are entirely man-made. They consist of laws, customs and practices, some that have endured for ages, some of recent invention. The law of primogeniture was introduced into England by William the Conqueror; VAT was adopted in 1973. Clear principles alone will enable them to be eradicated.

Economic Justice

'Freedom from avarice and a sense of justice'. Plato's dictum cannot be improved upon as a remedy for our economic diseases, but it needs to be interpreted for our time. To the individual civil duties of refraining from violence to person or character must be added the economic duties to keep land in good order, to support oneself and one's family by work, to leave others in quiet possession of land and, what is today most ignored, to pay the full rent to the community. On its side the community, apart from enforcing the civil law against all, including its own public servants, must maintain unused land, care for those unable to care for themselves, enforce security of tenure and collect the full rent from all who use or live on land within its juris-diction. Such are the prime economic duties. From their observance follow economic rights.

Plato has many lessons for our times. In Britain the slowly evolved system of representative government has not yet given way to the democracy that the 'Republic' so vividly describes, though there are many signs of the crude power of mass opinion, in the media and in election campaigns, for example. Plato's model of the descent from aristocracy to tyranny should remind us there is no equality in the fitness for power, however much we should aim at equality before the law and equality of opportunity. Those who are suited to govern are very few and always will be, and representative government takes wise account of this. Real economic reform would enable men and women of knowledge and virtue to emerge, unhindered by the poverty and privilege induced by a monopoly of land and wealth. Plato's aristocratic guardians possess no property of their own. So too the real entrepreneurs, people of acumen and enterprise, skilful, energetic, able to create wealth for all, not for themselves alone, would come to the fore, when the barriers of access to land and credit were removed. Of course, some such men succeed today, but their efforts are distorted by the structure of industry, which may turn them into managers or technicians in large companies controlled not by wealth creators so much as by creators of monopoly power, of claims on land values, of advertising techniques, of stock market manipulations. How often are the real experts in a modern business the paid servants of the men who can organise the finance and the complex claims of shareholders and the rest? As for the majority of the population, many of whom now live frustrated lives in tedious employment or take advantage of present opportunities to live unnecessarily off the labour of others by means of rent, 'capital' gains, dividends, interest or welfare payments would all alike face the prospect of fulfilling and well-rewarded work. By nature, not by privilege, men and women would find their place in society according to their talents, virtues and effort. The vision of justice is not an illusion.

APPENDIX

Rent and Landlord's Claim

I N THE ANALYSIS used throughout this book a difference arises between the economic rent of land and the amount which actually falls into the hands of landlords. This difference arises for three reasons. The first is that economic rent of land is defined as the potential rather than the actual excess of output on a site over output on the marginal, or least productive, site (see pp.72). The second is that there are other claims on the economic rent of land, in particular interest, taxation and monopoly profits (see Diagram 72, p.182), which are prior to those of the landlord. The third is that scarcity rent emerges when all land is fully enclosed i.e. in unconditional private ownership (see pp.77-8 and Diagram 75, p.189). Scarcity rent is not part of economic rent of land. It is received by landlords as a consequence of the limitation placed on available land at the margin.

This threefold difference between economic rent and what may be termed the landlord's claim would be exceedingly cumbersome to maintain explicitly throughout the whole analysis. Hence the term 'rent' is used with some latitude to include both. The purist, however, should not find it difficult from the context to see which precise meaning is intended.

The situation is analogous to the difference between the wages that measure labour's contribution to value added and the wages that are actually paid to labour. The term 'wages' is used throughout to refer to both, whereas strictly a distinction should be made by using different terms, such as 'wages' and 'labour's claim'. Scarcity rent is the measure of the difference, for it represents the transfer to landlords of part of what labour contributes to value added (see Diagram 50, p.106 where the full output on the marginal site is labour's contribution and WR2 – after deduction of scarcity rent – is labour's claim). Strict adherence to this distinction in the text would again be cumbersome.

Select Bibliography

Begg, D., Fischer, S. and Dornbusch, R. *Economics*. McGraw-Hill, 1997.

Blaug, M. *Economic Theory in Retrospect*. CUP, 1996.

Burda, M. and Wyplosz, C. *Macroeconomics*. OUP, 1997.

Burgess, R. *Public Revenue without Taxation*. Shepheard-Walwyn, 1993.

Buxton, T., Chapman, R. and Temple, P. *Britain's Economic Performance*. Routledge, 1998.

Carter, W.H. and Snavely, W.P. *Intermediate Economic Analysis*. McGraw-Hill, 1961.

Cahill, K. *Who Owns Britain?* Canongate, 2001.

Chamberlin, E.H. *The Theory of Monopolistic Competition*. 1933.

Daunton, M.J. *Progress and Poverty*. OUP, 1995.

Eaton, B. Curtis and Lipsey, R.G. *On the Foundations of Monopolistic Competition and Economic Geography*. Edward Elgar, 1997.

George, H. *The Land Question*. Robert Schalkenbach Foundation, 1965.

— *Progress and Poverty*. Robert Schalkenbach Foundation, 1962.

Glautier, M. *The Social Conscience*. Shepheard-Walwyn, 2007.

Harrison, F. *The Power in the Land*. Shepheard-Walwyn, 1983.

Harrison, F. (ed). *The Losses of Nations*. Othila, 1998.

Heilbroner, R. and Streeten, P. *The Great Economists*. Eyre & Spottiswoode, 1955.

Heilbroner, R. and Milberg, W. *The Crisis of Vision in Modern Economic Thought*. CUP, 1995.

Heiman, E. *History of Economic Doctrines*. OUP, 1964.

Hertz, N. *The Silent Takeover*. Heinemann, 2001.

Hill, C. *The World Turned Upside Down*. Penguin, 1991.

Hudson, M., Miller, G. and Feder, K. *A Philosophy for a Fair Society*. Shepheard-Walwyn, 1994.

Huhne, C. *Real World Economics*. Penguin, 1990.

Isard, W. *Locations and Space Economy*. MIT, 1956.

Keynes, J.M. *General Theory of Employment, Interest and Money*. MacMillan, 1957.

Krugman, P. *Development, Geography and Economic Theory*. MIT, 1997.

Locke, J. *Two Treatises of Civil Government*. Dent, 1962.

Lipsey, R. and Chrystal, K. *Positive Economics*. OUP, 1995.

MacLaren, L. *The Nature of Society*. School of Economic Science.

Marshall, A. *Principles of Economics*. MacMillan, 1956.

Marx, K. *Capital*. Dent, 1957.

Maxwell, D. and Vigor, A. (eds). *Time for Land Value Tax*. IPPR, 2005.

Mill, J. *Principles of Political Economy*. OUP, 1998.

Monbiot, G. *The Captive State*. Pan, 2001.

Ormerod, P. *The Death of Economics*. Faber & Faber, 1994.

Plato. *Republic* (trans. Jowett, B.) Random House, 1937.

— *Laws* (trans. Jowett, B.) Random House, 1937.

Ricardo, D. *The Principles of Political Economy and Taxation*. Dent, 1962.

Roll, E. *A History of Economic Thought*. Faber, 1962.

Schumacher, E. *Small is Beautiful*. Abacus, 1974.

Schumpeter, J. *The Theory of Economic Development* (trans. Opie, J.) OUP, 1961.

— *History of Economic Analysis*. Routledge, 1994.

Scitovsky, T. *Welfare and Competition*. Allen & Unwin.

Smith, A. *Wealth of Nations*. Dent, 1953.

Tideman, N. *Land and Taxation*. Shephead-Walwyn, 1994.

Index

Boom Bust
House Prices, Banking and the Depression of 2010

Fred Harrison

On both sides of the Atlantic economists, bankers and politicians have convinced themselves that they have tamed the business cycle through monetary policy. In his 2007 Budget speech Gordon Brown even went so far as to claim: 'We will never return to the old boom and bust.' Alan Greenspan was believed to have similar powers.

Harrison, on evidence going back more than 200 years in both the US and UK, reveals that there is a remarkably regular 18-year property cycle which enabled him to predict the peak of the current cycle in 2007, two years before it happened. He argues that monetary policy is not able to iron out these property cycles. It requires a major fiscal reform that would be enormously beneficial to enterprise.

'He does make a case for the existence of an 18-year business cycle, which he links to speculation in the property market' **Samuel Brittan in the FINANCIAL TIMES**

'... does Harrison really know something we don't?' **Ross Clark in the MAIL ON SUNDAY**

300pp **ISBN 978-0-85683-254-3** **£17.95 pb**

Ricardo's Law
House Prices and the Great Tax Clawback Scam

Fred Harrison

Fred Harrison reveals how taxpayers' money is channelled behind the scenes, through 'the invisible hand', from poor to rich people and from poor to rich parts of the country.

Public spending, for example on roads, railways, schools and hospitals, makes a major contribution to rising land values. These benefit house and other property owners, rich ones more than poor ones, desirable locations and asset-rich parts of the country more than poor ones, but those who rent their properties do not share in the windfall gains. In fact, they have to pay rising rents.

'This is the fundamental reason, Mr Harrison says, why the welfare state of the past 60 years has not worked.' **Ashley Seager in THE GUARDIAN**

320pp **ISBN 978-0-85683-241-3** **£18.95 hb**

Location Matters
Recycling Britain's Wealth

Tony Vickers

Land rights confer wealth, but not uniformly. Location matters – building Canary Wharf in a desert without the associated infrastructure would not have made anyone richer. The same effort and investment on a prime site yields a far better return than on a marginal one. Who benefits?

The author argues that the current tax regime fails to take account of the growing proportion of wealth conferred on landowners by the combined efforts and enterprise of industry and the public sector as the British economy grows. To enable Britain to prosper in the modern world, Vickers advocates a complete shift in the burden of taxation, *off* enterprise and *onto* resource usage, to ensure that those who now benefit from Nature's contribution pay and not future generations.

'*This book is a primer for anyone who wants to create a more equitable, efficient and sustainable Britain*'
Chris Huhne MP

112pp   **ISBN 978-0-85683-251-2**   £8.95 pb

Public Revenue without Taxation

Ronald Burgess

The author argues that taxation is a primal cause of both inflation and unemployment. The development of Keynes' general theory of employment leads to the conclusion that an open trading economy is likely to be most competitive, and therefore most prosperous, when all taxes are abolished.

Regardless of this, the freely elected governments of contemporary trading economies – with the acquiescence of their electorates – persist in raising most of their revenues by means of taxation. The immediate cause of such action by governments, and for the acquiescence of their electorates, is ignorance of any acceptable alternative method of raising sufficient public revenue. The author reveals an alternative and shows how reform may be introduced, with a minimum of disruption, so that politicians, with an eye to re-election, can achieve measurable results during the lifetime of a parliament.

128pp   **ISBN 978-0-85683-135-5**   £12 hb